Panicked Parents' Guide to College Admissions

Sally Rubenstone & Sidonia Dalby
Smith College

THIRD EDITION

THOMSON

PETERSON'S

Australia • Canada • Mexico • Singapore • Spain • United Kingdom • United States

About The Thomson Corporation and Peterson's

With revenues of US$7.2 billion, The Thomson Corporation (www.thomson.com) is a leading global provider of integrated information solutions for business, education, and professional customers. Its Learning businesses and brands (www.thomsonlearning.com) serve the needs of individuals, learning institutions, and corporations with products and services for both traditional and distributed learning.

Peterson's, part of The Thomson Corporation, is one of the nation's most respected providers of lifelong learning online resources, software, reference guides, and books. The Education Supersite[sm] at www.petersons.com—the Internet's most heavily traveled education resource—has searchable databases and interactive tools for contacting U.S.-accredited institutions and programs. In addition, Peterson's serves more than 105 million education consumers annually.

For more information, contact Peterson's, 2000 Lenox Drive, Lawrenceville, NJ 08648; 800-338-3282; or find us on the World Wide Web at: www.petersons.com/about.

ISBN: 0-7689-0927-9

Printed in Canada

10 9 8 7 6 5 4 3 2 1   04 03 02

CONTENTS

Acknowledgments

To Our Children: Jack, Betsy, and Christina

Special thanks to Janette Young at Peterson's for being a supportive stepparent to this book and to Ann C. Playe, friend, colleague, and financial aid wizard extraordinaire.

Thanks, too, to the many folks at Smith, especially Laurie Fenlason, Lisa DeCarolis, Lynn Oberbillig, Laura Rauscher, Karen Kristof, Deb Shaver, Sabrina Marsh, Erika Laquer, Sheri Peabody, and Pat Graham, and to the two Bills and Steve—in Technical Services. Other pros who really went the extra mile for us include: Jane Gutman, Lee Stetson, Dave Berry, Katie Fretwell, John Boshoven, Ann Wright, Frances Yelen, Bill Risley, Ed Wall, Joan Dorman Davis, and Kathy Roos.

From Sally:

Thanks to my wonderful family (Chris Petrides, Eddi and Al Simon, Liz Rubenstone, and Liria Petrides) who supported me when I needed them and left me alone when I didn't. As my mid-life miracle baby, Jack Christopher Petrides prepares to head off to school himself (kindergarten, that is), I realize that his college decisions will be here before I know it.

From Sid:

While editing this book, I began the college search with my older daughter. I'm not panicking yet, thanks mostly to Betsy for assuring me there's no need to get nervous about picking a college. Christina, I'm sorry I missed so many of your games. I want to thank Fred, Mary, Mother, and Jim for their everlasting support. My gratitude also goes to the custodian at Granby High School who found me a quiet place to write at the tournament between games.

So many people were generous with their time and their thoughts while we wrote that we wouldn't have enough room for the chapters if we listed each of their names. They know who they are, and we thank them for sharing their experiences to help others. We parents stick together. See you at parents' weekend!

Introduction

You're sending a child to college, and you're bound to be concerned—or maybe more like anxious or yes, even panicked. And whether this is the first child to go, or the last, another child or an only child, you recognize that life as you know it will never be quite the same again.

In today's world, you don't have to be breathing into paper bags to qualify as a panicked parent. You realize that a higher education is a huge investment—of time and money; of emotion and energy. You worry that your child won't be accepted by a favorite school or, worse yet, will get in, and go, and be miserable there. You wonder if you'll ever again be able to afford a new car, or *any* car, or a restaurant without a drive-through window. You question if the teenager who can't decide what movie to see on a Saturday night will be able to move hundreds of miles from home and make choices that may influence him or her for decades to come.

As a parent, your part in the whole process is important, yet can, at times, be especially confusing. You've reached a turning point. Your child is going to college. You're not. You think that your voice should be heard, but you're not always sure what to say. There are a myriad of forms to fill out, tests to take, trips to make, and bills to pay. You want to provide support and assistance but you don't know what will help, and you're scared of what may hurt.

Can parents contribute to prudent college selections and to favorable admission decisions? What can Mom or Dad do to realize (or ruin) a child's dream of attending a certain special school?

First, relax; you're in good company. There are nearly 15 million students in college. That means—with parents, stepparents, and grandparents included—billions of people share your questions and concerns.

In the pages that follow, you will find practical tips on how to take the perplexity, and the complexity, out of the college admission process. You will learn what college officials really look for in a candidate, and what you and your child should look for in a college. And you will have many questions about the admission process answered, such as:

- *Is there such a thing as a college match made in heaven?*

  God only knows! See Chapter 2

- *Can a private college cost us less than a state school?*

  Very possibly. Check out Chapter 5.

- *Can preparation improve standardized test scores?*

  Yes. See Chapter 3.

- *Will a good interview get my child into a long-shot school?*

  Maybe. See Chapter 4.

- *Do some colleges give preference to certain groups or types of students?*

  Often. See Chapter 7.

- *Will we all still be speaking when this is over?*

  We hope so. Quick...read Chapter 1.

CHAPTER 1

All in the Family: Decisions and Dynamics

I. How Involved Should Parents Be in the College Selection Process?

➤ *THE GOOD NEWS:* Even kids who have barricaded you from their bedrooms since seventh grade are likely to welcome—or at least *expect*—your input at college admission time.

➤ *THE BAD NEWS:* Somebody in the family needs to be the organized one and stay on top of piles of paperwork and deadlines. Ideally, this should be the student. In reality, it is usually the parent.

You may already have been terrified by tales of parents who seem to make their kid's college admission a full-time occupation. One private school college counselor remembers such a mother who "created a personal scrapbook for her son, had it professionally typeset and printed, hired a writer to compose the essays, and had a secretary fill out all the applications. After submitting the completed packages to her son for his signature, she Fed Ex-ed the whole shebang to each college."

At the other end of the spectrum—but by no means alone—is the Brown alumna who recalls that her mother refused to take any part in the application process. "She sent me off on bus and train trips around the country to visit colleges by myself. In retrospect, I suppose it wasn't such a bad thing. It helped make me independent. But every time an admission interviewer asked me, 'Are you here today with someone who may have questions?' then it hurt."

As a parent, it is critically important that you don't become *too* involved in the selection and application process. After all, *you* are not the one who is going to college, and children should always feel that they have played a key part in this important decision about *their* lives. Since most will soon be living far enough away that you won't be there to constantly remind them about daily responsibilities, this is also a good time to make certain that they're ready to take the reins. Yet, don't err too much the other way and not give *enough* support—moral, financial, and even clerical—needed during this sometimes frustrating, always busy period. You should find the best balance between being overbearing and nagging and being apathetic and distant. Some choice, eh?

Colleges, by the way, don't give extra credit for parental involvement—nor for students who survive without it. Contrary to what the grapevine tells you, it doesn't matter who calls to request catalogues or directions, nor how many parents (or sets of parents) are downstairs in the waiting room during an interview. Admission officers only wince when it's clear that candidates are passing off Mom or Dad's efforts as their own, like the prepackaged prospect described above or the applicant who can barely speak English but submits an essay that sounds suspiciously like *Self-Reliance*.

II. Self-Assessment Surveys for Students and Parents

Magazines these days seem to be full of stress charts. They're designed to show you (as if sitting bolt upright in the middle of the night doesn't do it) how major life events can affect your arteries, your lungs, your heart, and your head. Even "good" stresses (births and marriages; moving to a bigger house or a better job) can propel you to the top of the chart. Well, guess what. Sending a kid to college gets you right up there, too, and if it's the first one to go—or the last—then congratulations, you earn extra points.

In only the past few decades, the college admission process has become a highly charged, often tense and disruptive experience for many families. Where does all this pressure come from?

- For starters, it comes from *colleges* themselves. Student recruiting is now a top priority. Schools print more publications and send them out sooner than ever before. They vie for hot prospects by offering free flights and campus weekends, complete with tickets to concerts and sporting events. Exacting application requirements, endless forms, essays, and deadlines all add to the stress.

- Likewise, it comes from *society*. We live in a designer culture, where name-brand cars, clothes, luggage—and *colleges*—assure us (and others) that we've "made it." The media, too, is relentless in reminding us of the importance of approaching college in the proper way, and of the capriciousness of admission decisions, even when we do. Stores are brimming with books aimed at enlightening us about the most arcane aspects of the process, while burgeoning businesses prey on fears of substandard test scores.

- *Students,* of course, put pressure on themselves. Where you live, where your child goes to school, and even the varying personalities that make one senior class different than the next will all determine how college admission affects your family.

- Finally, the really big-time pressure can come from *parents.* The current generation of upcoming college students is the first with a high percentage of parents who have attended college themselves. Those who went to renowned and prestigious places usually expect their children to do as well. Those from less-celebrated schools often demand that their children do better.

Moreover, with college costs skyrocketing, parents have become savvy and careful consumers. They consider a college education an investment and expect immense returns. They scrutinize schools more critically than their own parents ever did and have more specific questions—and *demands*—that can also mean more stress at home.

Family life, as well, is not always as simple as it was when Ward and Wally Cleaver conferred in the study, while June baked brownies for the Beaver. Today, some students have one parent; some have more than four. Many have two who barely speak, or who use the college application process as a weapon in their own power struggle.

➤ *THE GOOD AND THE BAD NEWS:* Both the strengths and weaknesses of parent/child relationships (and parent/parent relationships) will be amplified during the college search.

Below is a self-assessment survey that should help you and your child as you approach the college selection experience. There are no right or wrong answers, nor even any scores to tally at the end. The quiz has several purposes:

- To get the whole process up and running; to generate discussions; to foster awareness of some of the complex questions and issues that are part of college decision-making

- To recognize potential hot spots, where you and your child (or you and your spouse, or all of you) are likely to disagree, so that problems can be diffused before they *really* heat up

- To create pleasant surprises—those areas where you thought you'd disagree, but don't

- To pinpoint priorities that all of you will want to consider when you read Chapter 2 and start identifying "target schools" (So don't throw away your questionnaires.)

The Rules

Actually, there aren't many. There are two separate but similar tests: one for parents; one for kids. First, make copies. That way, you can do your own; your child's other parent(s) or guardian(s) can do their own, too. If your child is just starting high school, answer what you can, then retake the quiz in a year or so to see what's changed. Even parents of seniors who do the survey now and again in a few months may be amazed by the differences. A sociologist-to-be in September could be considering medicine by March.

Don't hesitate to add comments, as needed, or to make up your own responses if the multiple-choice options aren't multiple enough. When everyone has finished the quiz, call a meeting to talk about your answers, but respect the others' privacy. There may be some thoughts that each of you would rather keep confidential.

MOM AND POP QUIZ:
Self-Assessment Survey for Parents

I. Particular Preferences

Name three things your son or daughter is doing right now and you hope will continue to do in college (e.g., playing piano, flossing daily, learning Japanese):

1. _____
2. _____
3. _____

Name three things he or she is not doing now, but you hope will do in college (academic or otherwise):

1. _____
2. _____
3. _____

Name three things your child is doing right now that you hope won't continue in college (e.g., flunking English, taunting the dog):

1. _____
2. _____
3. _____

Name three things not mentioned yet that you think your child can't live without at college (e.g., vegetarian food, wheelchair ramps, a French-speaking dorm):

1. _____
2. _____
3. _____

Pretend there's a perfect college. We'll call it Fantasy State. In your opinion, it's the ideal school for your child. Keep it in mind as you answer the questions below and, if you really have no preference in one area—or have several—be sure to say so. Put an asterisk (*) by those preferences you feel very strongly about:

II. Location:

How far is it from home? (Within an hour's drive or a day's drive? In a foreign country?) _____

Are you comfortable with your child attending a school that is primarily reached by airplane from your home? _____

Do you prefer a big city? Suburb? Small town? _____

What type of climate is most appealing to your child? _____
How important is this? _____

Do you have other preferences or requirements? (e.g., near a ski slope, close to grandparents, close to a major medical center) _____

Do you have a specific location in mind? (e.g., Boston, California, New York City) _____

How will your child react if your expectations conflict? _____

III. Enrollment

Will your child do his or her best in a small college (under 2,500 students)? A medium-small one (2,500 to 5,000)? A medium one (5,000 to 10,000)? A large one (10,000 to 18,000)? A very large one (18,000+)? _____

How good is your child at asking for help (anything from directions to tutoring) when needed? _____

Do you prefer an institution that is primarily for undergraduates? _____ What advantages (if any) do you see in having graduate students on campus, too? _____

Would you consider a single-sex school? _____ Would you prefer one? _____ In a coed school, do you care if the male-to-female ratio is disproportionate? _____

Do you prefer a school with a religious affiliation (and/or a strong majority of one religious group)? _____ If so, which one? _____

Would a religious affiliation bother you? _____

Is geographic diversity in a student body important to you? _____

Racial/ethnic diversity? _____

What preferences (and prejudices) do you think your child has regarding the size and student composition of the college he or she will attend? _____

IV. Academics

Does your child have a major in mind? _____ If so, what? _____

How certain about it do you think your child is? _____

Does he or she have a career goal? If so, what? _____

How do you feel about his or her choice of major? _____

What other academic areas do you hope will be pursued in college? _____

Are there subjects that your child is likely to avoid that you think should be studied? _____

Do you think your child works better when challenged by tough classes and bright classmates, or when near the top of a less competitive group? _____

How hard do think your child works in high school? See choices below:
a. Very hard (maybe too hard, at times?)
b. Hard (especially the night before tests and term papers)
c. Somewhat hard
d. What's work?

How hard do you think your child expects to work in college? (Use the same choices as above) _____

Do you think a college should have a core curriculum (distribution requirements)? _____

What other special academic focus or programs appeal to you? (e.g., military, agricultural or technical, study abroad opportunities, etc.) _____

Is having your child attend a prestigious college important to you? _____

Is it equally, more, or less important to your child? _____

V. Finances

Will cost influence where your child attends college? _____

Do you plan to apply for financial aid? _____

How much money, if any, have you set aside for college expenses for your child? _____

What amount do you expect your child to contribute from earnings and assets? _____

How is your credit rating? _____

How much do you expect to borrow to pay for college? _____

How much do you expect your *child* to borrow? _____

VI. Campus Life

What extracurricular activities do you hope your child will pursue in college? _____

How do you feel about fraternities and sororities? _____

How do you expect weekends will be spent? See choices below. Check all that apply:

a. Coming home (with the laundry)	e. Partying
b. With the high school honey	f. Working
c. Studying	g. Playing/watching sports
d. Some study; some socializing	h. Other_____

Would you prefer a college with a reputation for being a conservative school? _____ Liberal? _____ A high-pressure school? ___? A party school? _____ Other?_____

VII. Living Situation

Would you prefer your child live at home? _____ In a single-sex dorm? _____ In a coed dorm? _____ In a fraternity or sorority? _____

Has your child ever shared a bedroom? _____ How will your child do with a college roommate? _____ How about more than one? ___

Does dorm size matter? _____

Would you mind an off campus apartment? ____

Where do you think your child prefers or expects to live? _____

VIII. Getting Personal

What are your child's SAT I scores (or ACT or PSAT)? _____

Will your child retake the SAT?_____ If so, when?__/ ___/ __

What is your child's GPA? _____ Rank in class? _____

On a 1-to-10 scale, how demanding were his or her high school classes compared to the toughest ones the school offers? _____

Using the same scale, rate your high school for competitiveness and difficulty compared to others. _____

If 5 is Most Selective and 1 is Not at all Selective, to which level of colleges do you expect your child to apply? _____Which do you think are likely to accept him or her? _____

Why do you want your child to go to college? _____

Do you think she or he should go straight from high school? _____

Do you have specific schools in mind now that you'd like your child to consider or attend? If so, which ones? _____

Which aspects of the college admission process and of having your child actually going to college are you most apprehensive about? _____ Which are you most looking forward to? _____

Which aspects of the college selection/admission process are likely to cause friction between you and your child?

1._____ 4._____

2._____ 5._____

3._____ 6._____

Do you think your child feels pressure from you to attend a specific school or type of school? Explain: _____

Who do you think should decide which college your child should attend? See choices below:

a. She/he should—Period.

b. She/he should—With *strong* parental input.

c. She/he should—With *some* parental input.

d. Parent(s)—With some input from kids.

e. A guidance counselor

f. The Psychic Friends Network

KIDZ QUIZ:
Self-Assessment Survey for Students

I. Particular Preferences

Name three things you are doing right now that you hope to continue to do in college (These can be anything from studying science to shaving your head; playing polo to playing piano):

1. _____
2. _____
3. _____

Name three things you're not doing now but hope to do in college (academic or otherwise):

1. _____
2. _____
3. _____

Name three things you are doing right now that you don't want to do in college (e.g., sharing a bathroom with your baby brother, conjugating German verbs, singing alto):

1. _____
2. _____
3. _____

Name three things you haven't mentioned yet that you can't live without at college (e.g., vegetarian food, wheelchair ramps, a French-speaking dorm):

1. _____
2. _____
3. _____

In general, how do you want your college to be different than your high school? _____ How do you want it to be similar? _____

Pretend there's a perfect college. We'll call it Fantasy State. Keep it in mind as you answer the questions below and, if you really have no preference in one area—or have several—be sure to say so. Put an asterisk (*) by those preferences that you feel very strongly about:

II. Location

How far is it from home? (e.g., within a hour's drive or a day's drive? In a foreign country?)_____

Are you comfortable selecting a school that is primarily reached by airplane from your home? _____

Do you prefer a big city? Suburb? Small town? _____

What climate is most appealing? _____ How important is this? _____

Do you have other preferences or requirements? (e.g., near a ski slope or major medical center, close to your boyfriend or girlfriend, grandparents) _____

Do you have a specific location in mind? (e.g., Boston, California, New York City)_____

In what location do you think your parents want you to go to school? _____

How will they react if your expectations conflict? _____

III. Enrollment

Do you prefer a small college (under 2,500 students)? A medium-small one (2,500 to 5,000)? A medium one (5,000 to 10,000)? A large one (10,000 to 18,000)? A very large one (18,000+)?_____

How good are you at asking for help (anything from directions to tutoring) when you need it? _____

Do you want an institution that is primarily for undergraduates? ____What advantages (if any) do you see in having graduate students on campus, too? _____

Would you consider a single-sex school? _____ Would you prefer one? _____

In a coed school, do you care if the male-to-female ratio is disproportionate? _____

Do you want a school with a religious affiliation (and/or strong majority of one religious group)? _____ If so, which one? _____

Would a religious affiliation bother you? _____

Is geographic diversity in a student body important to you? _____

Racial/ethnic diversity? _____

What preferences (and prejudices) do you think your parents have regarding the size and student composition of the college you will attend? _____

IV. Academics

Do you have a major in mind? _____ If so, what? _____ How certain about it do you feel? _____

Do you have a career goal? If so, what? _____

How do you think your parents feel about your choice of major?
_____

What other academic areas do you hope to pursue in college?
_____

Which subjects do you hope to avoid like the plague?
_____

Do you think you work better when you are challenged by tough classes and bright classmates, or do you do prefer to be near the top of a less competitive group? _____

How hard do you work in high school? See choices below:

a. Very hard (maybe too hard, at times?)

b. Hard (especially the night before tests and term papers)

c. Somewhat hard

d. What's work?

How hard do you expect to work in college? (Use the same choices as above)
_____

Do you have objections to a college with a core curriculum (distribution requirements)? _____

What other special academic focus or programs appeal to you? (e.g., military, agricultural or technical, study abroad opportunities, etc.)
_____

Is attending a prestigious college important to you? _____

Is it equally, more, or less important to your parents? _____

V. Finances

Do you think cost will influence where you attend college? _____

Do you plan to apply for financial aid? _____

Do you know how much money, if any, your parents have set aside for your college education? If so, how much? _____

How much do you expect to contribute from your own earnings and assets?
_____

Are you willing to assume loans in your own name that must be repaid after college? _____

Do you plan to have a job during the school year while in college? _____ A summer job? _____

VI. Campus Life

What extracurricular activities do you plan to pursue in college?
_____

How do you feel about fraternities and sororities? _____

How do you expect to spend your weekends? See choices below:

a. Going home (with my laundry)   e. Partying

b. With my high school honey   f. Working

c. Studying   g. Playing/watching sports

d. Some studying; some socializing   h. Other _____

Would you prefer a college with a reputation for being a conservative school? _____ Liberal? _____ A high-pressure school? _____ A party school? _____ Other? _____

VII. Living Situation

Would you prefer to live at home? _____ In a single-sex dorm? _____ In a coed dorm? _____ In a fraternity or sorority? _____

Have you ever shared a bedroom? _____ Do you want a roommate? _____ Could you handle more than one roommate? _____

Does dorm size matter? _____

Do you prefer an apartment off campus? _____

Where do you think your parents prefer or expect you to live?
_____

VIII. Getting Personal

What are your SAT I scores (or ACT or PSAT)? _____

Do you plan to retake the SAT?_____ If so, when? ___/___/__

What is your GPA?_____ Rank in class? _____

On a 1-to-10 scale, how demanding were your high school classes, compared to the toughest ones your school offers? _____

Using that same scale, rate your high school for competitiveness and difficulty compared to others. _____

If 5 is Most Selective and 1 is Not at all Selective, to which level of colleges do you plan to apply? _____ Which do you think are likely to accept you? _____

Why do you want to go to college? _____

Do you want to go straight from high school? _____

Do you have specific schools in mind now that you'd like to consider or attend? If so, which ones? _____

Which aspects of the college admission process and of actually going to college are you most apprehensive about? _____

Which are you most looking forward to? _____

While at college, will you worry about the situation at home? (e.g., parents' relationship or welfare, problems with siblings, etc.) _____

Which aspects of the college selection/admission process are likely to cause friction between you and your parents?

1._____   4._____

2._____   5._____

3._____   6._____

Do you feel pressure from your parents to attend a specific school or type of school? _____

Who should decide which college you attend? See choices below:

a. Me—It's my life.

b. Me—With *strong* input from parent(s).

c. Me—With *some* input from parent(s).

d. Parent(s)—With some input from me.

e. My guidance counselor

f. The Psychic Friends Network

II. Pressure Points

Since going to college is a major life event (and there aren't that many for most of us), sitting down with your completed questionnaires should be a special occasion. Schedule a time in advance. Make sure that other pressing obligations (and younger siblings) are out of the way. Consider heading to a quiet restaurant or to a favorite secluded spot. This will underscore the importance of the meeting and often make it possible to discuss conflicts clearly and calmly.

Emphasize the positive aspects of the process—your mutual hopes and dreams, the excitement of a wide range of opportunities and options. Remember that you are sharing an experience that is the culmination of many years of schooling and parenting, and that no decisions need to be made overnight; no disagreements have to be resolved instantly; and "compromise" may be an important watchword along the way.

For example, Althea's parents envisioned her at a small, rural Catholic women's college. She was sold on Boston University—large, urban, and certainly coed. She agreed to investigate both and, in doing so, discovered Wellesley, which became her first choice and pleased everyone.

Of course, not all stories have such happy endings. But there are some other points for parents to keep in mind that will ease tensions and help to precipitate a fruitful and usually peaceful college search.

Are you able to let go?

Ask yourself this question early on. Are you pushing Pomona because it's a great college or because it's around the corner? What fears do you have about how family life will change when your child leaves for college? Will there be a family left at all? Are you anxious about how to fill the time you once devoted to this child?

Letting Go: A Parents' Guide to Today's College Experience, by Karen Levin Coburn and Madge Lawrence Treeger, and *Don't Tell Me What to Do, Just Send Money: The Essential Parenting Guide to the College Years,* by Helen E. Johnson and Christine Schelhas-Miller, are two books that offer insight and advice to parents dealing with the emotional side of sending a child to college.

Whose idea is this, anyway?

If you have always wanted to be a podiatrist or a psychologist, an accountant or a registered nurse, and are now pushing an unwilling child in that direction, consider going back to school *yourself.* (The federal government even gives a small financial aid break to applicants with a parent in school.) Likewise, don't insist on a college that offers football or physics, Theta Chi or Sigma Xi, just because it was right for you. Try to keep your own goals or needs separate from what your child wants. It's tough. Eighteen-year-olds don't always *know* what's best for them. They may choose to study archaeology, astronomy, French, or fashion design only because that's what a friend is doing. Meanwhile, you worry that history majors end up waiting tables; that art school graduates sweep floors (see "Major Dilemmas" in Chapter 2).

Ask your child to explain choices and try to point out when plans seem outrageous, but never deny a dream just because it's not *your* dream. Some parents live vicariously through their children, just as some children live for their parents' approval. Each of you must learn to recognize whose voice you're really hearing.

Questions & Answers

Q: Help! Our son has a list of college choices that don't sound at all like ours. He won't even consider the schools we're urging him to see. Who has the final say?

A: While parents are often considered the most influential people in students' choices of colleges, it's not always clear if that influence is positive or negative. Marc, for instance, felt that his mother had been ramming Harvard—where his dad had gone—down his throat since he was a toddler. As a result, he stubbornly refused to apply. Your son, too, may be rebelling against you and exerting his independence by bucking your authority. Or, your son may know better what he wants and what he needs in a postsecondary school. Talk with him. Ask him for specific reasons he is choosing the schools he is. Are his reasons valid? Perhaps you'll learn something about him that you don't know. If money is the root of this evil, call the financial services offices at the schools under debate and ask about payment plans and aid options. Even early in the search process, most colleges can give you a ballpark idea of what the bottom line will be for your family. Don't let misconceptions about college costs create conflicts. By the way, when parents refuse to pay (or complete aid forms) for schools they don't endorse, no one ends up happy.

Whose life is this, anyway?

While parents may anticipate arguments over college choices and career goals, and may also be on the ready to cajole and plead at deadline time, some are mystified when their children refuse to cooperate at all. The once-conscientious student now insists, "I'm not going to college, period" or, in essence, relays the same signal by ignoring the stack of catalogs and applications that is multiplying on the kitchen counter. In order to best respond, you'll have to translate the message. Is this just your basic garden-variety procrastination? Is your child afraid of failing to meet high expectations or fearful of breaking away? Is college the right move now—or even at all? First, try a bit of nagging and dragging (i.e., a few ultimatums and college visits that *you've* arranged). Sometimes, this is enough to break the ice. If not, consider other options: a year off (see Chapter 9), or even another route altogether. Your child may be a talented carpenter, an inspired chef, or a compassionate nurse's aide. These professions all require training, but not necessarily college.

Is prestige at the top of your priority list?

Many parents put pressure on students to apply to those colleges that will increase their *own* status or self-esteem. Such parents may be unwittingly setting their kids up for rejection or—if accepted—for frustration. "Students tend to be more realistic than their parents when it comes to college choices," notes Roger McC. Eastlake, director of college guidance at Germantown Academy in Fort Washington, Pennsylvania. "Applying to college involves complex decisions that should be based on thorough research, not on what decal you want on the back of your car," agrees Doran Morford, director of college guidance at Greens Farms Academy in Westport, Connecticut.

While many alumni insist that their years in Ivy League or equivalent institutions were worth the all-nighters and extracurricular efforts that it took to get there, some studies suggest that these super-school graduates are no more successful down the road (whether success is measured by earnings or self-proclaimed satisfaction) than those from the less-prominent places.

Applicants from impoverished communities and from working-class or lower-middle-class homes may benefit most from the opportunity to attend a college where they will rub elbows with the upper crust. Yet the students whose parents seem to care passionately about prestige institutions are those whose birthright has already secured them a spot on the top rung of the social ladder. Ironically, these children, who have typically been treated to more privileges than most, might get a truer "education" at a good, but less prestigious, place.

So, encourage your child to seek a challenging college experience, but don't attach unrealistic importance to name schools. Above all, never confuse what kind of *student* your child is with what kind of *person* he or she is. There are hundreds of thousands of high school students who are clever and kind, reliable and even remarkable, who won't be heading to Harvard next fall—but who will still lead happy and productive lives that make their parents proud.

Is this a split decision?

Although we've spent a lot of time talking about parents as if they are a united front like Ozzie and Harriet or NATO, the truth is that you and your mate may not see eye-to-eye on this college business at all. Don't expect to always agree. Pick your battles and respect your child's role as a tie-breaker.

Questions & Answers

Q: What happens when parents are divorced?

A: Divorced or separated parents must be especially sensitive to the hurtful issues that college planning can stir up. Anna's dad insisted he could not afford to send her to a private college, while she watched him splurge on luxuries for his second wife and new family. Sharon's father believed that his wife had abandoned him when she found feminism. He promised his daughter he'd pay her tuition, as long as she didn't attend her first-choice school—a *women's* college. Don't let your child become a pawn in your games.

As a divorced parent, you may be especially susceptible to the hard feelings that college selection can create. Perhaps you assumed your son would want a close-by east coast institution, but he's off to college near Dad in Des Moines. Try not to feel competitive when your child bypasses *your* alma mater for your ex's.

College admission and financial aid offices do not function in the Dark Ages. There is room on most forms for all kinds of combinations and permutations of blended families. Officials are accustomed to parents who are AWOL or uncooperative and can usually offer advice. Your own situation may seem confusing, but you should never feel uncomfortable about explaining it or about requesting special considerations where appropriate.

Finally, divorced or separated parents often both expect to take an active role in the college search. Sometimes a noncustodial mother or father will seem to spring out of the woodwork at admission time (though many disappear at *tuition* time). It is important that you, your ex, and your child communicate as clearly as possible and, especially, define your roles. Who will go on college visits? Who will oversee applications? Who will pay college costs? (Don't overlook application fees, either. At about $50 a pop, they can be a big-ticket item.) Also, who gets to go to parents' weekend when all of this is behind you?

What's the sibling situation?

Beginning a college search means reminding yourself again and again that, if you have more than one child, they may be very different. Just as Brenda was a beautiful ballerina and Tammy couldn't get into the tutu, you are likely to find that the college (or *type* of college) that is a perfect match for your first child may not fit the second one at all. Commonly, younger siblings are fearful of disappointing Mom and Dad after a superstar older brother or sister attends a big-name school. On the other hand, just because three kids have already trooped through the local state college, don't assume that it's the certain spot for number four as well. And parents of twins often find that college marks a turning point when a once inseparable pair heads in different directions.

Likewise, even if *all* of your children are seeking similar schools, you can practically count on different approaches to the process. Danny, for example, may have dragged you on a dozen campus tours, insisted that you read every essay, and never met deadlines without nagging; now Audrey wants to do it all alone. She visited Vassar with her boyfriend, canceled *your* Greyhound ticket to Grinnell, and may ultimately end up at a college where you never even knew she *applied*. Shifting gears among different children is one of the signs of brilliance among parents.

And speaking of siblings, although you may have to tuck the little ones away during summit meetings with the college-bound student, don't forget that this may be a confusing time for them, too. They recognize that change and anxiety are in the air. They know they will be losing an ally and mentor, tennis partner, math tutor (and occasional tormentor). Make sure you don't keep them in the dark—high school-age siblings, especially, can learn a lot from observing—and set aside time for special treats or attention.

Can't you just chill out?

With advice about the admission process swelling exponentially each year, a convoluted procedure can become an overwhelming ordeal for those who feel that they somehow have to do it all. Instead, parents and students should often remind themselves that there will always be another book they haven't read, another Web site they didn't visit, or another college they could have considered. You can't do everything and, frankly, an overload of information may only serve to cloud your decision-making capabilities.

You also won't be able to forestall every fight or heal every hurt that the college admission process will engender. You can help, however, by heeding the suggestions above and in the pages that follow. You can also help by stepping back sometimes. Don't let college consume your lives. Make a dinner date with your spouse; take your son or daughter to a movie (if they'll be seen with you in public). Make a list of off-limit words like "application," "acceptance," and "SAT," and see who can get through a day (or a meal or a minute) without saying them.

One top prep school offered students a workshop on dealing with their parents during the college search, and the room was packed. Sadly, several seniors confessed that they thought their parents would love them less if they didn't choose to apply to—or weren't accepted at—Mom or Dad's top-choice college.

Remember, *wherever* your child ends up, it's likely to be a place with thousands of books and hundreds of computers, with swimming pools and squash courts, and three square meals a day on the table. So above all, enjoy the adventure.

CHAPTER 2

Choosing the Right College

➤ *THE GOOD NEWS:* Picking a college is, in some ways, like picking a mate. Finding the right match is all-important. Research alone is not enough; chemistry plays a big part, and exploring your options ought to be exciting.

➤ *THE BAD NEWS:* One out of every two marriages ends in divorce. Far fewer college students drop out or transfer due to discontent. (This is only bad news if you're married. If your child is off to college, it's more *good* news. The odds favor a successful choice.)

By the spring of your child's junior year, it's time to start thinking seriously about college choices (or at least to *sound* serious when you're actually completely clueless). Making good matches is, indeed, the most critical part of the selection and application process. In some respects, it's also the hardest. There are no formulas to follow. A lot depends on circumstance and serendipity, on legwork and on luck.

There are approximately 3,500 colleges in the U.S., and more than one will be right for your child. Your goal then should not be to find *the* college but to find *several* of the many places where your son or daughter can be happy and productive.

I. What Kind of School Am I?

Before deciding on which colleges to choose, you and your child should give some thought to what *type* of college you prefer. There are two-year schools and four-year schools, liberal arts colleges and universities. Some are public, which means that their fortunes are tied to the shirttails of state budgets. (Nearly 80 percent of all college students attend public institutions.) Others are private, supported by tuition, endowment, and the generous gifts of friends and alumni parents. Although many students mix and match and don't restrict their applications to only one type of institution, it's useful to have a hunch which way you're heading and to understand the differences you'll encounter.

Two-Year Colleges

Decades ago, almost all two-year schools were known as "junior colleges." Some were bastions of wealthy young women who bided time before marriage; others enabled far less well-heeled students to get a low-cost education close to home.

Today, two-year schools are known as junior, community, or technical colleges. Of the nation's more than 1,500 two-year institutions, about three-fourths are public, and their tuition is traditionally far lower than that of four-year schools. Most offer programs that can lead to transfer, as well as occupational programs designed to prepare students for careers in such fields as secretarial studies, automotive technology, or computer programming, which demand specific training beyond high school, but not necessarily a bachelor's degree. The associate's degree is awarded at such institutions, and it is the terminal—or highest—degree required in certain job fields.

Some (primarily private) two-year colleges have a selective admission process and require standardized test scores. Many others offer "open" (or "noncompetitive") admission to all applicants with a high school diploma or its equivalent. Be aware, however, that even noncompetitive schools may have academic prerequisites for certain departments. Technical majors or nursing programs, for example, usually require preparation in math or science.

Four-year colleges frequently flaunt their diversity as a selling point, but it is the two-year school that truly attracts students from wide-ranging backgrounds and of varying ages and ability. Two-year schools are ideal for students who are eager to get out into the working world quickly and for those who are reentering academia after time away. Flexible scheduling, convenient locations, and low costs can make them wise choices for those who must live at home, who have families of their own, or who hold full-time jobs.

They can also be a way for students who struggled, or *vacationed*, through high school to test the waters of college or to prove themselves before "trading up." In fact, although two-year colleges aren't for status-seekers, and you'll rarely find students wavering between Brown University and Bunker Hill Community College, they are often a first step to a more selective school. Some of the top private institutions in the country take transfers from community colleges and provide ample financial aid to applicants who would have never made it in as freshmen or who were scared off by the private school price tag.

Conversely, there are also stories like Peggy's. She attended an elite private high school, earned a B.A. at Stanford, but, years later, returned to a nearby community college to learn real-world skills in film production. As parents, don't limit your sites to *only* the local community college but, on the other hand, don't be too quick to dismiss it—or any two-year school—as an inappropriate choice for your child. For more information on two-year schools and programs, visit Web sites like http://www.cset.sp.utoledo.edu/twoyrcol.html, check out guidebooks like Peterson's *Two-Year Colleges*, or contact:

The American Association of Community Colleges
One Dupont Circle NW
Suite 410
Washington, DC 20036
Phone: (202) 728-0200
Web site: www.aacc.nche.edu

Liberal Arts Colleges

Although the liberal arts have been around at least since the days when Socrates held court at the old agora, parents and students are still often confused by the term. Some envision left-wing enclaves of aspiring sculptors, actors, or musicians. In fact, liberal arts colleges can be far from liberal and may provide only minimal instruction in the arts. They do, however, enable their students to sample from a wide range of disciplines, with the aim of preparing them to reason and to communicate based on the lessons of history and literature, philosophy and physics, and dozens of other disciplines. While not career-oriented in the strictest sense (e.g., no certificate programs in dental hygiene or criminal justice), liberal arts schools insist that today's changing high-tech world demands not narrowly trained specialists but thinkers and problem-solvers who have learned how to learn.

Whether or not you buy into this is up to you. You may still be sold on Arnold's accounting college or Selma's speech pathology studies. Even some liberal arts schools now hedge their bets by offering programs like engineering and journalism with a vocational ring to them. Yet, Latin majors go to law school, music majors work on Wall Street, and many of the nation's greatest leaders (as well as wealthiest business tycoons) are products of a liberal arts education. Liberal arts colleges are generally geared toward undergraduates, although some may offer graduate study, too (see "Major Dilemmas" later in this chapter).

Universities

A university usually includes a "school of liberal arts" but also offers other "colleges" with a more professional orientation (e.g., The College of Engineering, The School of Allied Health Sciences, or The School of Hotel Management), as well as programs of graduate study. On the plus side, universities often provide a range and sophistication of facilities that liberal arts colleges can't equal, along with the opportunity to take advanced-level graduate courses. On the down side, undergrads sometimes complain that they are an afterthought at universities where faculty research and graduate students take a front seat.

Questions & Answers

Q: There are schools we've never heard of that cost as much as Princeton. Is a private college a better investment than a public one?

A: Some parents assume that private schools are better than public schools because they cost more. Others wonder why anyone would pay exorbitant tuitions when state colleges abound. While many people seem to agree that big-name colleges can be worth the big-time bucks they require to attend, what about the lesser-known spots that still carry high sticker prices? Are they worth the price of admission? What about state schools in other states that up their fees for outsiders?

"There are no simple solutions," says college counselor Roger Eastlake. "Each student and family situation is different. The not-so-famous colleges don't usually have the same ability to offer the kind of financial aid that the well-known, well-endowed schools do. Still, are they worth scrimping and sacrificing for? One really has to look at intangibles and ask, 'Can this college provide a quality of life, a more personalized experience than its public equivalent? What will work best for *this* child?' Parents commonly say, 'Well, how is my child going to get a job after graduating from this college that nobody has heard of?' And I remind them that even the 'old boy network' isn't what it used to be. I try to guide students to select the most broadening experience possible, to find the greatest opportunity for growth, which in some cases may be at a private school and, in others, at a state college or university."

Claire and Joe spent more than $150,000 to send three children to college. Their oldest daughter thrived at Hartwick College, a competitive but hardly prominent private school in upstate New York, and then earned a master's degree in a prestigious graduate program. Next, their son was thrilled with his choice of Springfield College in Massachusetts, enjoying small classes and individual attention. The youngest child, however, did not like the costly college she attended and felt that her parents' money would go farther at a state school. "She transferred to the University of

Massachusetts and loved it," Claire recounts. "Each child is different. What's right for one isn't always right for the other. Sometimes we asked ourselves, 'Are we crazy to be spending this kind of money,' but looking back on the positive experiences our kids have had—and at the ten years of loan payments still ahead —neither of us has any regrets."

II. List Value: The Long and Short of It

To how many colleges should your child apply? Is three enough? Is six too many? It really depends. Some students have their sights set on only one school. If it seems like a sure thing and offers *Rolling* or *Early* Decision (see Chapter 6) so if the news is bad you'll have time to turn elsewhere, then there may be little need to file more than one application. On the other hand, students shooting for highly competitive schools may have to sow many seeds with the hope that at least one will blossom.

Your child should aim to apply to five or six colleges that include:

- One or two long-shot or "reach" colleges

- Two or three likelies (at least a 50 percent chance of acceptance)

- One sure thing or "safety school" (If this choice guarantees admission but not necessarily affordability, your child should apply to an additional "financial-aid sure thing.")

Admission expert Ed Wall, former dean of admission at Amherst College, Lawrence University, and The University of Southern California, college counselor, and author, has seen the process from every angle. He advises his charges that safety schools should always be those where they are "satisfied to go, if not deliriously happy."

In order to end up with a short list that looks something like the one above, your child should begin with a long list of 20 or so "target" colleges that you will then explore via publications, the Internet, campus visits, videos, etc. The long list should include both familiar schools as well as those that are discovered during the search.

Begin by brainstorming. Buy a notebook. We'll call it your "College Bible." Start a page for every school you want to consider. Make it a family affair. When it comes to creating a long list, there's no reason to go to war. If Junior is saying "Pepperdine," and Dad's saying "Panhandle State," put them both on the roster. (Maybe only one will make the short list later on; maybe neither will.) Don't try to fill up all the pages; save some for some unknown schools that may crop up later. This is not the time to be narrow minded. No matter how long Sam has been set on Santa Cruz or Mom has been touting Tennessee, it's important to explore a range of options, even if it's just to see how the first choice will stack up against the competition.

III. Identifying Target Colleges

Just what, exactly, are you looking for? How do colleges land on your list? If you haven't yet completed the questionnaire in Chapter 1, do so before continuing. Your child should fill it out as well. Examine the priorities that emerge from your answers. Consider inconsistencies. Perhaps your son wants to attend a large school but admits to being shy about asking for help. That's a sign that a small college may be a better match. If prestige is important but your daughter has only average grades, then status schools are going to be far reaches. In other words, be practical. Fantasy State may offer year-round golf on one edge of its campus and year-round skiing on the other. However, your child's college probably won't.

Location, Location, Location

One of the questions that demands your closest scrutiny is the "where" issue. It can be the most emotional of all college-related decisions. Parents are often torn between wanting their children to take advantage of exciting but faraway opportunities while, at the same time, hoping that Sunday family dinners won't be out of reach.

The key to deciding where a child should attend school lies in thinking about the reality of a choice. While it is a great learning experience to study in another part of the country, travel costs can be quite high, and it may be very lonely not to be home for Thanksgiving. Likewise, a week of camping out west was Stacy's favorite summer vacation, but at the University of Montana, where only about one-quarter of the student body comes from outside the state, Stacy, a Connecticut native, felt like she was in a foreign country. Scott, on the other hand, another New Englander and an avid outdoorsman, fit in right from the start. Before romanticizing distant schools, see how many out-of-staters attend, and consider how your child would adapt to being in the minority.

Other location points to contemplate: Is your child an urban animal or a country mouse? Even those who are psyched to try something new should anticipate a big adjustment. Ask too, "Where is this college *really* situated?" Alexis, from Illinois, applied to a Massachusetts school that appeared to be close to Boston on the map. In fact, it was nearly 50 miles away, with little public transportation—not exactly what she had in mind for an afternoon cappuccino in Kenmore Square.

And how far is not far enough? Joo-Hee chose a college less than two hours from her family. Every Friday, her parents would arrive in their station wagon, bring her home for the weekend, and return her to the dorm on Sunday night. "They just assumed that was what I wanted," she reflects, "and I never questioned it. If I had it to do over, I'd pick a school farther away and make myself have a campus social life. When I talk to friends now, I realize that I missed out on one of the most important parts of college."

Amy, on the other hand, went to school in her hometown in order to take advantage of a special scholarship for local students. She lived in a dorm, met classmates from all over the world, and usually even did her own laundry. "I saw my parents about once a month," she notes, "and I saw my hometown from a completely different point of view." Likewise, Lucy's parents couldn't afford to let her live on campus, but she took an active role in several clubs and practically camped out in the commuter lounge. After four years, she too felt she'd had an authentic college experience.

Again, be realistic. Will your child be able to establish her own identity by attending college nearby? Is going far away too much of a challenge for this child at this time?

Sizable Differences

A large university can be exciting—or impersonal. A small school can be supportive—or stifling. Among the most common reasons for transferring, size is near the top of the list, with "too big" and "too small" getting pretty even play. Small colleges commonly translate into smaller classes and more faculty contact. They can, however, be too homogeneous or lack specific curricular offerings. Large schools may offer opportunities such as editing a daily newspaper or studying Swahili that a smaller school can't equal. Extroverts and self-starters may thrive on a big campus. Students who are shy or who lack the self-discipline to work when there are endless temptations to do otherwise will probably be better served by a small college where they won't be as likely to fall through the cracks.

Reach or Realistic?

A list of target colleges shouldn't be top heavy with places that aren't likely to admit your child. When you start to consider a school, look carefully at its freshman profile. These profiles offer a range of statistics about an institution's entering class and are typically found in viewbooks and general guidebooks (see "Using Publications" later in this chapter), and often on Web sites as well.

Pay attention to grade point averages, class ranks, and test results. Compare the numbers with your child's grades and scores. Is this college a long shot? If accepted, will your child be at the top of the heap or burning the midnight oil to keep up? Selectivity ratings found in most general guidebooks are also an aid in evaluating schools you've never heard of before. Some of the most competitive colleges in the country, like Cooper Union, Rice, and Harvey Mudd, attract the same upper-echelon students as the Ivy League but with a fraction of the fanfare. However, be aware that selectivity statistics can also be misleading. The U.S. Coast Guard Academy, for example, accepts only approximately 9 percent of its applicants. Dartmouth takes more than twice as many at 21 percent, yet boasts average combined SAT scores that are about 150 points higher.

When comparing SAT scores, be aware that the tests were "recentered" in 1995, adding about 100 points to combined verbal and mathematical tallies (see Chapter 3). Using out-of-date freshman profiles can make what is really a long-shot school seem like a likely one. For example, a college that routinely welcomed students with verbal SAT scores of 580 prior to 1995 may expect scores of 650 on today's test. Some highly competitive colleges no longer require standardized test scores, but most still do—and they weigh them more heavily than many admission officials are willing to admit.

When compiling target colleges, it's important to not only be wary of colleges that are too competitive, but also of those that may not be competitive enough. A student whose grades and tests scores far surpass those on the freshman profile may end up unchallenged and bored. On the other hand, some students do best in less stressful environments.

Questions & *Answers*

Q: I've heard that a common (and painful) mistake that parents make is being too impressed by their child's achievements. My nephew Jeffrey was second in his high school class, president of the literary club, and first violinist in the school orchestra. His SAT scores were over 1500 yet, much to his family's surprise, he was denied admission to every Ivy League college on his list. What went wrong? Should I discourage my son from applying to such places?

A: There are a handful of colleges in this country—the Ivy League schools among them—that are so *hyperselective* that their offices of admission ought to be renamed offices of rejection. Parents who for years have puffed up with pride at a child's academic and extracurricular achievements are shocked when first-choice colleges say, "We're sorry..." in April.

It's easy to underestimate just how difficult it is to be admitted to these top schools. Columbia takes about one applicant in every seven; Harvard, one in nine. While the statistics alone don't seem too daunting, consider the fact that nearly *every* student who applies to such schools is pretty well qualified to attend. Harvard, in fact, receives more applications from valedictorians alone than there are places in the freshman class.

Your nephew may be what we call the "average outstanding kid." Yes, it may sound like an oxymoron, but the Ivy League colleges and a few others have their pick of the most accomplished high school students in the nation. Jeffrey was competing not only with other literary club presidents but also with virtually thousands of student government presidents, and with young musicians who may have been selected for orchestras on the state or even national level. Sure, his grades and scores were excellent, but at top colleges, that's simply expected.

Sadly, many high school students have their hearts set on only the Ivy League (or equivalent) institutions and they believe that if they do everything right, they'll get there. At this rarefied level, however, the outcome can be unpredictable. Jen and Jan, for example, were good friends and friendly competitors since grammar school. Jen was admitted to Brown, but not Wesleyan; Jan got into Wesleyan, but not Brown. Go figure.

If your son is an outstanding student and has other strengths and successes on his record, he should certainly be encouraged to apply to the most selective schools if he wants to. He should, however, also be encouraged to seek out those other colleges that may be slightly less competitive but which might meet his needs just as well as the Ivies will—if not better.

It's never a mistake to be impressed by your child's accomplishments. Parents with high-achieving children have every right to be proud, but those going through the admission process—especially for the first time—simply lack the perspective to realize just how many other strong contenders are out there.

Major Dilemmas

In choosing a college, academic offerings should be a key consideration. Yet one misconception (particularly among parents) is that a student must have a major in mind before applying. Too often, high school seniors are pushed into picking a direction before they are ready. Many simply have no idea of what they want to do, and even those with minds made up should have the freedom to change them. Ideally, college is a time when teenagers are exposed to new ideas and career options, and it's not surprising that the number of transfer students climbs every year, as would-be doctors become museum curators or physicists turn to film studies.

➤ **THE GOOD NEWS:** Many successful graduate school applicants and Ph.D. recipients selected their majors after nearly two (or even three) years of experimentation.

➤ **THE BAD NEWS:** Universities (and some colleges) may insist that students apply to specific "schools," departments, or programs. Admission to some areas is quite competitive, while others are scarcely selective at all. Years ago, canny candidates figured out that at many institutions it was wise to apply to undersubscribed departments and then to switch to the popular ones, once admitted. Today, however, that little maneuver can backfire. Such an "internal transfer" may be difficult. Always ask admission officials what a change of intended major will entail; don't expect to pull the wool over their eyes with the old bait-and-switch trick. Counting on an internal transfer is a dangerous game; hoping for one may make sense.

Another typical parental problem is the belief that if Junior does have a field in mind, it's the *wrong* one; that philosophy majors or classics majors aren't employable; that only areas like physical therapy, architecture, or computer science will evolve into jobs. In Arthur's family, though, the shoe was on the other foot. He hoped his son Joshua would follow in his footsteps to a small, prestigious liberal arts college, but Josh would only consider business schools. "My generation doesn't have the luxury of experimentation that yours did," he told his disappointed father. Fear not. Many studies show that college majors have only limited ties to career selection and success. Law schools love liberal arts graduates; advertising executives may have biology backgrounds.

Moreover, at most colleges, a major takes up only about one-third of the total number of courses that students elect over four years. Astronomers have time to take theater and dance; pharmacists study Shakespeare; social workers may learn Swedish. "I have been in both liberal arts environments and in large state universities that offer programs like business, engineering, and agriculture," explains Bill Wright-Swadel, director of career services at Harvard University, "and I've seen some students choose a major because it fits with a life goal that they pursue following graduation, while others choose a wide range of careers that their major does not predict at all. Commonly, other experiences like studying abroad, internships, and extracurricular activities may be more likely than the major to influence the first job choice after college."

As you identify target schools, you should certainly aim for those with academic offerings in fields that your child enjoys—or wants to try. Even students who haven't made major decisions are bound to know of *something* that intrigues them and which warrants a closer look (and, if not, it may be time to consider postponing college altogether). If you and your child have different opinions, state your case and then back off. It's fine to remind an aspiring engineer that she hated math and physics or to tell a diplomat-to-be that he dropped both French and German. But, as you read in Chapter 1, you must listen to your child's voice and honor your child's choices.

Asking Around

Don't underrate the rumor mill when it comes to getting suggestions for target schools. Ask not only guidance counselors and teachers, but also your boss or your babysitter, your daughter's tennis coach, or your son's scout leader. Anyone who's been to college or has sent a child to one, whose interests you share, or whose opinions you respect is fair game. "Why did Molly pick Barnard over Bennington?" "What does Don like about DePaul?" "How are the dorms at Denison?" "...the food at Fairfield?" "...the chemistry classes at Colby?" Other parents, especially, love to share war stories about the admission process (and what they'd do differently if they got to do it again), so take advantage of an insider's experience.

And listen to the scuttlebutt. Your hairdresser's niece is doing an internship at Ithaca; your neighbor's nephew at St. Lawrence just spent a semester in Nairobi; your aerobics instructor got a scholarship to Bard. It's an excellent way to familiarize yourself with lesser-known colleges and unusual opportunities, and if a school sounds good, put it on the long list.

Something Old, Something New

The majority of applicants eventually end up at colleges they have already heard of through siblings or schoolmates, through reputation or location, or by virtue of a school's athletic program *before* beginning the search process. Of course, choosing an institution simply because last year's class president or next year's NBA first-round draft choice goes there can be a mistake if the school has little to offer *your* child. Yet such subjective factors do play a part in decision-making and aren't necessarily bad. Having a "good feel" about a place to start out with is an important initial step, as long as it's not the *only* step. The best matches are made when students (and parents) spend time snooping beneath the surface of a school, so put the feel-good places on the list and then look further.

The Love Connection

In Megan's mind, choosing a college was easy. She just waited to see where her boyfriend planned to go and followed suit. Her parents were perturbed. Meg was a far better student than her boyfriend and would be limiting herself to less selective schools. They actually liked Meg's boyfriend but questioned the wisdom of getting tied down at 18.

As parents, you may have to expect that some schools will land on a target list only because they're where a heartthrob is heading. Our advice? Stay cool, for starters. Once your child has taken a closer look, these colleges may end up on the cutting-room floor. If not, and you see your child courting disaster, then you must step in. If the beloved is bad news, if the relationship means abandoning long-held goals, then you have to point this out carefully but insistently. Sometimes, it's what children actually hope to hear. They realize themselves that it's time to go their separate ways. But breaking up, as we all know, is hard to do. A push from Mom or Dad is sometimes what's needed to help a child make the choice that he or she really *wants* to make.

Yet, be assured that a surprising number of love connections do work out—one way or another. Meg (and her sweetheart) went to a college where she was at the top of her class, doing research with a professor as a freshman. Her boyfriend, however, was history by mid-terms, and Megan—armed with a 4.0 average—had no trouble transferring to a more competitive college the following fall. But she still won't let Mom and Dad say, "We told you so." "It was a good learning experience for me," is the most Meg will concede. "In the future I won't be so quick to let someone else dictate my plans," she explains, "and the confidence I developed from being a star student stayed with me even after I transferred."

Good Sports

Some parents encourage their children to put sports programs (and the opportunity to take part in them) at or near the top of the list when making college choices. Others, however, fear that athletics may crowd out academics in a student's life. Whatever your views, there are always extra considerations for student athletes who hope to compete on the college level—*so* many, in fact, that you'll find an entire section on this topic in Chapter 9, "Special Situations."

Religious Differences

Since many colleges and universities have a religious affiliation, it's important to evaluate where this fits into college plans. For a student with strong religious beliefs, a school where others share these views may be a wise choice.

Conflicts may erupt when parents insist that an unwilling child must choose a sectarian school, yet, sometimes the opposite is true. Patti, a member of the Church of Jesus Christ of Latter-day Saints, wanted to attend Brigham Young University with a majority of students from similar backgrounds. Her family, however, prevailed upon her to experience a more diverse community.

When considering an affiliated institution, it is important to be aware of special requirements (e.g., religion classes or mandatory chapel) and rules or restrictions. Don't summarily dismiss a school because its religious orientation is different than your own. Ask admission officials what percentage of students on campus practices the prevalent faith. How well are outsiders accepted? What activities and attitudes are affected by the affiliation? Moreover, a college may label itself "nonsectarian" and still have a population of predominantly one faith, so many of the same issues will apply there. Reading student newspapers can be an especially useful way to put your finger on the pulse of a campus climate.

Questions & Answers

Q: What special considerations are there, if any, for minority students (or their parents)?

A: Be aware that some colleges do more to *recruit* minority candidates than they do to *retain* them, and it's important for prospective students to get a sense of what campus life will be like *after* they enroll.

Deborah Wright, who has served as an admission official at several colleges, including Columbia, Smith, and Simmons, cautions minority students to get beyond the statistical answers and to probe into the attitude and "feel" of the campus. She counsels students to ask, "How involved are minority students in campus life? Are they running for office? Are they resident advisors? Are they active in a variety of student activities (and not just the Black Student Association, etc.)? Are they contributing to the community as a whole? Is it an *inclusive* or an *exclusive* community?

Admission offices can give you the names of minority students to contact, if you need them. While these individuals are likely to be "ringers" who speak well of their school, they also tend to be those who are articulate and knowledgeable about the institution. In addition, admission offices commonly have publications and other information that is directed at minority students. If you're interested, just ask.

Of course, the questions and needs of minority students are wide-ranging and are often influenced by differences in socioeconomic and educational background, by gender, and by rural or urban upbringing, among other distinctions. You should feel free to inquire about *your* specific concerns, such as the graduation rate of minority students, special scholarship opportunities, campus organizations, multicultural courses or programs, whether there have been racially motivated incidents (and how they have been handled), etc. Most admission counselors can answer your questions. You may, however, be referred to a staff member in charge of minority admission or to someone else on campus. You also might want to ask college officials and high school guidance personnel about special events for minority students, either on campus or in your community.

African-American families may want to explore one of the more than 100 historically black U.S. colleges. An important advantage of attending such a school is the opportunity to emulate successful role models. For example, writer Toni Morrison and former Supreme Court Justice Thurgood Marshall are both Howard University alums. Similarly, tribal colleges have been established on or near Indian reservations and offer undergraduate and graduate degree programs that help preserve Native American culture. Even if an entire college career at such an institution doesn't seem like the right choice, your child may want to consider an exchange program down the road.

These days, many minority students are savvy enough to know that minority status can help them be admitted to "reach" colleges, but some are overconfident about the power of race or ethnicity. Anna, for instance, is a Miami native and the daughter of a successful doctor who was born and raised in Spain. She speaks fluent Spanish and checked the "Hispanic" box on her college applications. Several of the schools on her list courted her actively by inviting her to minority-student events before offering her admission. Others, however (including her first-choice college), did *not* consider her under the "minority" rubric—and did not admit her either.

In order to help calculate your child's chances of admission to a target college, it is okay to ask officials if he or she will be considered a member of a minority group and, if so, whether special consideration is granted. Yet keep in mind that admission personnel may choose words carefully when responding to such questions, and you may need to read between the lines to decide if your child will indeed get a "hook" at this school at decision time. (see Chapter 7)

The Graduate School Factor

Ariana was attracted to Georgetown University because she thought that success as an undergraduate there might give her a boost when applying to the school's Foreign Service graduate program later. Jason, on the other hand, viewed Georgetown as "a great place to go to graduate school," so he decided to apply to smaller, less urban institutions for his first four college years.

It's not unusual for high school seniors to cite "graduate school" as a post-baccalaureate goal, although for many the details can be pretty hazy. While graduate school ambitions should rarely play a huge role in selecting an undergraduate college or university, some students and parents find it useful to take a peek down the road and evaluate how target college choices mesh with long-term educational plans.

Status-seekers, too, should take solace in the fact that a strong undergraduate record at a not-particularly-prestigious college can lead to acceptance into a top graduate program. Even the snazziest universities endeavor to fill graduate school slots with representatives from a range of undergraduate backgrounds. In many career fields, graduate school credentials are all-important, and prospective employers race through the undergraduate details on a résumé to see where advanced degrees were earned. Thus, some students are better served by spending their initial college years in a less competitive environment where they can make a mark and best position themselves for an array of graduate school opportunities.

IV. Using Publications

➤ *THE GOOD NEWS:* Publications provide an excellent way to investigate target colleges and to add new schools to a list.

➤ *THE BAD NEWS:* The amount of propaganda that besieges the college-bound student today is mind-boggling, and it's important to have a handle on how to use it and when to take it with a *block* of salt. It's also helpful to understand the different types of publications you'll encounter.

- **Search Pieces** are short brochures that admission professionals call "throw-aways." Gazillions of these teasers are sent out to high school students as a result of the "Student Search," which identifies prospective applicants from information provided on standardized admission test registration forms (more on this in Chapter 3). Colleges tell "Search" what qualities they're seeking (e.g., women from Wyoming, African-American applicants, anyone with scores above 1,300, anyone who's breathing...) and "Search" responds with a list (names and addresses; not specific test scores). Soon your mailbox is swollen with pithy pamphlets from all sorts of institutions. "At first I was flattered," recalls Gina, an

Oberlin alumna. "I thought these colleges especially wanted me. Then I found out that everyone was getting the same stuff, or similar."

Search pieces are invitations to investigate or apply; not guarantees of acceptance. They *are* worth a second look and can, indeed, introduce you to colleges you hadn't previously heard of or considered. Keep in mind, however, that many are created by marketing mavens who know more about advertising than education. The slick results are designed to entice teenagers and tend to make all schools—from Hiram to Hamilton; from Florida State to Bismarck State—seem strikingly alike. All boast of "caring, sharing faculty," "fine facilities," and "a place to learn and grow." Sound familiar? So, let the teasers whet your appetite, then turn to a guidebook (see below) or a guidance counselor, a current student or recent alum, to get another perspective.

- **Viewbooks,** commonly confused with *catalogs*, are glossy magazine-style publications—like search pieces, only longer. They're usually full of color pictures and often offer upbeat anecdotal information about grateful students who have been piloted to prosperity by the institution in question, along with profiles of those caring, sharing teachers who have sacrificed lucrative high-tech careers to lovingly mold young minds. Viewbooks can also be valuable exploration tools for readers who are sufficiently astute and cynical to corroborate their lavish claims through other sources.

- **Catalogs** are book-like bulletins that list and briefly describe course offerings, academic programs, admission and graduation requirements, tuition and fees, etc. More functional than folksy, catalogs are aimed at a school's students and staff, not specifically at applicants, but are indispensable to your decision-making. Many colleges post their catalogs online.

Typically, after first contacting a college to request information, your child will receive a search piece or viewbook. You may find that other materials (e.g., catalog, application) will follow automatically. If not, should the school seem promising, then phone or write (e-mail is handiest in most cases—more on that later) and ask to have them sent. If your child is aiming for a particular department within a university— e.g., nursing, agriculture—be sure to say so. Some such "schools" publish separate literature. High school guidance offices and public libraries are often a good place to find catalogs, too, though some may be a bit out of date.

As colleges today compete for candidates, literature seems to be among their growing arsenals. Many schools now produce a myriad of specialized brochures on topics ranging from science departments to campus security, from the career counseling office to the crew team. If a search piece or viewbook doesn't list additional brochure options, ask the admission office what's available. While you may feel that you'll drown in the deluge that follows, it could end up being the biochemistry booklet or the baseball brochure that really gets your child fired up about a college.

- **General Guidebooks** are sold in most bookstores and list facts and figures on nearly every institution in the country. Academic offerings, admission deadlines, acceptance rates, test score ranges, student activities, and so on can be seen at a glance.

While the proliferation of college Web sites has made most of this information available on the Internet, most students (and especially their parents) still enjoy the convenient one-stop-shopping that these general guidebooks provide. Look for titles like Peterson's *Four-Year Colleges* and Barron's *Profiles of American Colleges.*

Peterson's *College and University Almanac* fits right in a purse or pocket (well, a *large* purse or pocket) and is easier to carry from campus to campus than the larger guides. General guidebooks are updated regularly, but never take them as gospel, especially where admission requirements and deadlines are concerned.

Narrative-style general guidebooks are less complete than the statistic-packed gargantuan guides—typically covering *hundreds* rather than *thousands* of institutions—but they offer entertaining tips about professors, campus hangouts, popular courses, parties, and student stereotypes that make schools come alive in ways that their bigger brethren do not. Try *The Insider's Guide to the Colleges* (compiled by the staff of the *Yale Daily News*) or *The Fiske Guide to Colleges* by Edward B. Fiske.

There are also some fun-to-read options around that are perfect for the bathroom bookrack. For instance, *The College Finder*, by Steven R. Antonoff, provides list after list of diverse and often amusing categories, from "campuses where movies were filmed" and those boasting the "top college fight songs," to schools with the highest retention rates or best computer science programs. You can likewise locate colleges with kosher kitchens, racquetball scholarships, windsurfing programs, or top-rated marching bands. (Remember that quiz question on what your kid can't live without?)

- **Magazine Ratings.** And speaking of lists, magazines everywhere are coming out with their college hit parades, from *U.S. News and World Report*'s best *colleges* to *Kiplinger's* best *buys.* Many admission officials and guidance counselors are up in arms over such insistence on comparing colleges as if they were cars or clock radios and fanning the flames of competition among parents and student status-seekers. "The reason that high school counselors and college people are so upset is because these rankings interfere with the counseling process that is so important in making the right match between a student and an institution," maintains B. Ann Wright, vice president for enrollment at Rice University. "They throw all the data in and they crunch the numbers, and whatever comes out they print without regard to the intuitive understanding of what really should be involved at all."

Magazine lists should be kept in perspective. After all, the *Motor Trend* "Car of the Year" may not be the one you want or need, and you may not even fit comfortably in its driver's seat.

V. Using Computers

In some families, Mom or Dad is the computer whiz. In some, only the kids know where the "on" switch is and, in a few, there is little or no computer access at all.

➤ *THE GOOD NEWS:* Thanks to modern technology, those with even rudimentary computer skills can "visit" target colleges, register for standardized tests, seek scholarship assistance, correspond with admission offices, students, and instructors, check out library holdings, and access multimegabytes of data and details in minutes. Families without computers in their homes can often go online at public libraries or in high school guidance offices or computer centers.

➤ *THE BAD NEWS:* There is now so much information readily available via the Internet that an already formidable process can become more overwhelming. How much time do busy high school seniors, or their parents, really have to e-mail prospective professors at target colleges, digest menus at a dozen dining halls, or take part in online chat sessions with dorm advisors and debate club presidents? And a student who gets lost in cyberspace may not earn the grades that first-choice colleges expect.

It would take an entire book to discuss all of the ways to use computers to help your child choose and apply to colleges (and if you want such a book, check out The College Board's *Internet Guide for College-Bound Students,* by Kenneth E. Hartman).

In typical households, students are at their keyboards far more than their parents are during the college search and application process, but even moms and dads who find that checking e-mail is a challenge (never mind downloading those attachments!) can get help on the Internet in several ways.

Home Pages and Web Sites

The vast majority of colleges and universities have their own Web sites that can be useful when choosing and exploring target colleges. From an institution's home page, you are sure to be able to link to information that might otherwise take weeks to arrive in the mail, like admission requirements, course descriptions, enrollment statistics, etc.

Especially helpful to parents making travel plans, Web sites usually list tour and information-session schedules, along with details about special programs for prospective students. However, it's always wise to double-check details by telephone before your itinerary is finalized, especially during college vacations (more on this in Chapter 4).

Many Web sites provide access to student (and often faculty and staff) publications, information about alumni, etc. They may also include lists of student organizations and, sometimes, links to the organization's home page. It's not uncommon for Web sites to provide e-mail addresses for the office of admission, academic departments, student organization leaders, etc., and many offer direct links to applications that can be completed electronically. (Computer application information is in Chapter 6.)

One private school college counselor tells the story of a student from Saudi Arabia who was at odds with his father about his first-choice college. The son wanted to attend the University of Rochester. Dad was pushing for Boston University, which he felt would offer more opportunities to be with other Arab undergraduates and to practice the Islamic faith. The son, however, had no trouble convincing Dad to come around once he accessed the University of Rochester's home page. From there he found links to information for Muslim students that even included menu offerings and prayer schedules.

Likewise, if *your* child comes home one day with a list of unfamiliar institutions, a quick trip to your computer can offer almost instant gratification and may help you become comfortable with your child's choices. Conversely, if you're having trouble convincing Junior that his favorite college isn't really right for him, the Internet may provide corroboration once he sees its foreign language requirement or mandatory senior thesis glowing on the screen.

While a college's Web site usually features pretty campus pictures (often an entire virtual tour) and some of the same statistics found in general guide-books, once you go beyond these, you'll be getting closer to the institution's real flavor. Student newspaper headlines, sports team highlights, fraternity and sorority happenings, local weather reports, and so on all reveal a bit about a place's personality. In addition, you may find links to departmental and faculty home pages that include news about specific courses and even syllabi. Student home pages are often accessible, too. These are likely to be entertaining—albeit rarely objective—looks at a college and its community.

Home page addresses (and, usually, e-mail addresses) can be found in viewbooks (and other admission office propaganda), in most up-to-date general guidebooks, or by calling admission offices. You can also visit your favorite search engine and type in the name of the school whose site you're seeking.

Most Internet aficionados know they have a good shot at finding a college on the Web by typing "www" followed by a dot, the college's name, another dot and then "edu." (Ithaca College, for example, can be found at www.ithaca.edu) but you may waste a lot of time that way (The University of Pennsylvania is at www.upenn.edu, which you'd not likely figure out on your first attempt), and if you're aiming for a place with a common name such as Saint Joseph's, you could easily arrive miles away from your intended destination. (www.sju.edu will take you to Pennsylvania, but if you try www.saintjoe.edu, you'll end up in Indiana)

More reliable are the numerous sites that provide lists of thousands of institutions and direct links to their home pages. Try a couple of these and add a "bookmark" to the one you like best. Keep in mind, however, that e-mail and Web site addresses can change. Those listed here were accurate when this book went to press.

- **www.petersons.com**

  Click on "Colleges and Universities" and then on "CollegeQuest." The handy "Name Search" allows you to type in the name of just about any college you can think of, and you'll get a link to that school's home page and, in many cases, to an online application and to an e-mail address for the admission office.

- **www.collegeboard.com**

  In addition to links to home pages and applications, this site offers a "LikeFind" function that identifies other colleges that are similar to the one you selected, as well as a "Compare" option that highlights the differences in several categories between two (or three) colleges that you choose.

- **www.mit.edu:8001/people/cdemello/univ.html**

This thorough, no-nonsense list enables you to link to college and university homepages. You can choose to view schools alphabetically or by state. The latter can be especially helpful to those with strong geographic preferences.

- **www.utexas.edu/world/univ/**

This site also offers alphabetical and state-by-state listings and includes U.S. community colleges.

- **http://geowww.uibk.ac.at/univ/**

Locate links to nearly 6,200 institutions in more than 160 countries. Even if your child will never study in Albania or Andorra, Togo or Tanzania, this site makes one realize that the World Wide Web is indeed worldwide.

- **www.universities.com**

This dizzying list leaves no school unturned. From Haagse Hogeschool (it's in Holland) to the His and Hers School of Hairstyling (Wasilla, Alaska), you'll find links to every place a kid might pick up a pencil after high school.

Matches Made in Cyberspace

Too many choices? Don't know where to start? There are also a number of Web sites that students and parents can use to help find colleges with particular traits (e.g., a Slavic studies department, an enrollment under 1,000, a location in the southwest, etc.). Your child enters specific interests and aims, and the computer spits back target schools. This is a good way to add new possibilities to the list but don't trust a machine to decide what really turns a person on. Moreover, computer-generated lists are rarely complete. Never eliminate a college just because it didn't show up in a cybersearch.

The Web sites listed below are among those that provide search services. Most offer other features, too, such as bulletin boards and chat lines, career and major data, and even off-to-college packing tips for when all of this is over.

- **Peterson's (www.petersons.com)**

    In addition to the "Name Search" described above, try a "Detailed Search." You'll respond to questions about preferred size, location, diversity, etc. and then reap a roster of colleges that might fit your needs.

Peterson's "Keyword Search" will provide a list of institutions that offer an area of particular interest. This works best for very specific choices. "Biology," for example, produced well over 2,000 options—far too many to explore. Even "Wildlife Management" netted 221. Keywords need not be limited to academic areas. You can use this search to find colleges with badminton teams or skating rinks, Model United Nation organizations or merit-aid scholarships.

- **College Board Online (www.collegeboard.com)**

    This matchmaking tool is similar to Peterson's "Detailed Search." Click on "Finding the Right College" or "College Search" when you reach the home page and respond to a list of questions. *Hint:* Too many preferences can lead to a "No Matches" conclusion. Eliminate a preference or two and your options may multiply.

- **The Princeton Review (www.review.com)**

    The "Counselor-O-Matic" helps students determine where they'll get in. (If you can't find it easily, click on the "Site Map.") Based on responses to a questionnaire that takes about 10 minutes to complete, the Counselor-O-Matic responds with a list of "Reach," "Good Match," and "Safety" schools. (There are no guarantees, of course, but it's fun. It's also a reasonable reality check for those who are aiming for tip-top colleges.)

Something for Everyone

If you've already explored some of the sites above, you've seen that many of them offer a wide range of additional services. The Peterson's site, for example, enables students to complete a "Colleges Want You" profile to elicit attention from potential target schools that you haven't yet considered. The College Board's extensive information includes a section aimed just at parents.

Below are several other sites that offer one-stop-shopping for the college bound student. Each offers a feature or two that is uniquely its own.

- ***U.S. News and World Report* (www.usnews.com/usnews/edu/college)**

    You'll find those controversial rankings here, of course, along with most of the other standard stuff (home page links, matchmaking questionnaire, etc.)

- **College Confidential (www.collegeconfidential.com)**

  College Confidential is a well-organized site with responses to many frequently asked questions, along with some you probably never thought to ask but might want answered anyway. While there is a sales pitch for their personal counseling business, it's not heavy handed.

- **College View (www.collegeview.com)**

  This site includes a special-interest section with such links as "Search for a Canadian University" or "Discover the Benefits of a Christian College."

- **National Association for College Admission Counseling (www.nacac.com)**

  The NACAC is really an organization for those on the other side of the admission office desks, but the "Parents and Students" section provides links to many resources, including college fair dates and locations.

- **College Link (www.collegelink.com)**

  College Link offers plenty of anecdotal search and application tips ("Small school blues," "Navigating the interview waters"), written by current college students and admission professionals. However, this site is best known as a jump-off point for students using its online application service.

Questions & Answers

Q: Won't all these online searches and other services cost us as much as a college education?

A: Don't worry, most of these services offer *free* advice—although sometimes you get what you pay for. Typically, it's the subscribing colleges and universities (and often an assortment of for-profit advertisers) that assume the costs of maintaining the sites. Sometimes site sponsors hope that students will be enticed to sign up for their courses, software, books, and other products after checking out the freebies on the Web.

In the earliest era of the Internet, when connections were usually sold by the hour, it was easy to run up a hefty tab during the college search process. These days, with flat fees and free hook-ups, the biggest cost to college applicants is likely to be their *time*. There's a lot of college-related information on the Internet that's more entertaining than it is essential.

Talk Is Cheap

If your child is a regular Internet user, chances are, he or she has already found ways to "talk" with peers via chat rooms and bulletin boards. Some of these are designed specifically for college-related subjects. Many colleges and universities, for example, take part in the Daily Jolt (www.dailyjolt.com). Anyone can select a school from the Jolt membership roster and log onto its site to check out topics that can include everything from dormitory floor plans to catchy faculty quotes. School searchers can eavesdrop on Jolt chats to see what campus topics are hot or can chat as guest users to ask current students about their school.

Go to www.collegeconfidential.com to find an easy-to-navigate, well indexed discussion site that focuses specifically on admission-related issues. (It's not just full of rumors and remarks from other perplexed parents and their kids. The College Confidential-facilitator pros weigh in regularly.)

Keep in mind, of course, that encouraging such behavior is tantamount to giving a teenager license to spend even *more* time than usual on the telephone. Remember, too, that many of the heard-it-through-the-grapevine responses espoused via the Internet will be subjective or, in some cases, downright inacurate.

"E" Is for Easy

E-mail is another way to communicate with college officials and students. Many wise parents have discovered that linking to admission office e-mail addresses can mean less tension at home. In lieu of nagging junior for weeks to find out whether tours are held on holidays or if all application materials have been safely received, Mom or Dad can fire off a quick message instead. E-mail is especially handy for answers to questions that may be specific to your situation. Don't worry about annoying admission officials with your queries, but do allow several days for replies.

Avid e-mailers may also contact faculty members, student organization leaders, health service professionals, etc. If addresses aren't available at a school's Web site, try calling the office of admission and ask, "Could you please give me the e-mail address of a student majoring in art history" or "... a freshman living in Parker Hall," "...a faculty member in the chemistry department," etc. When you can't get to campus, some of the questions listed in Chapter 4 may also be asked electronically. Again, the danger here is that students (or parents) can spend a lot of time gathering information that is very subjective and not always representative of the real scoop at target schools.

Et Cetera

As you continue to read this book, you'll learn other ways computers can be part of the college search. For example, in Chapter 3 you'll find out how to register for standardized tests and answer practice questions online. In Chapter 4, you'll make "virtual visits" to campuses. In Chapter 5, you can learn how to determine your financial aid eligibility and locate scholarship sources, and in Chapter 6 you'll see that there are a number of ways to apply to colleges online.

How much use is made of these options will depend largely on your child's computer access and interest level. And for those of you like us, who were born when Howdy Doody was considered a technological marvel, rest assured that it's still perfectly possible to complete the entire college admission process without ever touching a keyboard.

VI. Comparing and Contrasting

So what do you do when your pile of propaganda starts to resemble the Sears Tower? First, put it all in one place. If you haven't done so already, designate a specific and out-of-the-way spot for all of the books and forms that will be multiplying over the months to come. (In addition, several of the multi-purpose Web sites, such as www.petersons.com, include a section where students can store their online research results.)

As you and your child sort through your publications pyramid, save those (whether solicited or not) from colleges that seem appealing—recycle the rest. (Super-organized applicants start a folder for each college they're considering. It's a handy spot for catalogs, viewbooks, correspondence, etc.)

Now turn to a general guidebook for some cold, hard facts that may confirm—or refute—the pretty pictures and flowery prose. Do you want a diverse community? Politically correct brochure photos (often staged for recruitment reasons) can be misleading. Guidebooks will give enrollment breakdowns such as minority populations and in-state residents. Does your child expect to live on campus? Get housing options and availability from the guides.

Check also for special features such as study abroad opportunities, cross-registration with nearby colleges, pass/fail plans, and ROTC. Honors programs are a good way for outstanding students to find each other at a large university. Accelerated programs, like one offered by Coe College in Iowa, enable strong students to earn a bachelor's degree in just three years (a good money-saver for Mom and Dad). Syracuse University, on the other hand, has an unusual bachelor's of architecture program that takes five years to complete. A number of universities feature "3-2" options in such areas as engineering or business that allow participants to whiz through undergraduate *and* graduate school in five years.

"Student Life" sections of guidebooks include information on extracurricular activities, social calendar highlights, and telling statistics (e.g., how many students join sororities or participate in organized athletics).

Better yet, if you have the time and opportunity, go beyond the guidebooks and ask students at target schools how things *really* work. Whether you're visiting on campus or chatting in person, by telephone, or e-mail, the "Questions for Students" in Chapter 4 may give you some ideas of what to ask. (But beware— no single individual can speak for the experiences of an entire student body.)

While you've got your noses in the general guidebook—or your fingers on the keyboard—try to pick out new places to add to the target list. For instance, if Junior is keen on California, chances are he's heard of Stanford and UCLA, but how about Whittier or Occidental? Guidebooks are usually cross-referenced by state and size and selectivity—sometimes by academic offerings. Look for priority categories and see what clicks. The Internet can help you to conduct searches by major, location, etc., despite the limitations discussed in "Using Computers."

Now take out the questionnaires you completed in Chapter 1. What about those things your child can't live without? At which target colleges will you find them? In what other ways do target schools live up to the dreams of Fantasy State? Above all, look carefully at selectivity ratings and freshman profiles to gauge your child's chance of admission (see "Reach or Realistic?" earlier in this chapter).

Sooner or later, some schools are going to cry out, "I could be the one," while others will start to pale in comparison. Go back to your "College Bible"— that notebook where the target list was born. Encourage your child to use its pages to make an "exploration sheet" for every school that is still in the running. Otherwise, here's another job for *you*. Make sure that one page is labeled for all schools still being considered. Now add each mailing address and phone number (Web site and e-mail addresses are helpful, too), followed by "Dates to Remember" (deadlines, interview appointments, etc.). Below that, make two columns—one for pros (e.g., marine biology department, internship program, near Aunt Elaine) and one for cons (e.g., too big or expensive, foreign language requirement, near Aunt Elaine). Save the rest of the page (and the reverse side, if needed) for contact records and notes. (e.g., "Oct. 15: spoke to Ms. Muldoon, asst. dean of admission. She said okay to take SAT II in Jan.") This format, of course, isn't carved in stone (and doing it all on a PC may be a better choice for you), but you will surely find that life is simpler and more pleasant when all data and doodles are kept together.

VII. Getting Guidance: Public and Private School Counselors

Typical public school counselors handle hundreds of students with wide-ranging needs. Counselors must be equally informed about the Armed Forces and the Ivy League, music conservatories and hair-styling academies. They deal with scholarship opportunities and unplanned pregnancies, suicide prevention and drug dependency—all on any given morning.

➤ *THE GOOD NEWS:* Many are superheroes. They do all of it well.

➤ *THE BAD NEWS:* Unfortunately, due to budget cuts, some high schools have no guidance counselors at all; some have too few who carry unrealistic loads (and a handful are just downright inept).

Even in private schools, where loads are lighter and may be limited to admission advising alone, the situation can be far from ideal. Here, college counselors range from among the very best in the business to inexperienced, untrained generalists who may be teaching eighth-grade English and sophomore Spanish at the same time. Some private school counselors face pressure from administrators who insist that a list of acceptances to prestige colleges is the most important report card by which their institution will be judged, and from parents who insinuate that a thumbs-up from a big-name school is the reward they deserve for years of tuition bills.

No matter where your child goes to school, it is up to *you* to evaluate the strengths and weaknesses of the available guidance counseling and to participate in the admission process.

Questions & Answers

Q: What can parents do to get the most from school counselors?

A: **Have realistic expectations** about what is available to you and your child through the guidance counselor. If the counselor is not willing or able to go further than shepherding students through standardized test registration and distributing federal financial aid forms, you will have to take an aggressive role in the college search. If, on the other hand, the guidance counselor...

- offers thorough suggestions about college selection, application completion, and deadlines;

- is well informed about a range of institutions and urges students (and parents) to explore those they may not have heard of or considered;
- gives a realistic assessment of acceptance but doesn't discourage application to "dream" schools; and
- provides thorough financial aid information and doesn't insist that expensive colleges are only for rich folks.

Then you can relax and take a back seat.

"Travis had planned to apply to several state colleges," says his mother, Joanne. "His father and I knew little about other options, ourselves, but the school counselor pointed out two quite selective colleges that had academic merit-aid programs. She called both to see if Travis' grades and test scores would make him a contender, and the answer was yes. She also helped him fill out the required paperwork. I'd been told in advance by other parents that we'd lucked out and gotten the best counselor at the high school, and she certainly lived up to those expectations."

John, the father of another high school graduate, realizes now that he *assumed* his daughter's counselor would be taking a more active role than she did. "Perhaps because Kate was in a private school," he reflects, "I expected her counselor to make suggestions about where Kate should attend college and then monitor the process to be sure that deadlines were being met. With hindsight, I'd sit down with the counselor at the start and outline the responsibilities each of us would have. For example, someone has to play the 'heavy,' to make sure that the 17-year-old is getting everything completed on time. Someone should be reading the essays to see if they say what they should, and in an interesting way. Someone has to be deciding which schools should stay on the list and which shouldn't. I think the whole thing would have worked better for us if each of our roles and duties had been clearer from the outset."

Because guidance counselors' abilities and availability vary so widely, it's up to you, the parents, to determine how much support and useful information you will be getting.

Don't play hooky on Parents Night. Sure, the coffee is lousy and you'll have to endure endless questions from other parents who are far more panicked than you are, but even in the fanciest high schools, counselors simply do not have the time to repeat general information to everyone who stayed home to watch *Wheel of Fortune.*

Schedule a conference, if you feel you need one. While this is protocol at most private schools, at public schools it's often only for those who take the initiative. Most guidance counselors welcome parent appointments, but even good schools rarely have the staff to routinely contact every parent. If you don't arrange a conference, visit the guidance office to find out what resources are available: catalogs, guidebooks, computer software, etc.

Ask for a school profile. When sending transcripts to college admission offices, guidance staff enclose a brief "school profile" that details the curriculum available and explains the grading system at your child's high school. Profiles also commonly include information about the community in which the high school is located, the percentage of students who go on to college, where they go, etc. By reading through your child's school profile, you will learn what information admission offices will receive—and what they won't. For example, if British Literature is an Advanced Placement course at your child's school, is that clearly stated on the profile?

Ask your counselor to alert colleges to situations that may not be obvious from a transcript. If a standard-sounding course (e.g., earth science) is really one of the toughest on the roster, admission offices won't figure it out for themselves. If Mr. Snurd, the chemistry teacher, is convinced that C is a "to-die-for" grade, the counselor should be certain to put Brian's B- in perspective for Princeton.

Alert your counselor to situations that he or she might not be aware of that affect your child's school performance. The more candid you can be with your counselor about a messy divorce, a chronically ill sibling, and other home-grown problems that your child may be struggling with, the better the counselor can present your child's transcript to target colleges.

Don't be a pain in the you-know-what. Use good judgment to decide how often to contact guidance counselors. Although it is up to you to call counselors with questions or concerns (and don't wait by the phone for them to call *you*), do be sensitive to their unwieldy workloads. If you think you require a symbiotic relationship with a counselor, consider hiring an independent consultant. (See below.)

The other fine line that parents must tread is in recognizing that *good* guidance counselors really *do* know their stuff. Don't expect them to spin straw into gold. One of the worse things you can do to sabotage the entire process and to undermine your child's esteem is to insist on an unrealistic list of target schools. Be open to suggestions from the counselor, even if Stanford and Yale aren't among them.

VIII. Who Are Independent Counselors and How Do You Know If You Need One?

Also called Independent Educational Consultants, these individuals offer private, in-depth, college admission advice to students and their families...for a fee.

➤ *THE GOOD NEWS:* "Parents want unlimited and instantaneous access to information, and we provide that," maintains Jane Gutman, a Los Angeles independent educational consultant. "Even private school counselors have other duties and can't always be available. Our clients can pick up the phone any time."

➤ *THE BAD NEWS:* "Independents" are pricey. Top-of-the-liners can charge as much as $5,000 for conducting a complete college search. (One New York City big-wig charges $30,000 for her premier package!) Even on the low end, expect to shell out close to $1,000. Some counselors will provide pay-as-you-go services. Figure on about $100/hour for their advice. Many do offer pro bono work, but often only to those in dire straits. "The students who most need outside help—those in public schools where counseling budgets have been severely cut back or curtailed—are usually the ones who can't afford us," admits Gutman. The bulk of her clients attend private schools.

Independent counselors offer advice, not inside tracks to highly selective schools. Joan Dorman Davis, who served the Seattle area as an independent counselor for nearly two decades, spoke for many of her colleagues when she explained, "Sure, many of my clients apply—and are admitted—to the handful of colleges that are the toughest to get into, but my job is broader than that. I help protect kids from heartbreak, from operating under the assumption that top grades, test scores, and extracurriculars mean certain admission everywhere. I'm like a big red stop sign, constantly saying, 'Yes, you're good, but what if you don't make it? Let's see what else is out there.' Some of my most satisfied clients have gone to colleges I introduced them to."

Questions & Answers

Q: How does one pick a qualified consultant?

A: "Choose your independent consultant the way you would pick a physician or a lawyer," suggests Bill Risley, an east coast private educational consultant with a national clientele. "Ask around; get referrals from other parents." If you're stuck for leads, the **Independent Educational Consultants Association** (3251 Old Lee Highway, Suite 510; Fairfax, VA 22030; phone: (703) 591-4850) is a good place to start. They will send you a free directory of member counselors nationwide. Faster still is its Web site, www.educationalconsulting.org, through which you can view members' names by specialty or state.

"But," cautions Risley, "there are an awful lot of tinkerers and moonlighters out there. Even professional association membership doesn't assure quality. Ask for references and check them out thoroughly. Talk to prospective consultants before signing on to make certain that the chemistry is right." Risley suggests asking these question before choosing a consultant:

- **What related job experience have they had?** The best independent consultants have often done time as college admission officers and high school guidance counselors. Others claim qualifications as questionable as "I got both my kids into Brown."
- **How often and extensively do they visit campuses?** Risley insists that the best independent counselors visit up to 100 schools each year, not only seeing admission offices and facilities but haunting student hangouts to get the real scoop from insiders. "When a counselor suggests a college for your child," he advises, "the first question you should ask is 'Have you been there?'"
- **How else do they stay current?** Does the counselor attend meetings of the National Association of College Admission Counselors (NACAC) or other professional groups? What else does he or she do to keep up with changing trends in the business?
- **What is their specialty?** Educational consultants often offer wide-ranging services. If you ask them for their area of expertise, they'll ask you what you're after. Testing for a dyslexic third grader? Vocational training for a mentally handicapped teen? You want it, they've got it. Some consultants, especially in urban areas, focus on private elementary or high school placement. Make sure the expert you hire is a *college* specialist.
- **What promises do they make?** Good counselors give guidance, not guarantees. They make matches, not miracles, and they won't fill out your child's application form or write his or her essay because they're smart enough to realize that colleges will be onto them if they do.

Do you "need" an independent counselor? That's sort of like asking if you *need* a chauffeured limousine. In other words, it's nice to have someone taking you where you want to go with minimal hassle, but it's also a luxury that most families do okay without. So here are a few more questions to ask before you decide:

- Can you afford the additional expense?
- Do you feel like you require guidance that you're not getting elsewhere?
- Are the colleges that your school counselor suggested for your child *either* much less selective or much more so than those on your own list? Are the school counselor's suggestions significantly different in other ways: size, location, academic programs, etc.? (Some families find that a good private consultant will broaden a list offered by an inexperienced or limited school official. Other families, however, need to hear from yet another party that their own ideas are off base.)
- Do you need a mediator? "An independent consultant can prove essential in preserving family peace," maintains Miami-based counselor

Frances Yelen. "For example, if I tell a student that an essay requires a lot more thought and must be rewritten, the student usually thinks about it and rewrites it. If a parent says that to a student, the result is often a police action, if not an outright war."

- Have you already found a private counselor—either through reputation, recommendations, or your own research—who seems like a good match for your family?

If you answered "yes" to two or more of the questions above (especially the big one at the top of the list) then you may want to consider seeking the assistance of an independent college consultant.

Q: We can't find a private counselor nearby. What should we do?

A: While it's helpful to hire a consultant with an office near your home, many of the top guns, says Risley, work with families from afar. "I expect one face-to-face meeting," he explains, "but after that, everything else can be done by phone, fax, and e-mail. Young people these days are especially comfortable with electronic communication, even if their parents are not."

In fact, some independent college counseling services rely *only* on Internet communication. For instance, College Confidential (www.collegeconfidential.com) offers services that range from a "Stats Evaluation" (i.e., Where will your child's GPA, test scores, and writing skills make the grade?) for under $100 to a complete two-year advising package for about $1,500. There's even an "Ivy Guaranteed Admissions Program," for a select few. The fee, around $5,000, is refundable to those who don't get into one of two first-choice colleges. If your son or daughter is a star (and you read all the fine print), it's not a bad bet.

College Confidential counselor Dave Berry rarely meets his clients but insists that, as a "compulsive e-mailer," he's never far from a keyboard. "I'm constantly available to respond to parents and students," insists Berry, co-author of *America's Elite Colleges* (Random House), "whether they need to 'discuss' a major problem or just want to know if they can drive from Princeton to Haverford in a day. And the asynchronous rhythm of e-mail is the ultimate convenience. Mom may get home from a meeting at 10:30 at night with a question on her mind. She can sit down at her computer and write me, and she'll have an answer in the morning. " While Berry doesn't dismiss the value of personal contact, he notes that, for many families, his service is more affordable and pragmatic.

As high school counseling budgets decline and computer comfort-levels soar, expect to see such online services proliferate. If having a knowledgeable pen pal throughout the admission process lowers your stress level and fits your budget, don't dismiss Internet counseling as just another cyberscam. Do, however, carefully check out the credentials of anyone who will be advising you or your child.

CHAPTER 3

Testing, Testing

"We survived sleep-away summer camps and cheerleading try-outs; glasses, braces, drivers' ed, and the purple-haired prom-date-from-hell. But nothing upset the family equilibrium more than the day that Daria received her SAT scores."

"Miles agreed to take the tests because the guidance counselor says he's supposed to, but he insists he's not even going to try to do well and won't apply to any schools that require them. I think he's limiting his options, but he refuses to listen. I also think that he's terrified, and he is immunizing himself—and us— against disappointment."

"We had been warned to play the SAT thing real cool. I figured that if I didn't make a big deal about it, then Kevin wouldn't get all tied up in knots either. Wrong! He was putting all sorts of pressure on himself, and when I tried to tell him to relax, that it was only a test, he said, 'Get a life, Mom.'"

Every year, about two million high school students take SAT exams and almost as many take ACTs. Some take both. By the time a student arrives at an authorized test site, clutching sharpened number 2 pencils in sweaty palms, most families have already experienced the tension and apprehension; the myths and misgivings that the notorious process produces.

Decades ago, when standardized entrance testing was conceived, one goal was to create a more democratic system so that candidates from little-known public high schools could compete with those from the celebrated academies where a headmaster's handshake or the proper pedigree were passports to a big-name college career. Ironically, however, what was once intended to *open* doors is now capable of *shutting* them—on many bright, ambitious applicants whose numbers alone aren't up to snuff.

Through all of the hopes and heartaches you have shared with your child—basketball playoffs or ballet recitals, student council elections or state orchestra selections—you have undoubtedly learned that parenthood hardly grants you the power to shield those you love from humankind's incessant reminders of inequalities and insufficiencies. So, too, may the SAT or ACT tests separate your son from his favorite cousin, your daughter from her closest friend.

There are, however, measures you can take to assure that the testing process is approached in a positive frame of mind. The pages that follow address what parents most want to know about college entrance exams. So, learn what you can about test scores and how they are used, what you can do to affect them, and what you can't. Separate rumor from reality and then... relax. After all, *you're* not the one who has to take the darn things.

I. The PSAT/NMSQT

This is a test that is routinely administered to students in October of their junior year, and is frequently a family's first brush with college admission examinations.*

The PSAT/NMSQT has several purposes. They are:

- To serve as a practice or warm-up for subsequent SAT testing

- To give students, parents, and counselors some indication of future SAT performance

- To determine eligibility for several scholarship programs discussed below, including the prestigious (but not typically well-paying) National Merit Scholarships. (Their qualifying test is the "QT" part of this exam's title.)

- To allow students and colleges to find each other through the Student Search Service, also discussed below

Early in your child's junior year, PSAT/NMSQT registration information (the *Student Bulletin*) should be distributed in school. The test will ordinarily also

---

* In some parts of the country, the ACT Assessment (and its preliminary test, PLAN) are administered in most schools in lieu of the SAT program. These tests will also be discussed in this chapter.

A growing number of schools give the PSAT (or PLAN) as early as junior high as a method of evaluating their own effectiveness—not as a college admission tool. Similarly, some programs (e.g. the Johns Hopkins Talent Search) use SAT scores to select participants. If your child has results from such tests, do your best to ignore them when you begin the college search process.

be given right in your child's school, usually during a school day; sometimes on a Saturday. (Home-schooled students who wish to take the PSAT can arrange to do so at a local high school.)

PSAT/NMSQT Scores

In December, scores will be mailed directly to your child's high school and distributed to students along with an explanatory booklet. Students will receive separate scores for verbal and mathematical test components. New since your day, too, is a PSAT Writing Skills component, so students now get *three* scores, not just two.

The scores range from 20 to 80, designed to correspond to the SAT score scale of 200 to 800. Thus, by adding a zero to the verbal and math PSAT scores, you will get a rough approximation of future SAT results. Nationwide average PSAT/NMSQT scores for high school juniors are typically in the high 40s—just shy of the midpoint of 50— in each of the three skills areas, but your region (or school) may post very different results.

Note that in the fall of 1994, the scoring of PSAT tests was "recentered," adding roughly 10 points to a typical student's combined verbal and math tally. (SAT scores were recentered in spring 1995.) Recentering is explained more thoroughly in the SAT section in this chapter.

➤ **THE GOOD NEWS:** Colleges do not use PSAT results as admission criteria. Good scores can help to take the trauma out of upcoming SAT tests. Poor scores may help identify weaknesses in time to remedy them or, at least, to take some of the sting out of sad SATs. (You will read more about SAT preparation at the end of this chapter.) PSAT scores usually improve due to what is known as "maturation." In other words, by the time the SAT I is taken, the student is more aware of what to expect, has completed more schooling, and (dearest to parental hearts) is even a tad more grown up.

➤ **THE BAD NEWS:** When an honors student with high aspirations scores below 50 on a PSAT section (a not-so-uncommon occurrence), it is a rude awakening to parents and their progeny. While maturation will probably lead to a stronger SAT I performance, score improvement is unlikely to be significant enough to allow admission to the *most* competitive colleges and universities (without a huge "hook"; see Chapter 7).

Scholarships

Several scholarship services determine award recipients on the basis of PSAT/NMSQT junior year results. Most well known of these is the National Merit Scholarship. Other programs which use PSAT/NMSQT results include: the

National Achievement Scholarship Program for outstanding Black American students; the National Hispanic Recognition Program; the National Scholarship Service and Fund for Negro Students; and the Telluride Association.

Some of these programs offer monetary awards; others provide college counseling or match qualified students with appropriate institutions. In each case, if a student qualifies for such recognition on the basis of PSAT scores, he or she will be notified.

The Student Search Service

Students who check the appropriate box on the test registration form become fair game for colleges participating in this service. These schools—which range from renowned to obscure—ask the service to give them names of appropriate candidates who may fall into one or more of a range of categories: e.g., all prospective science majors; students from the South; Native Americans; those who scored above 130. Much of the information that colleges receive is based on the Student Descriptive Questionnaire, which is completed by all test-takers. The College Board does not send specific scores to Search colleges. As you may have read in Chapter 2, all students who take part will receive information in the mail from a variety of institutions.

Some scholarship programs, in addition to those described above, also use Search. If your child is eligible, these services will automatically contact you. (Search also locates students through information provided on SAT and Advanced Placement Test registration.)

PSATs and Parents

The first thing you will probably wonder is if your child should be doing something special to prepare for the PSAT/NMSQT. While there are commercial prep courses available which will be discussed at length at the end of the chapter, we recommend that students get ready for this test simply by using the sample materials and instructions that are provided in the *Student Bulletin* and/or those found at the College Board Web site (www.collegeboard.com). Try not to make a big production about the PSAT, but if your child is interested in obtaining a test preparation guidebook (or computer software), it's a worthy investment. Because the PSAT/NMSQT is essentially an abbreviated version of the SAT, don't feel you need to purchase material specifically designed for the shorter test.

You may need to intercede in the PSAT process if your child wishes to try this test in grade 10. There is really no down side to taking a trial PSAT/NMSQT in the sophomore year. Like the 11th-grade test, it serves as a good warm-up and an indicator of academic weaknesses—and with more time left to work on those shaky spots. Though most schools don't typically test sophomores, many will do so if parents prod. (The test can still be retaken the next fall. Only junior year scores are used by the National Merit Scholarship Program.) Frankly, we recommend it, as long as it's presented to your child as a laid-back, non-threatening option—and if Junior balks anyway, don't push.

Once scores have been received (and especially if results are disappointing) parents and students can use this advance warning to discuss varying strategies for improvement. It can also be a time for parents to spearhead exploration of target schools with test-score ranges appropriate to their child, and perhaps it is a time, as well, to loosen your grip on long-held college dreams.

II. Just What Is the SAT, Anyway?

The SAT Program includes:

- The SAT I: Reasoning Tests (formerly the SAT)*

- The SAT II: Subject Tests (formerly Achievement Tests)

In your day, the "A" in SAT stood for "Aptitude"; now it means "Assessment," a change designed to reflect increased emphasis on skills learned in school rather than on innate abilities.

The SAT I focuses on verbal and mathematical skills. Students receive separate scores for each of these two areas. The SAT II offers one-hour exams in subjects that include English and math, as well as foreign languages, history, and natural sciences.

The aim of the testing program is to assist college admission officials in comparing applicants from different educational backgrounds and to predict their academic performance in the first term of college. How well these tests fulfill these aims is a subject of ongoing and often heated debate.

Both ETS (the company that creates these tests) and The College Board (the folks who administer them) maintain Web sites that offer a wealth of information and links to countless other sites—and even more information. Students can now sign up for tests online, tackle sample questions, request score reports, access school and college codes, etc. (You'll find a Web ad-

---

* As this book went to press, the College Board announced SAT I format changes to be implemented in the spring of 2005. A separately scored hour-long writing test will include a handwritten essay plus multiple-choice grammar and usage questions. Word analogies will be dropped from the verbal component (which will be renamed "critical reading") in favor of additional reading passages. The mathematics section will cover more advanced material (specifically, Algebra II). The test will become somewhat longer and more costly, and a perfect score will jump from 1,600 to 2,400.

dress reference page at the end of this chapter and another Web site page in the appendix.) But if you came of age when the hula-hoop was king, fear not. The information available electronically is also covered in several free College Board publications. These can be easily ordered by telephone. Details are at the end of the chapter.

SAT I: What Parents Really Want (and Need) to Know

Questions & Answers

Q: When and where should the SAT I be taken?

A: The SAT I: Reasoning Test is offered on Saturday mornings in October, November, December, January, March, May, and June. Arrangements can be made for those who require special accommodations due to religious beliefs or physical disabilities. See your counselor or call the all-purpose number that you'll find later in —and again at the end of—the chapter. The SAT I and SAT II are generally administered concurrently, so students *cannot* plan to take both on the same day.

Ideally, a student will take the SAT I test for the *first time* in May of 11th grade. This allows near maximum course work to be completed, but also leaves the June date open for the SAT II: Subject Tests. Because the summer following junior year is an excellent time to explore colleges, don't postpone testing until grade 12; scores serve as an important guide in selecting target schools. Junior year testing also facilitates "early decision" or "early action" application options, which will be explained in Chapter 6.

Another important consideration in picking an initial test date is *where* the test will be administered. If possible, your child should take the test at a familiar place—his or her own high school—with its own friendly feel and smell (in many schools that means sweat socks; in others, it's chicken à la king). Some schools serve as authorized test centers for every test administration; some for selected dates only; some not at all. Your child may have to register to take tests at a nearby school. The *Registration Bulletin*, available from guidance offices or by calling the College Board, lists all tests sites and dates, as does the College Board Web site (www.collegeboard.com). Plan ahead. The *Registration Bulletin* and the Web site (look under "Registration") also explain procedures for those who live more than 75 miles from a test center, on how to change test sites or dates, and on what to do if your child is ill and misses a test.

Q: How often should tests be retaken?

A: If junior year scores are satisfactory, there is no reason to retake the test, but nearly half of all college-bound students will go for it at least once more, in the fall of their senior year. (October or November test dates are best; December will work for colleges with deadlines in January or beyond. Later test dates may mean that scores don't reach colleges in time or parents pay for pricey "Rush" reporting.) The College Board maintains that the majority of students who take the test in 11th and 12th grades will improve on the second testing, without any special coaching, showing an average growth of 15 to 20 points on both the verbal and mathematical sections. We do not recommend taking the test more than two times, because rarely is there anything to be gained.

➤ *THE GOOD NEWS*: If your child has taken the SAT I more than once, many colleges will consider only the best two scores (verbal and math), even if they come from different test dates. Some will use the highest total score from a single testing.

➤ *THE GOOD and/or BAD NEWS:* SAT score reports always include both new and old test scores. So, even if a 540 verbal is the one that counts, admission officials will probably see last spring's 460. Conversely, they'll also see that a 530 math score was once a 600 and, maybe, chalk it up to an off day.

Questions & Answers

Q: How do we register?

A: There is hardly a more thorough reference work around than the official SAT *Registration Bulletin*. (Most guidance departments always have them; the College Board information number, just below, provides an order service, too.) A registration form and envelope will accompany it. The *Bulletin* is clearly written, covers most imaginable contingencies, and will guide you or your child through filling out an otherwise intimidating form. (Make sure you also get the free companion publication called *Taking the SAT I.*)

You or your child can also sign up for the SAT tests electronically by accessing the College Board Web site (www.collegeboard.com). You'll need to have a major credit card handy to register. Like the *Bulletin*, the Web site provides a wealth of information that is well presented. (*Hint*: Click on the "site search" icon if you get lost or overwhelmed.)

The *Bulletin* and Web site both clearly explain test fees (figure on about $25 for the SAT I) and various add-ons (e.g., late charges, site changes), which must be paid at the time of registration.

For students who have already taken SAT tests, telephone re-registration is available. Call (800) SAT-SCORE for automated service. In addition, during east coast business hours, you can talk to a real person at the College Board SAT Program headquarters by calling (609) 771-7600.

Some points to keep in mind when you begin the registration process:

- A Social Security number, while not required, will make score reporting and record retrieval easier and more error-proof. If your child doesn't yet have a number, this is a good time to get one.
- Urge your child to say yes to the Student Search Service (described in the PSAT section above). Again, it's an option on the registration form.
- Take advantage of Score Reports to Colleges and Scholarship Programs. The SAT fee entitles you to four free reports. Use them. Don't wait to see if scores are good enough, because later score reports will include all previous scores, anyway. (Exception: a child who is considering a college with no testing requirement may want to see scores before sending them to that school.)
- Treat registration deadlines with reverence. Deadlines for "regular registration" are about five weeks before each test date. There is a "late registration" option that buys nearly two weeks more for a $15 surcharge. Of course, the sooner you sign up, the greater your chances of getting your first-choice test site. Stragglers may be assigned to locations in unfamiliar communities or neighborhoods, and getting there alone can be enough of a "test" for one day. "Stand-bys" will also be admitted to tests on a space-available basis (for a $30 stand-by surcharge). For those with registration forms already on file, telephone sign-up is available for another small additional fee (plus test costs). Deadlines are the same as those for mail registration.
- Guidance counselors can obtain "fee waivers" for low-income students, but only two are granted per applicant, regardless of how often the SAT I is taken. (Two SAT II waivers are also granted per applicant.)

Prior to the test date, an "Admission Packet," which includes an "Admission Ticket," will arrive in the mail. Your child will not be admitted to the test site without this ticket and one of the forms of identification outlined in the *Registration Bulletin*. If the packet hasn't appeared at least a week before test time (or if the dog eats the admission ticket), call the College Board information number at (609) 771-7600.

Q: Our guidance counselor has recommended a "nonstandard SAT administration" for our daughter who has special needs. What does that mean? Will it affect admission decisions?

A: The SAT Program provides accommodations for students with many different special needs. Examples of such accommodations include large-print test booklets and answer sheets, Braille or audiocassette test materials, and permission to bring snacks or medication to the testing room. The test center can also provide sign-language interpreters for test instructions and even a writer to record test answers.

At www.collegeboard.com, there is extensive information about how students qualify for special tests, what forms they must complete, application deadlines (be sure to apply well in advance), and the types of assistance available. (You can also send for a brochure by writing, College Board Services for Students with Disabilities, P.O. Box 6226, Princeton, NJ 08541-6226.)

Some of these accommodations give students extra time to complete tests; some do not. When scores are reported, an asterisk indicates that there has been a "nonstandard administration" of the test only when extra time has been allowed. Other forms of special accommodations are *not* indicated on the score report.*

In recent years, a growing number of students have requested nonstandard administrations that allow extra time. Typically, these tests are for students who have been diagnosed with dyslexia and other learning disabilities, and they offer an extra 90 minutes to complete what is normally a three-hour exam.

Some admission officials have expressed concern that this extended-time option is being abused by students with minimal dysfunction and easy access to psychologists and other specialists. Occasionally, admission personnel will question a student's need for nonstandard scores, which might (though they're loathe to admit) be reflected in their evaluation of the candidate.

However, in the vast majority of cases, special accommodations on standardized tests do not affect admission decisions. What is far more important for you to consider is whether the special support your daughter requires will be available at the college she chooses, and not just on test days beforehand.

Q: *What is the test format?*

A: Questions within each section go from easiest to hardest. Because all carry equal point value, students should concentrate on those they are most

---

* *This policy has been under scrutiny. Check with a guidance counselor or consult the College Board for updated information.*

sure of. Those who answer only 50-60% correct will still receive average (or slightly above-average) scores. Scores are computed by totaling correct answers and then subtracting a fraction of a point for each incorrect answer. There is no gain or loss for omitted answers. Thus, students should make educated guesses but never random ones.

Including registration and break time, the entire test will take about three hours.

Q: Who knows the score...and when?

A: Approximately three weeks after the test date, scores will be mailed to your home. Your high school guidance department and all colleges or scholarship services specified on the test registration form will also receive them. For an additional fee, scores can be reported to your child over the Internet or telephone about two weeks after a test. And, yes, for yet another extra charge, "Rush Reporting" can get *new* test scores in the mail about three weeks after tests are taken, or can launch *old* scores in two working days after a telephone request is made. It does *not* mean that you child's new tests will be scored first or faster, and thus there are better ways to get scores to colleges quickly (see "How Do Colleges Get Test Scores" below).

The opening of the score envelope is an excellent time for you to practice keeping your cool. After all, if Junior pulled down some big numbers, dancing around the dining room is still premature—he hasn't actually been accepted anywhere yet. On the other hand, if the scores are really low, then you must summon all of your Academy Award-winning abilities. Chances are, the test will be retaken, and you don't want to turn up the heat in the pressure cooker any more than it already is. Cursing or complaining on your part is only going to jeopardize your child's performance on the next test. (And not to bring up a sore point, but scores are addressed to your child, not to you. Occasionally, the Educational Testing Service receives calls from parents who can't pry test results from their kids. ETS won't tell *you* either, but a guidance counselor will probably squeal. If not, then you'll just have to work it out with Junior—or, suggests one ETS employee, off the record, "Beat 'em to the mailbox!")

Q: What do the score reports mean?

A: Your child will receive separate scores for the verbal and math components of the SAT I test, each ranging from 200 to 800.

The score report also includes percentiles which compare your child's scores to those of college-bound seniors, both nationwide and in your state, a record of up to six previously-taken SAT I and SAT II tests, a regurgitation of information reported on the Student Descriptive Questionnaire section of the registration form, and some rather superficial admission data provided by those colleges to whom score reports were sent.

High schools and colleges receive similar report forms. College admission officials cannot tell from score reports where *other* reports have been sent.

Q: **My son is gloating that he outscored his oldest sister on the SAT I, but we've heard that the scores were adjusted since our daughter took the test. What does that mean?**

A: In June 1994, the College Board announced that the SAT I and II scoring scale would be "recentered" to increase national test score averages. Students who took the SATs in or after spring 1995 were scored on this new scale, which typically added about 80 points to verbal scores and about 20 to math. In other words, the same performance that once generated a verbal score of 520 will now net about a 600; the "old" math score of 530 has jumped to roughly 550.

National averages for high school students who took the SAT I in 1992 were: Verbal–423; Math–476. According to the College Board, the goal of the new system was to bring average scores back to the 500 mark where they began, and the recentering has indeed met that aim. The insiders insist that—despite claims of critics that the whole business is a cover-up designed to compensate for downward spiraling high schools—falling averages reflected a larger and more diverse pool of test-takers, not dumber kids.

But what's confusing for parents—many of whom took the SATs themselves and feel like it was just yesterday—is that scores which once opened doors to top-tier colleges (i.e., anything over 600) are now no longer so impressive. For instance, before recentering, fewer than 250 students per year achieved 800s on the verbal section of the test. Now 4,000+ hit the perfect mark.

What's also confusing is that, while recentering has added points to *most* test scores, the number of points is not consistent (e.g., what was once a 270 math score is now a 290, but the old 370 has become a 420) and—here's where you'll really go nuts—many of the math scores at the high end of the scale (i.e., above 650) actually go *down* when recentered.

For the first couple years after the recentering, most general guidebooks offered both original and recentered averages, which was especially helpful to us older folks. Today, however, the majority of publications list only recentered scores. Initially, after the recentering, all PSAT and SAT score reports included an "R" next to each number, but in the fall of 2001 that designation also disappeared.

So, tell your son to stop gloating, and as you explore college options, make certain that you are not comparing his recentered scores with outdated statistics.

Q: **How do colleges get test scores? What happens if our scores are late or lost?**

A: In addition to the four free score reports (to colleges or scholarship services) that are included in each test fee, the registration form allows space for four additional reports (with a charge for each, of course). If you paid properly, these reports will all be in the appropriate hands even before scores arrive at home. Extra reports can be ordered at any time. Your child will have received (and perhaps already lost!) an "Additional Report Request Form" that is mailed out with test admission tickets. Requests for extra reports can also be made online or by telephone. Allow five weeks after your request for these additional scores to reach their destinations, although "Rush" reporting will cut that time by nearly two weeks.

Most colleges that require standardized tests will tell you that the scores must be sent to them directly from the test administrators, ETS. What many college officials *won't* tell you, however, is that there are several other ways they *may* accept test scores during the hectic decision-making period. If your child comes up with a last-minute target college (or has simply overlooked sending scores to a target school), or if your child takes tests at the eleventh hour (especially common for the SAT II), all is not lost. Colleges *want* as many applicants as they can get and will go out of their way to obtain official scores through a variety of means.

For instance, many high schools routinely include standardized test scores on all transcripts. Since these scores then become part of a student's permanent record, colleges *may* accept their validity, as if the scores had been mailed to them from ETS. Keep in mind, however, that transcripts won't include scores from tests *just* taken. (**Hint:** If a college on your child's list does *not* require test scores, and you don't want that college to see them, you should find out if the scores appear on the high school transcript. If so, most counselors will agree to remove them from the transcript that is sent to designated colleges, but you or your child will have to orchestrate this process.)

Many admission officers, particularly in smaller colleges, will also accept SAT scores over the telephone from guidance counselors, if they haven't received them by decision time. Usually, students or counselors will be asked to follow up with an official written score report, but without the pressure of a looming deadline. This is especially useful for seniors who have opted for January test administrations.

Score reports that come directly from students or parents, whether in print or by phone or fax, are not considered suitable.

Thus, before you lose sleep over a score-report oversight or pay for "Rush" reporting (that is far less speedy than the name suggests), call the college(s) involved and ask if scores have been received on the transcript (and, if so, are they sufficiently official?) or if can they be obtained in another way (e.g., via counselor phone call) in order to keep your child in the running.

Q: How do colleges use test scores?

A: Almost every college that requires standardized tests will be quick to insist that scores are *not* the most important factor in an admission decision and that the secondary school record is far more significant. While this is true in theory, it is also crucial to keep in mind that many applicants to colleges (at all levels of selectivity) have very similar high school records and so test scores can—for better or worse—become the tie-breakers. At the most selective institutions, SAT scores are usually *far* more critical than many admission officials want to admit.

➤ *THE GOOD NEWS:* Once you have received test scores, it becomes easier to identify colleges where your child will be accepted.

➤ *THE BAD NEWS:* If your kid's scores are not at least in the ballpark at your top choice colleges, without unique talents or special circumstances (see Chapter 7), then it's time to turn your interests and efforts elsewhere. Remember that "average" SAT scores reported by colleges may be skewed by alumni children, athletes, economically disadvantaged applicants, and other "hook" cases. Out-of-state students applying to public universities are also typically held to a higher standard than in-staters. All this must be kept in mind as you compare your child's SAT scores to norms at target colleges.

Below are samples of some approximate middle 50 percent SAT I scores. (All scores are on the recentered scale.)

College	Verbal	Math
Princeton	680-770	680-770
Swarthmore	650-780	660-750
Harvey Mudd	660-770	730-800
Carleton	650-740	640-720
Duke	640-740	660-760
Notre Dame (IN)	620-710	640-720
Georgetown	620-730	630-720

College	Verbal	Math
U. of Virginia	600-700	610-710
Colorado College	590-680	590-680
U. of Michigan (Ann Arbor)	560-670	600-710
Syracuse	540-640	560-660
U. of Vermont	510-610	520-620
Seton Hall (NJ)	480-580	480-580
U. of California (Riverside)	440-570	480-620
U. of West Virginia	460-560	460-560

Source: The Insider's Guide to College *(Yale Daily News Pubishing Co.)*

As you can see, many of these ranges are broad, and an applicant may be at the low end of the verbal scale and the high end of the math—or vice versa. Just as you will use such ranges to roughly determine how your child stacks up against other applicants so, too, will colleges use standardized test scores in several manners to see if one candidate is comparable to others. Here are some of the ways that admission offices use standardized test scores:

- **To choose among students from seemingly similar backgrounds with seemingly similar records.** The most selective schools get loads of amazing applicants, but test scores show some to be just a bit more amazing than others. Likewise, there are lots of nice "B" (and "C") students around. Standardized scores are one factor that admission officers use to make distinctions.

- **To see how top-performing students from weak or disadvantaged high schools may fare when placed with those with stronger academic backgrounds.** A valedictorian with 350 SATs could get eaten alive at a highly competitive college; a salutatorian with 500s will probably hold her own.

- **To give the benefit of the doubt to students in first-string high schools.** Admission officers recognize that there are some schools out there where Albert Einstein himself would be lucky to land a "B" in physics or to fall in the top of his senior class. SAT scores can help put such super schools in perspective.

- **To see how hard a student is working.** An "A" student with mediocre SATs may be viewed as a go-getter or a poor tester, but high test scores combined with middling grades suggest that the candidate is an underachiever. Most schools will favor the former.

- **To make cut-and-dried decisions.** The majority of colleges and universities are not beholden to rigid score cut-offs, but some do screen out prospects whose tests don't meet minimum requirements. Even within an institution, cut-offs may vary from school to school or from major to major. However, most institutions or departments with minimums usually check applications for special circumstances and unusual talents or offer an appeals process for those with inadequate test results.

- **To award scholarships or merit aid.** Increasingly, colleges are trying to lure top prospects with financial incentives that are based on academic ability, not need. Usually, contenders for these awards—which range from full scholarships to token grants—are identified on the basis of both school record *and* test performance.

- **To determine college-class placement.** This is especially true in areas like foreign language, math, and writing.

- **To determine athletic eligibility.** NCAA eligibility depends on test results. (See Chapter 7.)

Questions & *Answers*

Q: What if "our" scores are awful?

A: One of the pluses of PSATs is that they serve as a warning of SAT scores to follow. If SATs are significantly *lower* than PSAT results, then you should be concerned. Was your child ill, upset, or preoccupied on the test day? Was the score on one section of the SAT consistent with the PSAT, while the other section was not?

The College Board Question-and-Answer Service is available to all students who took the SAT I on several—but not all—of the national test dates. It can be ordered online or by mail, phone, or fax, and it provides a copy of the actual test, a copy of your child's answer sheet, the correct answers, and scoring instructions. It is an excellent way to help identify recurring errors for future tests or to ascertain if the test was scored correctly.

If the Q & A Service isn't available for your child's test date, there is a "Student Answer Service" option. This report lists which questions (and *types* of questions) your child answered correctly and incorrectly (or omitted). But, because it does not include the questions themselves nor your child's answer sheet, few test-takers find it helpful.

If you believe that a scoring error was made on your child's test, you can request a "Hand Scoring" service for $25. Of course, most unwelcome scores are *not* (unfortunately) the result of administrative slip-ups. So, then what?

- **If this is the first time your child took the SAT I, he or she should plan to retake it.** Remember, the best first testing is in the spring of 11th grade; the re-test should wait until the fall of 12th.
- **Consider one of the preparation options** discussed at the end of this chapter.
- **Does your child have a diagnosed learning or physical disability?** If so, did you already take advantage of extended-time tests or other special accommodations? If a disability is suspected, consider a professional evaluation before the tests are retaken.
- **Reset your sights**. To a great degree, "good" and "bad" test scores are relative. For example, a combined score of 1,200 is certainly very respectable. Yet, while in one household, it is cause for celebration; in another, it could sabotage hopes for a long-shot college. "An applicant with below 1,250 and no special connections, 'hooks,' or unusual talents is *unlikely* to get into Yale," admits Associate Director of Admission Patricia Wei. "There are simply too many applicants with similar qualifications and better tests."

If your child's test scores fall below middle range at target schools, you may be barking up the wrong ivy. The most competitive colleges will admit some applicants who don't hit 1,250, but usually these are kids with special clout. Without it, you'll need bigger numbers. There are just too many kids around who are as wonderful as yours (well, almost) and who have stronger test scores, too.

"High reach" applications are fine, but make sure that you use SAT results to make *realistic* choices, as well. There are lots of excellent institutions that don't expect astronomical numbers.

- **Ask if test scores are playing a diminishing role**. You've probably stumbled on stories in the media that question the merit of standardized admission tests and cite the growing list of colleges and universities (or even entire state systems) that no longer demand them. Some institutions, while still requiring SATs (or ACTs), are willing to admit they've devalued their importance. At such schools, this means that applicants with admissible grades and extracurricular activities are less likely to get turned away now due to low SAT scores than they might have been in recent years.

"Smith College has de-emphasized the use of SATs in the selection process," notes Debra Shaver, senior associate director of admission. "The reason is simple: SATs are not a good overall predictor of success in college, and often first-generation college-bound students and students from low socioeconomic backgrounds do not score well on such tests. Since making SATs a lower priority at Smith, we have not seen the quality of our entering classes decline. On the contrary, there's been a significant *increase* in the percentage of students who are in the top tenth of their high school class."

If your child's SATs look too low for a target college, don't ask admission officials if the tests are truly important. You may get a rehearsed response that's confusing or downright misleading. Do ask, instead, if the importance of test scores has changed in recent years, is under scrutiny, or on the wane. Try this approach, and you'll be likely to receive a more revealing answer.

• **There are also excellent institutions that don't expect any numbers at all.** SATs or ACTs are optional at some well-respected schools. Good scores will work in your favor, but if you don't send them in, the colleges don't automatically assume they were horrendous.

If your child's scores are truly disappointing, one of your first stops might be the FairTest Web site, www.FairTest.org (or phone (617) 864-4810). This Massachusetts organization, which contends that admission testing is biased and unreliable, maintains an updated list of the hundreds of colleges and universities that do not use SAT or ACT scores to make admission decisions. Among them are:

Antioch (OH)
Bard College (NY)
Bates College (ME)
Bowdoin College (ME)
College of the Atlantic (ME)
Dickinson College (PA)
Franklin & Marshall (PA) (SAT/ACT is used only when minimum GPA or class rank is not met.)

Hampshire College (MA)

Mount Holyoke College (MA)

Muhlenberg College (PA)

New England College (NH)

St. John's College (MD & NM)

Wheaton College (MA)

Some colleges (e.g., Middlebury College in Vermont; Union College and Sarah Lawrence College, both in New York; and Connecticut College) allow students to substitute three SAT II Subject Tests for the SAT I.

Hint: If one (or more) of these colleges is on your short list, don't have SAT I scores sent to them until you have seen them first, and if they're not so hot, tuck them under the mattress.

Colleges that don't require test scores *will* probably use them for those candidates who submit them anyway. If you don't want colleges to see scores, make sure they are not included on your child's high school transcript.

Questions & *Answers*

Q: Are tests biased against females and minorities?

A: Some experts say yes; some say no. Others say they were, but they aren't any more. Arguably, even if the tests themselves are perfect, there are still societal problems that penalize many girls and minorities when it comes to standardized tests. Some females are brought up to believe that math and science are male domains. By the time they get to high school, they may have fallen behind in these areas. Many of the most problem-plagued high schools in the nation are those that serve primarily people of color. These students, too, may approach standardized admission tests with poorer preparation and expectations.

Most colleges will, to some degree, give extra slack to students from disadvantaged communities and put emphasis on class rank, not test scores. They recognize that scores may be lower for some students—both male and female—whose parents didn't attend college and/or whose first language isn't English.

Young women, however, don't get much leeway, except at single-sex schools. The outstanding women's colleges (e.g., Smith, Wellesley, Barnard, Bryn Mawr) have somewhat lower SAT averages than their coed Ivy (and the like) counterparts, but they attract bright, serious students and can be a smart college choice for those whose test scores lag behind their proven abilities.

SAT II: Subject Tests

Still sometimes called by their erstwhile name, "Achievement Tests," these hour-long College Board exams are not as widely required as the SAT I, but many highly competitive colleges do demand them. (Often, however, the ACT can be substituted for *both* the SAT I and SAT II. In some cases the SAT II can replace the SAT I, as described above.)

It's nearly impossible to stay on top of which colleges want what but, typically, most (of those who expect subject tests at all) require three, though some ask for fewer. Because many stipulate that Writing and/or Math* be among those selected, a safe bet is to elect both of these, plus one more from the other subjects listed below:

Writing (includes multiple choice questions on language usage and an essay)

Literature

English Language Proficiency (for non-native speakers)

Math Levels IC & IIC

United States History

World History

Biology

Chemistry

Physics

Chinese with Listening

French (reading only or with listening)

German (reading only or with listening)

Modern Hebrew

Italian

Japanese with Listening

Korean with Listening

Latin

Spanish (reading only or with listening)

Subject Test Hints

- **Plan ahead.** There are six SAT II dates annually. Registration information is offered online (www.collegeboard.com) or in the same *Bulletin* that is used for SAT I. (Make sure to pick up a separate free publication called *Taking the SAT II*.) Remember, the SAT I and II cannot be

---

* *A few specialized institutions (e.g., Cal Tech) expect or prefer Math Level II and one science test.*

taken on the same day. Some SAT II tests are not offered on every test date. Up to three tests can be taken on one day. There is a base registration fee and additional charges for each test.

- **Schedule tests as close as possible to course completion.** For instance, if your daughter takes biology in 10th grade and does well, she might want to take the Subject Test that spring, not a year or more later when she wouldn't know a stamen from a pistil if it turned up in her cereal.

- **Foreign language tests are designed for those with two to four years of study. (European language tests are often tough for those with only two years of prep.)** Colleges, however, tend to take bad language scores less seriously than those in other areas because so many districts have weak language programs. Comprenez?

- **Science and history test questions are designed for students who have taken a one-year introductory course (at the college prep level),** not just for Advanced Placement aces.

- **English Literature DOES NOT require knowledge of specific authors or their works.** It presents reading passages and questions on them (and is, perhaps, the easiest test to do well on for those who are reasonably bright but haven't learned much in school).

- **Students with solid backgrounds (and grades) in trigonometry and/or pre-calculus should probably take the Math II test.** If you're not sure which math test is most appropriate for you child, you'll find the tests compared in the SAT II section of the College Board Web site and in *Taking the SAT II.* High school math teachers can also offer advice. Some students who qualify for Math II decide to take the "easier" Math I instead, believing that they are certain to score well, and are surprised when classmates taking the harder test get better results. Why? One theory is that the Math II test covers material that is more current to advanced students.

- **Biology students must choose between "M" (molecular) and "E" (ecology) versions of this test. The choice is made at the test site, but make sure your child understands the differences ahead of time.** Again, both the information booklet and the Web site offer comparisons.

- **A parent's primary job is to make sure that students have the proper equipment for certain SAT II exams.** Both Level I and II math tests require a calculator. (See the registration bulletin or Web site for recommendations and restrictions.)

  Students taking language tests with a listening component should bring hand-held cassette players with earphones (and don't forget those extra batteries).

*Q*uestions & *A*nswers

Q: My daughter Kelly is not applying to colleges that require SAT II tests. Is there any reason she should take them?

A: Is Kelly strong in subjects that the SAT I doesn't cover, such as foreign language, science, or history? If so, her SAT II scores may show off this strength. High scores on the SAT II can also help compensate for a weaker SAT I performance.

While most students take no more than three SAT II tests (the maximum for a single test date), those with talent in a range of specific subjects may opt for additional SAT IIs.

Keep in mind, too, that SAT II results may be used for placement purposes, and good scores might help Kelly skip introductory-level classes, if she wants to.

III. The ACT Assessment

The ACT Assessment is best known to families living in the Southeast, Southwest, and Midwest, but it is administered practically worldwide. Even elite eastern colleges, former SAT strongholds, will now accept ACT scores instead. In fact, many colleges that require SAT I *and* II permit the ACT to be substituted for both.

In the majority of cases, the decision to take the ACT versus the SAT is left to the hands of fate. If you live in a state—or your child attends a school—where one test is more prevalent, then that is the choice that is probably your best bet. However, some reasons to buck the trend will be listed later on.

In ACT regions, many high schools administer the PLAN assessment test to 10th graders. Like the PSAT, this test also serves as a warm-up for the ACT, but its primary purpose is to provide families and, especially, schools with a way to evaluate their curriculum and instruction so that appropriate changes can be made. As a result, the PLAN test is usually not a high-pressure experience for sophomores.

The ACT test itself, like the SAT, is best taken in the spring of 11th grade, and again in the fall of 12th, if desired. (Few students take it more than twice.) The registration and testing processes are also very much like those for the SAT Program, so make sure you have read the SAT I section above, even if your child will not take that test. As with the SAT, there are provisions for students with disabilities and for stand-by testing, fee waivers, etc.

Also, like those who take the SAT, ACT students can opt for a "search" service (the ACT version is called the Educational Opportunity Service) and can order copies of completed tests and answer sheets (for specific national test dates only).

The ACT has a Web site (www.act.org) that offers online registration, lists test dates and centers, provides test-content details, sample test items, testing hints, etc. Telephone numbers (for general customer service or automated re-registration) are listed at the end of this chapter.

Two free booklets, *Registering for the ACT Assessment* and *Preparing for the ACT Assessment*, will also tell you everything you need to know. Both should be available at your child's school; otherwise order online or by phone. ACT service charges are similar to most SAT fees. Here, however, are some differences that you might want to note:

- There are up to six ACT administration dates annually, depending where you live, but in some states where the SAT reigns supreme, you may have to travel to reach an ACT test site.

- Ordinarily, ACT score reports are mailed to schools, not home, but students can choose where they prefer them to be sent. (All June test date scores go to the home address automatically.) ACT score reports are not cumulative. This means that students can decide which scores colleges see...or *don't* see. There are three types of mail-order additional score reports: "Regular" will arrive within a month; "Priority" will arrive within four days, and "Mailgram" will arrive within about 36 hours. (There are fees for each, and telephone requests are honored for an additional service charge.)

ACT Format

The ACT includes four main parts: English, Mathematics, Reading, and Science Reasoning. Each is divided into sub-sections.

ACT questions do not progress from easiest to hardest, as SAT questions do. The entire test lasts three hours, plus about 45 minutes for breaks and registration.

Calculators are permitted but not imperative.

ACT Scoring

The ACT is scored on a 1-36 scale. There is no penalty for wrong answers, so guessing is encouraged. Colleges are most concerned with the Composite Score, which is an average of the English, Mathematics, Reading, and Science Reasoning tallies. The national average composite score is about 21.

Students who grow up in ACT-land often have a sense of what these scores mean. They know, for example, that a 31 Composite is something to brag about. (It's around average at Stanford and M.I.T., among others). A 28 is nothing to sneeze at either (and is an approximate mid-point at places like Oberlin and West Point); while a 22 or 23 is the going rate at many state universities. But if your brain only functions in terms of 100s, then try this highly unofficial formula to compare ACT scores to SATs:

Multiply the ACT composite by 40, then add 150. The result will be a crude equivalent of an SAT I Verbal & Math total (on the recentered scale).

Example: 24 (ACT Composite) x 40=960 +150=1,110

A student who scores 24 on the ACT would be likely to score about 1,110 on the SAT.

Questions & Answers

Q: Which test should "we" take?

A: Only a handful of colleges insist on one test and not the other, and the list is dwindling rapidly. (Most of these, in fact, are schools that draw largely from one geographic region and require the test that is most popular in that region.) Even colleges that claim to prefer one test above the other will never discriminate against applicants who took the wrong one; most will scarcely notice. Thus, it's fine to go with the flow and sign up for the test that prevails in your area. Why, then, would anyone want to swim against the testing tide?

Reasons to go out of your way to take the SAT

- Actually, it's the PSAT that is a qualifier for the National Merit Scholarship Program (and several other scholarships) which ACT (or PLAN) students aren't eligible for. Most other scholarship services accept scores from either, and the registration booklets include lists where score reports can be sent directly.

Reasons to go out of your way to take the ACT
- Students who are unduly anxious about taking SATs may feel less pressure attached to a lesser-known test.
- In many colleges, the ACT replaces both SAT I and II. Of course, students with strength in foreign language and history won't get to strut their stuff with the ACT.

Other test differences
- The ACT has trigonometry questions in the math section, but math accounts for only 25 percent of the Composite Score. The SAT I has no trig questions, but math makes up half of the aggregate.
- The ACT tests grammar; the SAT does not, but it puts more emphasis on vocabulary than the ACT does.
- The ACT has a science section; the SAT does not.
- All ACT questions are multiple choice; some SAT questions are not.

Those who take *both* tests (and use the formula above to compare them) commonly find that there isn't a significant difference in their scores. Indeed, recent changes have brought the two exams closer together. Still, there are some score-watchers who insist that the SAT puts more focus on aptitude (smart kids with fair grades will shine here), while the ACT emphasizes achievement (i.e., it tests what students have learned in their classes). "I have observed that when conscientious (but perhaps not brilliant) students do poorly on the SAT I, their scores are better if they then try the ACT," claims independent college counselor Jane Gutman. "The ACT is primarily a reading test where questions follow passages. Even the 'science' section really requires only minimal science background (although some avowed non-scientists will still freak out at the first sign of saline solutions or biomasses). There is no out-of-context vocabulary on this test, an area that trips up many SAT I-takers."

Some students will insist on taking both tests, but only rarely is this a necessity. If admission literature does not state that the exam your child has chosen is acceptable, check directly with an admission counselor.

IV. TOEFL

This exam is required or recommended for students whose native language is not English. It is most commonly taken by those living outside of the United States or who have only been in the U.S. a short while. In some cases, colleges will accept TOEFL in place of required SAT or ACT tests. However, the reverse is also true—if a student has spent more than two or three years in a school where English is the primary language of instruction, then some colleges will not count TOEFL results at all and, thus, taking the test is a waste of time and money. If your child's situation is not clear-cut, check with individual colleges to see what they expect.

TOEFL is administered worldwide. The standard paper version, which is still taken by students in some locations, was the only one available prior to 1998. It includes three sections—listening, sentence structure, and reading—and is scored on a scale of 310 to 677. (Until 1998, the range was 200 to 677.) Those who take the paper TOEFL should also expect to demonstrate their writing proficiency with the 30-minute Test of Written English (TWE), but this is graded separately and not included in the overall TOEFL result.

Now, however, students in many countries can elect a computerized TOEFL. As in the past, it is still necessary to report to a test administration center—one does not take this test at home—but many of these test sites are permanent and thus able to offer convenient, ongoing test dates.

The computer-based test is scored on a very different scale: 0 to 300. The test format is somewhat different as well and includes a mandatory essay. The essay is graded separately but the results *are* also included in the overall TOEFL score. The test begins with an untimed "tutorial" to help familiarize students with the computer and test software. Students can choose to compose the culminating essay on the computer or on a sheet of paper provided at the center. One big advantage of the computer-based test is that students will get an approximation of their score before they leave the test center. (This score is not finalized until the essay is evaluated by two readers.) Unsatisfactory results can be immediately canceled at the student's request, and the test can be repeated at a later date.

If your child needs to take a TOEFL test and you have Internet access, your first stop should be the TOEFL Web site, www.toefl.org. From there you can determine if your area offers the computer-based TOEFL or if you child will take the standard paper-based test. You will learn about test sites and dates, registration and payment procedures, and identification requirements. You can even download complete information bulletins for both the computer-based test and paper test.

Without Internet access, you may find TOEFL bulletins and other information at your child's school, at educational advising centers, or at local universities. Otherwise, contact:

TOEFL Services
PO Box 6151
Princeton, NJ 08541-6151
USA
Phone: (609) 771-7100
Fax: (609) 771-7500

Allow up to eight weeks for bulletins ordered from outside the U.S.

TOEFL scores are mailed about a month after the test is taken (sooner for computer-based test-takers who wrote the mandatory essay on the computer). Scores are also available by telephone four weeks after the test. (See the end of this chapter for numbers.)

You and your child can use TOEFL results to help make college choices. The more competitive institutions usually expect scores above 600 on the paper test or 250 on the computer-based version. Many schools indicate that students scoring below 550 (paper version) or 213 (computer-based) are not prepared to follow a college curriculum in English; however, there are some colleges that will accept students with far lower scores. Some even offer special English programs for non-native speakers. Unlike SAT scores, which are archived until the end of time, TOEFL test results are only kept on file for two years.

Your child can prepare for the TOEFL by ordering or downloading the free bulletin described above. You can purchase practice materials in bookstores or order software at www.toefl.org. Some of this software can be downloaded (with a credit card payment) directly from the Web site. Preparation classes offered in many parts of the world. The pros and cons of these various approaches are discussed in the next section.

There are a few other tests that some colleges will accept in lieu of TOEFL, such as the English Language Proficiency Test (ELPT), an SAT II exam. Check with admission officials before registering.

V. Preparing for Standardized Tests

Admit it. You probably skimmed through most of the chapter to get to this section. The only thing you *really* want to know about admission testing is whether you should fork over the big bucks for a commercial prep course. Perhaps you're also wondering what other ways there are to prepare or if preparation is even possible at all.

Both College Board and ACT officials maintain that the *best* way to get ready for standardized tests is through following a challenging high school curriculum and staying abreast of assignments. It is no secret, either, that bookworms significantly outscore less avid readers— often even on mathematical tests (those questions have to be read, too).

The market is flooded with books, software, videos, courses, and even flashcards (remember them?) that all promise to improve standardized test scores and, to some degree, they do "work." The catch, of course, is that your kid has to work, too, to get anything out of them.

Take the quiz below to see how (or if) you should invest your time and money:

1. How eager is your child to prepare for college entrance tests? She/he...
   a. is the one who insists on doing something.
   b. is willing to do what we suggest.
   c. thinks it's probably a waste of time.
   d. makes gagging noises when we bring it up.

2. How much time do you think she/he can devote to taking a class?
   a. Three hours a week or more
   b. Two hours a week
   c. One hour a week
   d. Every second is already scheduled

3. How much time will she/he spend preparing at home?
   a. About eight hours per week
   b. About four hours per week
   c. About two hours per week
   d. About 10 minutes per week

4. Does she/he tend to see projects through to completion?
   a. Yes, sometimes compulsively
   b. Most of the time
   c. Only if they are interesting
   d. If we threaten

5. Does she/he get anxious at test times?
   a. Extremely—the whole family is off the wall
   b. Usually—these college tests seem to do it
   c. No, test scores are often above class achievement
   d. No, as long as the mall will still be open when the test is over

6. What is his/her approximate junior or senior year average?

   a. A

   b. B

   c. C

   d. Don't ask

7. What were his/her combined PSAT scores? (Or use "PLAN" or "ACT" scores & conversion formula or SAT scores with a 0 added to choices below.)

   a. Between 80-110

   b. Between 110-140

   c. Over 140

   d. Below 80 or didn't take them yet

8. Which statement comes closest to your child's reaction to the PSAT (or other entrance tests already taken)?

   a. It took a while to get in the swing of it.

   b. I kind of went blank.

   c. It was easy.

   d. It was too hard.

9. What's the likelihood that you (or another adult) could prepare with your child on a regular schedule of two to four hours per week, over 10 weeks?

   a. We could probably pull that off.

   b. If we really made an effort and organized in advance.

   c. Sounds like a long shot.

   d. We haven't finished that soapbox racer we began in 1997.

10. How big of a bite would $900 take out of your budget?

    a. It's small change compared to what college will cost.

    b. It's a big chunk of change, but we've spent more money for worse reasons.

    c. It would mean some real creative financing.

    d. Are you crazy? We had to *borrow* to buy this book!

11. Your child seems to absorb information best when:

    a. in a classroom situation.

    b. reading independently.

    c. working one-on-one.

    d. watching the Home Shopping Channel.

The best time to get serious about SAT or ACT preparation is in the winter of junior year, before the "real" test is taken for the first time. (For practical purposes, the summer of that year works better for many, and tests can be retaken in the fall.)

If you answered "a" or "b" to questions 1 through 8 above, then your child is probably a good candidate for some sort of preparation program. Despite raging debate over the effectiveness of such programs and the validity of claims of titanic score surges, common sense can tell you that preparation means practice, and practice makes...well, if not perfect, then at least improvement.

Especially helpful is the administration of an entire timed test. This can be done at home, but it's one area where coaching *classes* clearly have the edge because they can best simulate genuine testing conditions (complete with sneezing, belching, groaning, and furious scribbling).

Any form of preparation will enhance your child's familiarity with the testing process and that, in turn, is bound to boost confidence. The pros and cons of several preparation methods are listed below. Use your quiz results to determine which is best for you.

Freebies in Print

➤**THE GOOD NEWS:** Excellent booklets (*Taking the SAT I; Taking the SAT II;* and *Preparing for the ACT Assessment*) are available at no cost at most high school guidance departments or by contacting the appropriate offices listed at the end of the chapter. These booklets are not the same as registration bulletins but usually accompany them. They provide some test-taking tips, preparation strategies, and complete practice tests. **At the very least, your child should be thoroughly acquainted with this material before taking an exam.**

- If you answered "c" or "d" to questions 1, 2, and 3, and "c" to questions 7 and 8, then this may be the way to go.

➤ *THE BAD NEWS:* While brevity makes these booklets manageable, it also means that they lack information that might be helpful. The longer manuals described below provide study aids such as vocabulary lists and mini-math lessons. The good ones also offer insight into the different types of test questions and how each is best analyzed or approached.

Test Preparation Manuals

➤ *THE GOOD NEWS:* Most bookstores offer a broad selection of preparation books—and tomes for every existing major test are available. One good investment is Peterson's *Panic Plan for the SAT*, which offers a step-by-step two-week study plan, along with lots of helpful tips about common SAT I stumbling blocks. ACT-takers might try *Getting Into the ACT* (Harcourt Brace). In general, look for volumes that:

- are written in a user-friendly style that seems fun to read (well, sort of, anyway);
- include several complete practice tests that mimic the real McCoy;
- provide not only practice test answers but also *explanations* of answers;

- explain test structure and test-taking strategies;
- offer comforting advice about quelling anxiety; and
- are up to date. (Test formats are revised periodically; library or school copies may not be current.)

➤ **THE BAD NEWS:** *Buying* the book is not enough. If your child is not likely to systematically read the material and do the lessons and practice exercises provided, then this prep method will flop. Likewise, while last-minute cramming can help students understand test-taking strategies, that same information can be had for free from the College Board or ACT booklets.

Computer Software

➤ **THE GOOD NEWS:** Preparation programs are widely available for both Macintosh and PC use. For computer buffs, these interactive exercises can be entertaining. Most of the big names in the college-search industry sell decent test-prep software. Both the SAT and ACT folks also peddle their own materials on their Web sites and in registration booklets. Look for software that includes complete practice tests, explained answers, and other features listed under "Test Preparation Manuals" above.

➤ **THE BAD NEWS:** Like books, this method won't work if the software is harboring six species of spiders on the shelf.

Online Assistance

➤ **THE GOOD NEWS:** There are a burgeoning number of ways to prepare for tests online. These range from entire test-prep courses and practice tests to helpful hints and sample questions. Many are free.

For instance at www.collegeboard.com, your child can take a timed mini-SAT with real questions, along with an analysis of weak spots and a personal study plan. There is always a sample "question of the day" with immediate feedback (a bit of fun for Mom or Dad to try, although the thrill of victory is quickly diminished when you are told that the question you struggled to answer correctly was only an "easy" or "medium" one!) The ACT home page (www.act.org) offers a limited number of free practice questions for that test as well, with answers supplied and explained.

One-stop-shopping sites, such as www.petersons.com generally include test preparation advice and free practice questions. If you type "free SAT preparation questions" into your favorite search engine, you'll get a long list of the other most current sites. Many, like www.powerprep.com offer both free questions and advice along with the opportunity to pay for more.

Noted test-prep titans *Kaplan, Inc.* and *The Princeton Review* offer everything from free materials to entire classes online. There are several options (and prices) available. Visit www.kaptest.com or www.review.com for details. The online programs combine the benefits of self-paced study with those of a structured course. The most complete ones cost hundreds of dollars but are still far cheaper than their classroom counterparts.

➤ *THE BAD NEWS:* You or your child can fritter away a lot of time jumping from link to link as you investigate online preparation options and tackle sample questions. Sites sometimes provide information only to those who are registered and, although registration is free, it takes…yep, you guessed it…even *more* time.

- Try the book or computer approaches, above, if quiz answers included: 1a; 4 a or b; 7 b or c; 11 b.

School-Based Coaching Courses

➤ *THE GOOD NEWS:* Unlike most commercial courses (they're next; we're working up to them), classes offered in school (either as part of the curriculum or as an after-school option) are either inexpensive or cost-free. (Similar classes may also be available through local adult-ed programs or community colleges.) To some extent, these programs will force students to be aware of test formats and strategies, although good results require effort (and homework).

Even College Board literature concedes that short-duration familiarization courses (20 hours or so) seem to increase scores an average of 10 points on the verbal section and about 15 to 20 points on the math. Longer courses (40 hours), which stress skill development, can bring total gains of up to about 40 points. The literature also suggests, however, that such improvements may be largely due to continued academic growth and test-taking practice; not the result of exclusive insiders' information.

➤ *THE BAD NEWS:* Quality of instruction and course content in such homegrown classes can vary tremendously. Some are taught by moonlighters with little experience. If the class is boring or disorganized, it will be of limited use. If your child is not especially motivated in regular school classes, you can bet that he or she will *really* snooze through this one. (Commercial courses can be better prepared to deal with reluctant pupils. See below.) The time would be far better spent participating in a club or sports or other more meaningful activity.

On the other hand, in-school classes may be actually taught by pros. *Kaplan, Inc.,* for example, places trained instructors in some public schools or trains the school's own staff to present their course. School districts pick up the entire tab for these programs or offer them to parents at a significantly reduced cost.

Before committing your child to a school coaching program, get the particulars on its teachers. "There is a proliferation of coaching courses all over the country," notes ACT official Patricia Farrant. "We don't endorse or participate in any one of them. It's really a 'buyer beware' situation. Some are fine. Some are less-than-fine."

➤ *THE GOOD AND/OR BAD NEWS:* When a student who balks at taking a coaching class learns that several friends have already enrolled, he or she may be suddenly eager to sign up, too. Whether this is great news or not depends on if you think such a class would be beneficial to *your* child.

- Is a school course right for your child? Look for quiz answers 2 a or b; 10 c or d; 11 a.

Commercial Coaching Courses

➤ *THE GOOD NEWS:* Some private companies devote much of their efforts to college test preparation and, as a result, they know their business and understand their market. They stay on top of test changes and they've learned how to keep teenagers alert and engaged, even on Saturday mornings. Of course, all of this expertise doesn't come cheap.

If you decide to go with a pricey prep class, then it's your turn to do the homework. Investigate which firms have the best reputation in your area. Some commercial programs are regionally based; some are national. *The Princeton Review* and *Kaplan, Inc.* are the Coke and Pepsi of coaching courses. Both hold classes from coast to coast and claim to outdo the other. Both offer preparation courses for a range of tests, including the PSAT, SAT I & II, and the ACT. The SAT I class is the bestseller and most widely available, and its cost varies regionally. Expect to pay between $700 and $1,000+ for about 30 to 40 classroom hours. Both programs include several complete SAT tests taken under "authentic" conditions.

The Princeton Review "guarantees" a 100-point score increase (verbal and math combined), but claims that the average gain is 140 points, with the top 25 percent jumping 190. Kaplan cites an average increase of 120, with the top 28 percent gaining at least 170 points.

Kaplan will refund fees to those who show no score gains at all. The Princeton Review offers a special refresher class for those who have not made a 100-point improvement despite fulfilling attendance and homework requirements.

➤ *THE BAD NEWS: Kaplan* and *The Princeton Review* courses require home study, and students are clearly told that score increases are linked to output. "Most will get better scores by osmosis from simply sitting in our classroom," maintains one Kaplan official, "but each extra hour of work means more dramatic improvement." As parents, you've surely learned by now that buying the top of the line baseball bat doesn't mean your kid is Willie Mays; music lessons don't often make Mozarts.

And the winner is... Whether you pick *Kaplan* or *The Princeton Review* should hinge largely on convenience and schedule and, especially, local reputation. For class offerings and locations (and an overload of other information) go to www.kaptest.com (for *Kaplan*) or www.review.com (for *The Princeton Review*). By phone, call (800) KAP-TEST or (800) 2-REVIEW, respectively.

Although both firms keep close watch over materials, teacher training, and evaluation, with so many classes and instructors, quality will inevitably depend on where you are. Ask around, and—while you're at it—check into lesser-known companies that may be successful in your area.

• Look for 2a; 3a or b; 7a or b; 10 a or b (a must) and 11a.

Et Cetera

If you've already earmarked the family fortune for a coaching course, you might consider a private tutor instead. A guidance counselor or independent educational consultant can probably tell you if there is an individual nearby who has had appropriate experience. Look for someone who plans to administer an actual test to your child and then zero in on weak spots. Tutoring won't be as much fun as a commercial course but, for kids who work best in one-on-one situations, this could be the way to go. *Kaplan* and *The Princeton Review* also offer private-tutorial courses with their instructors. Their fees range from about $100 to $200 per hour for a 10- to 35-hour program. (Did you choose 10 a and 11 c?)

For a few (and far between) families, the private tutor can be *you*. A preparation manual (or software) is the real teacher; you are primarily the enforcer. (If you answered "a" or "b" on question 9, but "c" or "d" on 10, then you may be candidates for "home schooling.")

Read, Read, Read. Many studies have proven the benefits of regular reading to young children—and of insisting that they read to themselves as they grow older. Even if this has never been a habit in *your* household, some experts argue that the months that might be devoted to test prep programs can be equally well spent curled up in the corner with a good book. Even reluctant readers who fought through *War and Peace* or drowned in *Moby Dick* can find a friend in Tom Clancy or Robert Parker, Alice Walker or Amy Tan. It doesn't have to be Shakespeare or Steinbeck—it just has to be every day. (Did you answer "c" on question 4?)

A Word to Wise Parents

No matter which preparation methods you elect, never lose sight of the importance of keeping test anxiety to a minimum. Be an ally, not an antagonist.

Instead of nagging about completion of registration forms or score order reports, stay on top of deadlines yourself and help your child complete tasks on schedule. Leave test weeks free of other obligations and try to put controversial family issues on the back burner during those times, too.

On testing mornings, be sure that your child eats a healthy breakfast (well, *some* breakfast, anyway), and keep in mind that an extra smile or a favorite family joke on the way out the door can make a difference in a potentially stressful day.

Above all, don't make your child feel that his or her value as a person is in any way linked to scores—or that *your* status at the country club or coffee klatch is on the line. Try to implant in your own mind the seemingly disparate beliefs that, yes, test results may affect where a child goes to college; but, no, that really won't determine future happiness or success.

VI. Information Numbers

The SAT and ACT registration bulletins contain all sorts of useful information that you may want to refer to repeatedly, even months after the last test has been taken. Put them in a safe place (with the passports and car titles; not the dog food coupons and garbage disposal warranty). But for handy reference, detach the page that follows and hang it where it won't be missed (the refrigerator door, the bathroom mirror, or the TV screen?).

Information Numbers

SAT Program Information

College Board SAT Program; P.O. Box 6200; Princeton, NJ 08541-6200; www.collegeboard.com

Customer Service: (609) 771-7600 (Mon.-Fri. 8 a.m to 8:45 p.m. Eastern Time) for test date or center changes, publications, etc.

Automated Service: (800) SAT-SCORE (24 hours, daily; touch-tone phone & credit card required) for re-registration, scores by phone, score reports, "Rush" service

Special Needs: (609) 771-7137 or TTY service: (609) 882-4118 (or ssd@info.collegeboard.org)

PSAT Information: (609) 771-7070

ACT Information

ACT, Inc. P.O. Box 414; Iowa City, Iowa 52243-0414; www.act.org

Customer Service: (309) 337-1270 (Mon.-Fri. 8 a.m to 8 p.m. Central Time) for test date or center changes, lost or delayed admission tickets, publications, etc.

Reregistration (24 hours, daily; touch-tone phone & credit card required): (800) 525-6926

Score Reports: (319) 337-1313

Universal Testing (Special Needs): (319) 337-1332 TDD: (319) 337-1701

TOEFL Information

TOEFL Services PO Box 6151; Princeton, NJ 08541-6151; www.toefl.org; (e-mail: toefl@ets.org)

Customer service (general information, publications): (609) 771-7100; Fax: (609) 771-7500

Scores by phone: (in U.S., Puerto Rico, Virgin Islands, Canada): (888) 863-3544; (all other locations): (609) 771-7267

CHAPTER 4

Finding Out More: Campus Visits & Inteviews; College Fairs & Reps

Forget those robins and daffodils. For many years, the surest sign of spring in one New England town was counselor Ed Wall loading his 11th-grade advisees onto a bus and taking them on a college tour. The junket always included one nearby private college, one small public school, and then a huge state university. Never mind that few of his traveling companions would actually end up at the stops on this itinerary. "I simply wanted them to get an idea of what a college campus looks like," Wall explains, "and an idea of some of the differences among various types of schools. Many sixteen- and seventeen-year-olds have never really seen a college up-close."

Parents, too, notes Wall, should organize outings to area schools early in the search, even before target colleges are identified. By summer, he suggests, students ought to be planning visits, tours, interviews, or information sessions at target schools and finally, by fall of 12th grade, should arrange to spend the night, whenever possible, at top-choice campuses.

I. Campus Visits

Undoubtedly, a visit to a campus is the best way to make college matches. Sure, there are bound to be those random moments that may make or break a school unfairly. One young woman determined her favorite college before even getting out of the car. "I saw this guy who looked just like Tom Cruise," she told her admissions interviewer later, "and I knew right away that this was the place for me." Conversely, eager applicants have been turned off by rainy weather, campus construction, or by the crabby graduate student who gave bad directions at the front gate. Nonetheless, if a picture is worth a thousand words, then a morning or afternoon on campus surpasses a million catalogs, viewbooks, and Web pages. Sometimes it doesn't take much more than a snack in the student lounge to determine if a school is a good fit.

Where to Visit

Take a look at the long list. Has your child read the appropriate publications for every target college? There's no point in getting all the way to William and Mary before discovering that there's no journalism major, nor in trekking to Temple if you want a rural campus. Eliminate the colleges that only sound so-so, then try to see the others. When cost and distance permit, schedule trips to each front-runner school.

➤ *THE GOOD NEWS:* The more colleges you visit, the easier it will become to discern differences and to pinpoint priorities. "It wasn't until I had seen seven schools," Leah recounts, "that I realized that some libraries had 'open stacks,' where I could look among the shelves myself for books I needed, while others had 'closed stacks,' which meant that titles had to be first picked from a card catalog or computer, then ordered at a main desk. I didn't want to do research that way. I like to browse."

➤ *THE BAD NEWS:* If it's Tuesday, this must be Brandeis. And two dozen colleges later, you can't remember where you've been at all. Pragmatism may dictate that you see too many schools in too short a time. If you live in Oklahoma, you're simply unlikely to get to Ohio more than once. Try to limit stops to only two schools per day, and no more than 10 colleges on a single trip. In fact, 10 colleges in an entire year *is* plenty for any applicant—or applicant's parents—to digest. (And be sure that notes get written down during—or right after—every visit to avoid confusion later. Some farsighted families even tote camcorders for the express purpose of campus identification films.)

When to Visit

Again, the ideal world and the real world don't always coincide. Aim to see schools with students on campus, mainly during September through mid-May. Even some colleges with year-round sessions are not in full swing during the summer, but for many families, summer is still the best time to hit the highways. You'll just have to use your imagination if a campus (or an entire town) seems dead (and perhaps visit again at "crunch time"). Commonly, high-school and college spring vacations do not overlap, so if you are well-organized, March or April of your child's junior year can be a good time to see campuses in action. Before finalizing any visit, check with the admission office to see if you'll be arriving in the midst of autumn recess, reading period, or semester break. Web sites often include these schedules, too.

The timing of your visit to campus will also depend on what you plan to do once you get there. Many colleges offer group information sessions that usually include a question and answer period and often a video. These may augment or replace an on-campus interview, depending on policy and availability at your target schools. Some colleges schedule interviews six or seven days a week; some have none at all. The University of Pennsylvania, for example, encourages interviews by alumni in applicants' communities but does not hold them on campus.

In addition, you should ask admission offices about other special programs like the University of Iowa's "Hawkeye Visit Days" or The University of Texas' "Rise and Shine," which offer full days of tours, presentations, class visits, and campus cafeteria meals to prospective students and their parents. Some colleges may invite you to attend open houses sponsored by specific programs or departments.

Questions & Answers

Q: My daughter, a high school junior, hasn't done a thing about planning campus interviews, and it's almost April. When should these be scheduled? Is she missing the boat?

A: Few families are ready to march off to target colleges prior to spring of one's junior year, and many colleges refuse to interview applicants before then, anyway. (Of course, there are always extenuating circumstances. If you're heading from Hawaii to New Hampshire for Uncle Albert's wedding in your child's sophomore year, a sympathetic admission officer may agree to an interview—even after the receptionist has *insisted* that only juniors and seniors are granted personal sessions. Be sure to insist yourself—but nicely.) Most students begin the interview circuit in earnest in the summer between their junior and senior years and then continue in the fall. Colleges are generally willing to interview students until it's time to make admission decisions in the winter of the senior year.

While you may luck into a last-minute vacancy, interview appointments are best made at least two weeks in advance. Gone is the era when students were instructed to write a polite note to the director of admission in their best handwriting to request a meeting. While interviews can still be scheduled by mail, far more expedient are phone calls to admission receptionists who can tell you immediately if your desired dates and times are open.

Again, although Junior may learn from the experience of making the calls, it is usually Mom or Dad who has a better grasp of what will best fit into the travel plans, and colleges certainly don't care one way or another. Some colleges will schedule appointments by e-mail too, which is cheaper—but usually not easier—than a phone call.

Of course, while an interview can be an important aspect of the college selection process and a key part of a trip to campus, it can also be worthwhile to see a school without an interview appointment and, if the place passes muster, to return later for a more official visit. "We did a 'reconnaissance mission' in the summer after Kerry's junior year," recalls her father. "We drove up to New England and looked at about a dozen colleges. We took tours at some places and just walked around on our own at others. In October, Kerry had interviews at two of the schools we'd seen, stayed overnight at two more, and claimed that she wouldn't be caught dead at the others."

Other Visitors' Tips

While there are entire books available on college visits alone, even frequent revisions can't keep all information accurate. Better yet are Web sites, which typically include visit options and schedules. There are usually driving directions, too, and sometimes lists of other area attractions. But even Web pages aren't always up-to-date. A pre-departure phone call to double-check details can help eliminate disappointment.

It is usually not necessary to submit an application before having an interview, and the visit can be an excellent time to decide if a student even wants to apply at all. Guided campus tours are not only a good way to see a school but also an opportunity to grill a real student. If your child will be living there, don't miss a stop at the dorms. In fact, it's wise to pay particular attention to *every* place in which your child is likely to spend lots of time. Such hot spots could include the weight room or the music practice room, the language lab, or the chemistry lab.

Check out the bulletin boards along the way. They often say a lot about an institution's opportunities, ambiance, and attitude. Likewise, pick up student publications—especially the college newspaper—to get more of an inside scoop than admission office propaganda is likely to give. Most tours are available without advance notice, but some colleges require appointments even for group tours, so call ahead to check schedules and make reservations.

Overnight Stays

Colleges often welcome overnight visits from applicants, or even from those in the earliest stages of exploring, and it is an excellent way to get an inside glimpse at any school. The Bucknell University "Host and Hostess" program—typical of many—offers overnight accommodations on Sundays through Thursdays, when classes are in session. Guests, who must bring a sleeping bag or bed roll and pay for their own meals, are matched with Bucknell students who share similar academic interests. Appointments should be made two weeks in advance. At Antioch College in Ohio, special guest rooms in the dorms are available to candidates, and each dorm has a host in residence. Meal tickets are provided, and weekend stays are possible, if necessary. Ask each admission office about options and availability when you call.

"Networking" is another good way to find a campus host. Most college students enjoy showing off their school to visitors, so don't be shy about calling your dentist's daughter at Duquesne or last year's Pep Club president at Pomona. Similarly, coaches are often eager to pair prospective players with current ones (where NCAA regulations permit), or a call to the debate society chairman or literary magazine editor can likewise lead to an overnight invitation.

Questions & *Answers*

Q: We've heard that there are college visits conducted by private "escort services." Is this a good way to see schools?

A: Group touring of college campuses is a burgeoning business, and there are pros and cons to this approach—that is to say, some programs are indeed run by pros while others may be spawned by those with more mercenary motives.

Typically, tours are held in the summer or during school vacations, and high school students spend a week or so visiting a range of campuses, sometimes spending overnights and/or having interviews on several. The best of such outfits not only helps participants get the most out of these visits, but also offer tips on self-assessment, interviews, and applications along the way.

At $1,000 or more, this option isn't for everyone, but compared to the price of a comparable college trip for your family (be sure to factor in hotels, meals, and Rover's kennel costs), it may be worth a closer look. Always check out organizers and leaders and get references from previous participants.

College Visits (www.college-visits.com) or (800) 944-2798 is based in South Carolina and offers many different itineraries, with some tours heading as far from home as the Pacific Northwest and Canada. College Impressions (www.collegeimp.com) or (781) 828-6227 is a smaller venture that specializes in Northeast and Middle-Atlantic schools. Both services come well recommended. With each, your child is bound to see some schools that he or she has no interest in but, on the plus side, may also be introduced to new target colleges.

Crunch-Time Visits

Increasingly, applicants find that they like to see schools *after* they've received admission decisions, during that perplexing period when they have only several weeks to decide which college they'll actually attend. While campus visits early on do assist in determining where students ultimately apply, it also makes sense to avoid financing cross-country junkets to colleges where your child won't even be accepted. "We told Jeffrey that he could look at the University of California-Berkeley *if* he got in," Jeff's mother, Sandy, recounts. "The rest of his choices were all near us in the East. We certainly weren't thrilled when Berkeley rejected him, but we were glad that we hadn't paid for a plane ticket to San Francisco." Likewise, says Dylan, "I was desperate to go to Brown. I knew I couldn't be objective about another school. I applied to four colleges but didn't visit any other campuses in the fall. When Brown denied me, I collected myself and went to the three places that had said yes. As it turned out, I was really impressed with two of them, and I think it was helpful to visit with a mind-set that said, 'This isn't window shopping. These places all want me, and in five months I will live at one of them.'"

Colleges, too, can be eager to entertain on-the-fence accepted applicants. Most will offer overnight accommodations; some issue invitations to special "open campus" events. (See Chapter 8.)

In an ideal world, candidates would visit colleges before applying in the fall and again before making final decisions in the spring. Of course, if this were an ideal world, Ed McMahon would come to your house and give you a check for $10 million, which should just about cover four years of tuition and late-night snack attacks. In *this* world, however, you may have to decide between pre-acceptance and post-acceptance visits or make no visits at all.

*Q*uestions & *A*nswers

Q: How much time should we expect to spend on every campus we visit?

A: If you're planning on an interview and tour, you'll need a minimum of about two-and-a-half hours. Most tours last an hour or so; interviews range from 30 to 60 minutes. Colleges are pretty good about coordinating the two so that you don't spend all morning in the waiting room reading yesterday's *USA Today*, but there is usually some down time in between. Be sure to arrive 10 or 15 minutes before an interview appointment. There will probably be a short form to fill out. Colleges can't normally cater to latecomers, and you might find your child's interview time shortened or juggled if you're not prompt. (If you get lost or stuck in traffic, try to call ahead.)

It's always wise to check on estimated tour, interview, and overall timing when you call for an interview appointment. If you have specific questions about financial aid, you might need to see a financial aid officer (often separate from admission staff). Schedule these sessions in advance, when possible, and add extra time. You may also wish to inquire about sitting in on a class or eating a meal on campus. (If campus meals aren't available, the next best thing is the student snack bar or a nearby student hangout.)

Would-be college athletes might want to plan time with a coach. For top recruits, NCAA rules will govern meetings, but for most aficionados at the Division III level, a call from you or your child could make a coach's day. Don't be shy. (It's also effective if you get your child's coach to call ahead and chat with his or her collegiate equivalent in coachly vernacular. (See "Athletes" in Chapter 9.)

For some families, the infirmary, counseling services, or special needs coordinator should be on the schedule, too. A few seek out music teachers or, if a child has a strong interest and specific questions in a particular academic area, a professor. Just for the record, typical applicants *don't* run around meeting half of the campus personnel. Most stick with the standard interview and tour routine. If you do wish to see someone special, the admission office can give you names and phone numbers, but it's usually up to you to schedule the meetings.

➤ **THE GOOD NEWS:** Faculty and coaches are generally happy to meet prospective students and their families. Don't feel as if you're harassing them. They're glad to encourage a promising candidate to attend their school, and may even put in a good word with the admission office.

➤ **THE BAD NEWS:** Planning college visits can be more complicated than taking a family of five to Disney World, especially if you expect to see several schools on the same trip. Don't be timid about changing arrangements if one key person (e.g., the oboe instructor or tennis coach) isn't available.

Questions & *Answers*

Q: What happens at a campus interview? Do parents get interviewed, too?

A: An interview is usually a one-on-one session that involves an applicant and a member of the admission office staff. In "The Interview Itself" below, you will find more information about what goes on behind that closed door and how you can help your child prepare.

Parents are never *required* at admission offices but commonly choose to accompany their children. They are rarely invited to sit in on interviews and are almost always given a chance to ask questions afterwards. Often this question and answer period is brief and may be in the admission office waiting room where there is little privacy. Occasionally, parents may wish to speak to admission counselors alone (e.g., you may want to discuss your child's health problem or physical disability). In such cases, notify the admission office at the start of the session so that there will be time left in the schedule for your talk. (Remember, specific financial aid questions may need to be directed to a different department.)

➤ *THE GOOD NEWS:* Some parents, especially those who did not attend college themselves, may feel intimidated or overwhelmed in an admission office. Relax. We couldn't find one admission counselor who could think of a single thing that a parent *ever* did at an interview that botched a child's shot at acceptance. Neither Mom's Michael Jackson earrings nor Dad's John Wayne impersonation will fluster admission pros (though your child may want to vanish through the ceiling tiles), and no question should ever be considered too stupid to be asked.

➤ *MORE GOOD NEWS:* Just like your child, you may find yourself tongue-tied in the lobby and remember what you really wanted to know only when you're half-way back to Dubuque. Don't hesitate to telephone or e-mail admission officers any time you have questions or concerns. (Make sure you get each interviewer's card or name before leaving.)

II. The Interview Itself

While colleges don't often insist on personal interviews, many strongly recommend them and may look skeptically at candidates who live within two or three hundred miles and don't take the time to come to campus. Many colleges also offer official interviews with their alumni in an applicant's home city or state (and even in foreign countries).

An interview is a no-lose proposition. Well, almost, anyway—especially if you read the tips that follow. Yes, it's a remote possibility that your child will mess up so badly that he or she blows his or her chance of admittance but, insists a dean at Swarthmore College in Pennsylvania, "that doesn't happen very often." "It's highly, highly unlikely," concurs an official at Hobart and William Smith Colleges in Geneva, New York.

Parents often want to know how much an interview "counts" as if its value can be specified in percentage points. Most admission officers agree that the process is far too subjective to be so weighted. They'll tell you that the high school transcript is far more important and, indeed, it is. However, the interview can be especially helpful for borderline candidates. It gives them a chance to explain irregularities in their transcripts and to present themselves in a positive way that may not come across in the application itself. (In other words, your child has about 30 minutes to make that "D" in geometry look like a valuable learning experience and not a disaster.)

Moreover, admission counselors consider an interview to be an exchange of information, not the Spanish Inquisition. Their questions are not likely to put your child on the spot, nor will they have right or wrong answers.

In admission circles, interviews are said to have three main functions:

- to gather information about a student

- to evaluate the student and the student/school match

- to recruit the student by showing off the school's best side

*Q*uestions & *A*nswers

Q: Who will conduct the interview?

A: Your child may talk to the top-dog dean, to an underling on the admission staff, or even to a faculty member or student. The assignment rarely reflects the "importance" of a candidate. What *is* important is the skill of the interviewer and how well he or she relates to your child.

Alumni interviews may replace or supplement the campus interview. Sometimes they are longer or more informal than their campus counterparts, but not always, and quality varies markedly. Keep in mind that when it comes to getting questions answered, alumni may not be as up-to-date as admission officials or students, and no viewbook or video can replace a visit to campus.

Q: Do we need to bring anything with us to the interview?

A: You should ask before arriving, but the answer is likely to be no. However, unofficial transcripts and résumés are helpful to some interviewers—while others won't so much as glance at them. It's also helpful for your child to review this information before the interview. You'd be surprised by how many students freeze when asked what courses they took last term. It's useful, too, if your child knows his or her standardized test scores, GPA and, if available, class rank.

Art aspirants often appear with bulky portfolios, but most interviewers are hardly critics and, unless your child is applying to an art school or art program where a portfolio has been specifically requested, don't expect more than a fast flip-through. Consider bringing only one or two "masterpieces" instead. The only thing your child shouldn't leave home without is the "College Bible," a good place to record questions, answers, and impressions. (But while you've got the packing list out, don't forget rain gear—especially an umbrella—and comfortable walking shoes, if you're planning to take a tour.)

What to Expect and How to Prepare

One young woman recalls getting stuck with an interviewer who had recently spent some quality time in South America. "What do you think of Chile?" was the first question he asked her. "I'm a vegetarian," she replied, confused. "I won't eat it if it's made with meat."

Fortunately, interviewers rarely ask such questions, nor any that resemble science or social studies quizzes. Nonetheless, an interviewer may want to see if your child is aware of the world beyond the high school. Keeping abreast of what's going on in the world is a sound pre-interview strategy.

Interview formats will vary. Some are quite open-ended. The interviewer may begin by saying, "Tell me about yourself," and then expect the student to take it from there. Others might have a more specific list of queries, some quite straightforward ("What schools have you attended?"); some more provocative ("What character from a book would you most like to be?"). Don't worry, though, the former type far outweigh the latter, and your child isn't expected to come off sounding like Barbara Walters or Billy Crystal.

Commonly, questions arise from student comments, just like they would in a casual conversation. If your daughter says she's on the track team, the interviewer is apt to ask what events she does, how she fared last season, or perhaps what aspects of the training are most demanding. Here are some other typical interview questions:

- **What classes have you enjoyed most?** Your child should be ready to show enthusiasm for *something* (and it should be a recent course, not seventh-grade wood shop). Another spin on this is "What do you like best (or least) about your high school?" or "Who is your favorite teacher and why?"

- **What do you do outside of class?** Whether your child's passion is soccer or ceramics, community service or a part-time job, showing interest in—and a commitment to—an activity is far more important than *what* that interest actually is—unless the activity is watching MTV or playing laser tag at the arcade.

- **What do you do during the summer?** Some teenagers have the luxury of studying overseas while others have to work long hours. As above, interviewers expect your child to be doing something constructive. When planning ahead, make sure that your child does have meaningful summer activities scheduled, not only because they "look good" on applications and in interviews, but because summer choices can be an important part of an overall education.

- **What books have you found enjoyable but challenging?** This is an applicant's chance to show off academic acumen. Let's face it, Jane Austen will make a stronger impression than Danielle Steele; Stephen Crane surpasses Stephen King. Your child may have favorite books that were great for the beach, while others demand more intellectual exertion. The emphasis should be on the latter. Another pre-interview strategy: suggest that your child review recent favorite titles.

- **Whom do you admire?** Your child should be prepared to say why and to go easy on the soap-opera stars.

- **What are your post-college plans?** It's fine to be unsure, but a student should be prepared to discuss some options or interests. Rather than simply saying "I dunno," your child might continue, "I like art and computers, and graphic design seems to combine both, but I want to study Japanese and economics too, so maybe I'll end up in international business." (That covers quite a few bases, doesn't it?)

- **What are you looking for in a college and/or what brings you to this one?** Again, an academic emphasis is important. It's also fine to say, "I have a friend from home who loves it here," but applicants should add why a school seems right for *them* (size, location, majors, and extracurricular offerings may all be legitimate factors). Sometimes, however, the honest answer is, "My mother (or father) went here (or wants *me* to go here) and is bugging me." Our advice? A student can admit to admission personnel that someone else is behind this choice, but it should be *stated*—not *whined*—and applicants ought to cheerfully agree to keep an open mind until the interview and visit are over and the experience sinks in.

- **What will you contribute to this college?** Students may be asked this explicitly. If not, it's certainly something they should impart before they depart.

Interview Hints

Many high school students have never been interviewed before. They're bound to be nervous and unsure of how much to sell themselves and just what to say. In addition to anticipating common questions, as above (and mulling over answers ahead of time), help your child relax and get ready by offering these suggestions from the pros:

- **Prepare**. Before every interview, an applicant should jot down the key points he or she wants to get across and then end the interview by adding, "There's something else I'd like you to know about me…" This may be the only way that the admission office learns about a summer art scholarship or a role in an upcoming musical.

- **Explain**. One critical function of the interview is to enable admission staff to read between the lines of a transcript. Although the application will tell them about grades and other activities, it's bound to be an incomplete picture. For instance, a "C" in calculus may not wow them, but do they realize that no one in the class did better? Or that Junior had been out of school for three weeks do to an illness and had to keep up on his own? He may have only pulled a "B-" in biology, but the teacher praised his term paper as the best she's read in years. Admission officers won't know that from a transcript. It's up to the *applicant* to tell them.

  Admission personnel can get pretty jaded. They've seen more than their share of cultural exchange programs, regional orchestras, and debate awards. What makes your child special? Did she get a chance to go to China because Grandpa wrote a check, or did she have to submit an essay and be selected from hundreds of candidates? Was she the youngest flutist from her school to perform a solo with the state symphony or the first debater to make the national tournament?

Furthermore, although interviewers are not therapists, they are accustomed to confidential information and don't shock easily. If health or family difficulties have affected your child, they should be explained succinctly during an interview. Your child shouldn't go overboard with details but shouldn't be mysterious, either. This information is an important part of who an applicant is and may affect how a candidate is evaluated.

Problems, both academic and personal, can be sources of strength and self-knowledge. If your child doesn't feel comfortable discussing these in an interview but would like admission officials to know about them, consider a supplemental letter. (See Chapter 6.)

- **Boast**. Most of us have been taught not to, but at a college interview a bit of bragging is in order, and admission counselors welcome it. For example, if asked about a chemistry class, it's fine to say, "I was proud of the fact that I got the highest grade on the mid-term" or "the teacher picked me to help with a special research project." If your child *founded* the environmental club and didn't merely *join* it, he or she should say so.

- **Expound**. Interviewers hate to pull teeth. They expect applicants to do much of the talking. Good interviewers usually ask open-ended questions like, "What did you like most about your trip to Japan?" In any case, your child should offer detailed information.

On the other hand, as impossible as it sometimes seems, teenagers need to know when to say when. Especially when they're nervous, kids tend to rattle on about extraneous details. In particular, they should focus on events that occurred during high school. Unless they're extraordinary, fourth grade trials and triumphs are not appropriate.

- **Question**. An interviewer is sure to ask if your child has questions. Even those who have memorized the catalog and spent a week on campus are bound to have *some*. An interviewer may construe a lack of questions as a lack of interest, but your child shouldn't feel compelled to fabricate queries ("How many books are in the library?") to impress the interviewer.

Questions say a lot about the person behind them. The student who inquires about research opportunities in physics is bound to be viewed differently than the one who wonders if the dorms have cable television. Questions should also indicate that the candidate has done his or her homework. "What do students seem to like best about the geology department?" is a legitimate question. "Do you have a geology department?" is not. In general, good interview questions are any that *do* demand information that applicants genuinely want to know and that *don't* depict them as dingbats. The list of possibilities is almost endless. Some questions to ask during an interview include:

- Will my choice of major affect my admission?
- If I'm accepted into one department, how easy is it to transfer to another if I change my mind?
- What is the average class size (especially in my field of study)?
- How large are "introductory" classes?
- How easy is it to take classes in other fields or are there some departments that are too crowded to accommodate non-majors or underclassmen?
- What are your internship options?
- Where can I study or take classes off-campus?
- How competitive is admission to your study-abroad programs (or other special programs)?
- Will my financial aid "travel" with me?
- Are there research opportunities for undergraduates?
- Tell me about your career guidance office.
- What are the pros and cons of different housing options?
- Does this school have a stereotype? How accurate is it?
- What happens here on weekends?
- Do fraternities and sororities dominate the social scene?
- Who are the "minority" students here and are they comfortable?
- How does this college's religious orientation (where appropriate) affect campus life?
- Do students of other faiths fit in?
- What political and campus issues concern students most?
- What do students like best and least about this school?
- What do you like about living and working here? (This is a good catch-all question that turns the tables on the interviewer and bails out the tongue-tied.)

Interview Q&A Tips

- Encourage your child to make a *written* list of questions before each college visit, to leave a space after each one, then answer as many as possible using the catalog and other publications. Those left are fair game for the interviewer. (Your "College Bible" is a perfect place for question lists.)

- The list can go into the interview. When it's time for questions, they can be read right from the list. Interviewers appreciate organization, and your child won't forget anything (and should also feel free to jot down brief notes as each question is answered).

- The interviewer should be alerted to long question lists at the start of the session, so that time can be scheduled accordingly.

Questions & Answers

Q: Should we plan a practice interview at a college we don't care about?

A: One family tried this strategy and discovered that the daughter liked the "practice" school far better than the "first-choice" college she saw three days later. While interviewing at a college that your child will *never* attend is really a waste of time for all concerned, it does make sense to plan interviews at one or two "safety schools" before visiting the long shots. You might also try role-playing at home where *you* play the part of the admission counselor. Better yet, if your child is charming to your friends (but barely gets beyond a grunt with you), ask another adult to serve as a warm-up interviewer. Let this "coach" and your child read the suggestions above and then stage a mock session.

Q: How will an interviewer "grade" my child?

A: After the session, the interviewer will write a brief report. It will usually include objective details that will probably appear on the application later (e.g., "Is enrolled in 3 AP classes"), as well as other information that might not (e.g., "Dropped physics after hospitalization for hepatitis" or "organized city-wide clean-up campaign"). The write-up will become part of the student's "folder" and will assist admission officers in making decisions when the time comes. The interviewer is also likely to include some sort of personal evaluation such as "is articulate" or "reticent" or "will be a good candidate if senior grades continue to improve." At some colleges, interviewers also give a numerical or letter grade, and the vast majority of candidates get some version of a "B." Few fare poorly. Most interviewers are delighted to be on their own side of the desk and have enormous sympathy for their jittery victims. In fact, students tend to give *themselves* a lower grade than their interviewer will.

Moreover, an interview can go well, and an interviewer can be extremely impressed with a candidate who is still denied admission. "Jon loved his visit to Middlebury," his mother recalls. "He thought that he and the interviewer really clicked, so when he ended up on the waiting list, he was demoralized because it made him question his own assessment of the impression he makes on others. Fortunately, I was able to learn from a friend in the admission world that Jon had indeed impressed the Middlebury interviewer. Even a good interview couldn't overcome deficiencies in his other credentials, but at least the inside information restored his self-esteem." You, too, must help your son or daughter realize that a letter of denial doesn't mean that a seemingly successful interview session was really a flop. Some families expect to know a child's chances of admission by the end of an interview, but interviewers rarely give decisions in person. They may, however, point out if their college is a far reach.

Q: Does a long interview mean a successful one?

A: Parents and students often obsess when a session scheduled for 30 minutes lasts only 15—or celebrate if it drags on for an hour. In fact, "good" or "bad" interviews can be either long or short. Most commonly, an admission counselor's appointment roster—not a teenager's wit or wisdom—determines length, and a student can usually tell how things went without looking at the clock. Of course, there will be times when applicants and interviewers connect so well that they chat far beyond the projected period, but timing should never be used as a barometer of success. There was once a dean who was so unable to hold up his end of a conversation that he rarely saw students for more than 15 minutes, and many must have left the office downtrodden. On the other hand, one interviewer confounded her colleagues by keeping a prospect tied up for well over an hour on a busy Saturday. "She was such a boring, insipid kid," the counselor explained afterwards, "that I kept thinking there must be something *I'm* missing. I asked a million questions, tried every angle I could think of, and finally just decided I'd gotten a dud."

A Final "Note" on Interviews...

Someone (your Aunt Pearl?) may have told you that a thank-you letter to an interviewer is proper etiquette. While this is often true for job-hunters, it's polite, but hardly protocol, for college applicants unless *special* thanks are in order. One nice touch is for your child to follow up on an interviewer's suggestions. ("We tried *Jake's* for lunch and loved it" or "Professor Stein *was* interested in my bassoon composition.") It's also a great time to ask those two or three crucial questions that weren't remembered until the ride home. But most bread-and-butter notes get stuck at the back of folders and ignored, so don't insist that your child write thank-you notes to every interviewer with whom he or she had spoken.

Questions & Answers

Q: My son Sean is a strong student and a good writer but so terribly shy that I think he'll come across far better on paper than in person. He doesn't want to interview at any colleges. Should I force him?

A: Probably not. If interviews are recommended or target colleges are close to home, admission officials may question Sean's interest if it appears that he never made it to campus. However, Sean *can* skip what may prove to be a painful ordeal if he lets his evaluators know that their school is important to him. One good way to do this is to send a note or e-mail that says something like, "Although I wasn't interviewed when I visited Davidson in October, I loved the campus and even got to sit in on a philosophy class...." For those who never see a target school at all, a similar note can be sent to ask a question, request the name of a professor or student to contact, etc.

While it's true that students who are very reserved may not sell themselves in interview situations, they are also depriving themselves of a valuable one-on-one opportunity to learn more about their target colleges.

III. Second Opinions

Talking with current students is by far the best way to get to know a college, and any warm body is a likely source of information. Once you get to campus, put your inhibitions on hold. Feel free to approach passers-by with your questions. They'll probably be delighted. A range of perspectives will paint a more accurate picture than merely one or two. It can be especially enlightening to compare admission office "party-line" answers to what real students claim is the status quo. (Tip: Try this investigative-reporter routine while your child is being interviewed. Not only will it pass the time, but it also will enable you to engage in an activity that is potentially mortifying to your child.)

Questions to Ask Current Students

Classes

- What is the average size of your classes?
- Do professors know your name?
- Are professors easily available outside of class?
- How are advisors assigned/selected?
- Do they really *advise* you?
- Is it hard to get into popular courses?
- What's the workload like?
- What's most stressful here?
- Are students competitive or supportive?
- Do many students apply to graduate school and are they accepted?

Campus Life

- Would you call this a "friendly" campus?
- Is crime an issue?
- What's the social life like?
- Are drinking or drugs prevalent?
- Are there fraternities, sororities, or other social clubs?
- What happens on weekends?
- What are the most popular extracurricular activities?
- Where do cultural events fit in?
- What's dorm life like?
- How's the food?
- What are the strong points of the town/city where the college is located?
- Where do students hang out on- and off-campus?

Student Body

- Would you say the student body is diverse?

- Is there a stereotype here?

- What is the political climate?

- Who are the minority groups here and how are they treated?

Other Topics

- Are internships readily available?

- Is the career planning office helpful?

- What do students complain about most?

- Would you apply here all over again?

Accessing a Target College

Professors' opinions are important, too, and making appointments ahead of time is recommended if your child really wants to meet a faculty member. However, a useful way to assess a target college is to wander the corridors where professors have their offices. Are doors often open? Are students in evidence? Are office hours posted?

Below are some questions that you or your child might pose to professors:

Questions for Faculty

- How many students are assigned to each advisor?

- What is your average class size?

- Is the format lecture, discussion, or other?

- Do students question or participate often?

- How frequently do you meet with students outside of class?

- Do non-majors take your classes?

- How many classes do you teach per term?

- Who corrects and grades papers and exams?

- Do you offer special independent study or research opportunities?

- What can a student do if she or he needs extra help?

- How do you use technology in your classroom?

- May I see a syllabus from one of your classes?

- What are some of your former students doing now?

Remember, whether you're talking with professors or students, alumni or administrators, counselors or coaches, the manner in which they respond to your questions can be as telling as *what* they actually say. Are they amiable or aloof? Enthusiastic or apathetic? Well-spoken? Well-informed?

After all, a college is its *people,* as much as it is its catalog, classes, and campus, and without a visit to your target schools, it's difficult to determine just how your child will fit in.

IV. When You Can't Get to Campus

If cost or time constraints preclude a trip to campus, there are a few ways to "visit" anyway. They can't replace the real thing but can help to broaden your view of a college and promote your child's candidacy.

Take a Virtual Tour

With Internet access, students can "visit" almost every campus in the country. Hundreds of home pages will link you quickly to photographs, facts, and figures, as well as to other information that can range from course syllabi to cuisine. Look back to Chapter 2 to review some strategies for getting the most out of the World Wide Web without getting lost or tangled.

Some "virtual tours" are even set up to replicate armchair trips to campus. But keep in mind that just as travel brochures won't let you smell the coffee on the Champs-Elysées or feel the warm sand of Waikiki, photos found on typical Web pages can't compete with a real stroll through the library or dining commons. More telling, however, are student publications that can usually also be accessed from the Web. At many institutions, student organizations have their own home pages, too, and these student-designed sites may provide more insight into a school's culture and climate than the official offerings. At www.collegenews.com you'll find lists of—and direct access to—online college newspapers that will help you get the feel of a campus you don't see.

Make the Scene by Screen

Most colleges try to show off their best sides via video. Ask each admission office to mail you a copy of its own. High school guidance departments often have a range of tapes available as well. Although celluloid tends to bring out the sameness—not the "specialness"—of most schools, the video will give a view that even the viewbook can't.

Let the Campus Come to You

Ask your child's guidance office about area "college fairs" or "college nights" attended by representatives from a range of institutions. These vary from large and noisy all-comers occasions to smaller events, limited to students and parents from only one secondary school. Tables piled high with publications and festooned with catchy banners and displays are staffed by admission officials or by local alumni. Don't rely on fairs as a time for your child to really get to know a school nor for the school to know your child. Yet, you might get lucky on a slow night, have lots of questions answered, and allow your child to feel he has made a connection with a particular college. At the very least, a fair is a good time to browse and see what's out there and to get on (yet more) mailing lists. Parents, as well as students, should try to attend and "work the room" from your own unique vantage points. (**Hint**: Bring stick-on address labels to fairs, and it will save you and your child from writer's cramp.)

Schedules for fairs sponsored by the National Association for College Admission Counseling are listed at www.nacac.com. At this same site you can find information about, you guessed it, college fairs online. Yes, lest some Internet opportunity go unexploited, parents and students can "attend" these regularly scheduled events where a virtual visit hall features "exhibits" provided by participating colleges, and campus representatives "chat" live with guests. The cost is free, but whether these sessions are worth the price of admission depends largely on how much you or your child enjoy such e-enterprises. Perhaps for those who live in remote areas, this is the closest you'll ever get to a college fair.

In addition to visiting fairs, representatives from hundreds of institutions make visits to high schools during the day. The guidance office posts schedules in advance, and students may have to be excused from class to attend. Sometimes college representatives speak to a roomful of students; sometimes to only one. These talks are not official interviews and candidates are not judged by their comportment, but they do offer up-close and accessible looks at colleges. Parents should ask guidance counselors for lists of upcoming visitors and encourage their children to attend appropriate sessions. If a top-choice college is on the list, you can call that school's admission office to see if the visiting representative will be attending evening events where parents are welcome. Your high school may also permit interested parents to sit in on school-day sessions (and oh how your child will love that!).

Some college representatives conduct official interviews while on the road; a few will even do so by phone. Always ask admission offices what your options are.

Connect with an Alum

As you read earlier in this chapter, colleges commonly utilize a network of their graduates who help with the admission process. These alumni may conduct interviews that are just as official as the ones held on campus (complete with an evaluation sent to the admission office afterwards), or they may provide less structured ways to learn about their former schools. The admission office can give you the names of such alumni in your area. You may be surprised by how widespread—even international—these contacts can be.

Your child will go to the alumnus' home or office (or another mutually convenient spot) and should ascertain in advance if this is to be a formal interview and prepare accordingly. Be aware, however, that even when alums are trained to represent the college as interviewers, they are often better at answering general questions about their alma mater than specific admission-related queries. Alumni, too, are likely to paint a picture of the school that may be more subjective than factual. Recent graduates *should* have the up-to-date scoop on a range of topics, while other alums may offer enchanting anecdotes about the good old days but could have limited information about the campus that your child will encounter.

Connecting with an alumnus might also help your child's chances at decision time. Some influential and experienced alumni are eager to promote their favorite local candidates and may even have the ear of top-ranking admission officials.

V. Drawing Conclusions

You've paraded through dozens of campuses, sampled coffee from Carnegie Mellon to Kalamazoo, seen more gyms than Bobby Knight. Each time you fish for the phone book, you come up with a viewbook instead. The "College Bible" brims with your child's inscrutable scribbles: contacts and questions, pros and cons. Now what?

Now it's time to choose. The facts are in front of you, but there's more to this decision than the data. Sometimes, when all schools start to sound alike, it can be the little things that make a match work best. Cassie and Lissy, for example, were both strong students who wanted coeducational liberal arts colleges and considered several seemingly similar institutions. Cassie especially liked the honor code at Haverford. It reminded her of the one that worked so well at her high school, and she knew that it would make her feel at home from the start. Lissy appreciated Carleton's "No Cars" policy, believing that it would help to put everyone there on equal footing. While both young women selected their schools for a range of reasons, it was a small and special quality—not the list of majors offered nor the student/faculty ratio—which led them to their final decisions.

Moreover, don't discount gut reactions. Two colleges might look about the same on paper, but your child may feel good about one and not so great about the other. This is quite normal. A small, subconscious voice that whispers, "It just doesn't seem right" can be a perfectly fine reason to eliminate a college from the ledger.

Let that same small voice remind you of what's really best for your child. It's easy to be swayed by a prestigious reputation or a fabulous football team. If such factors are important to you and to your son or daughter, by all means, don't dismiss them, but *do* pick those places that will meet your *child's* needs and not yours or anyone else's.

As you read earlier, aim for five or six applications. As you finalize your list, also keep these tips in mind:

- **The most selective colleges should be considered long shots by almost everyone.** Too many candidates with 1,400 SATs, excellent grades, and other extras are turned away to make any of these schools a certainty. If your child is set on an Ivy (or the like), he or she may want to submit several more than the five or six applications.

- **Although your child may like one college far better than another, that doesn't automatically make the latter a back-up option.** "Just because a college is *your* second or third choice, doesn't mean that it's easier to get into," warns a former dean of admission at Colgate University. "That's a dangerous type of transferal that's commonly made." Make sure to use statistics to determine "likely" and "safety" schools.

- **These days, with so many families depending on financial assistance, no college is a sure thing until the tuition bills are paid**. Don't forget that a sure bet is not only a place where your child will definitely be admitted, but also one that he or she can afford to attend.

- **For many students, first-choice colleges will often be likelies, not long shots**. In such cases, fewer applications have to go in the mail—unless you need to compare financial aid packages.

Did somebody say "application" and "financial aid"? That's right, no matter how extensive (and exhausting) your college search has been, it's not over until it's over—which means that there's a lot of paper-pushing still ahead.

5

Money Matters: Financial Planning and Financial Aid

This is the chapter you have been waiting for, according to the responses from the questionnaires we circulated asking, "What are the major issues that you, as a parent of a college-bound student, are concerned about?" (The only item rated as more important was finding the proper fit between your child and college.)

In this chapter, the focus will be on financing. You'll be able to set up a budget projecting college costs, start to determine what aid is available and how to qualify, and learn more about financing options if your child is not eligible for—or is not awarded—financial aid.

I. Estimating College Costs

Questions & Answers

Q: Just how much does college cost?

A: If you take a look at current, published tuition fees for private and public colleges, you'll note that there is quite a range in cost. Some public colleges charge in-state students just a couple of thousands of dollars per year in tuition while many charge several thousand dollars; public-college tuition costs for out-of-state students can be two to four times more than tuition fees for students who are state residents. In some cases, public tuition costs for non-residents are comparable to private tuition costs.

Also, the range in private college tuition fees is wide. Many fine private colleges now exceed six figures for a four-year education. Check for up-to-date fees on Web sites and in current publications. If your child is an eager high achiever, he or she might want to consider accelerating and graduating in less than four years. However, at some colleges, there is an extra charge for a student enrolling in more credits than a standard full-time load. In addition, many schools award advanced standing for Advanced Placement credit and college courses taken in high school. Your child may be able to graduate a term, or maybe a year, early and invest the money saved into graduate education.

If your child will be living on campus, you'll need to plan for room and board charges. Often, there are variations in room and board fees based on whether or not your child lives in a single or triple room and what kind of meal plan he or she chooses. Published fees will give you a general idea of what to expect. Closer to enrollment time, you will get a bill with detailed information created specifically with your child's preferences noted.

In addition to tuition and room and board, you'll have to budget for books and supplies, as well as additional fees for activities and health insurance. Averages for books and supplies vary depending on major. Financial aid officers generally have a standard figure they use—$1,500 to $2,000 per year is not unreasonable for books, supplies, and personal expenses. Based on recent history, it's safe to predict 4- to 6-percent annual increases.

Read everything you can get your hands on about paying for college. The Internet, school guidance office, your local library, colleges, newspapers, and government publications have information for you. Read them, reread them, and copy and underline what's important to you. Be sure the sources are up-to-date. Remember, you will pay for college with your past income (savings, investments, etc.), current income, and future income (loans). Figuring out the money-end of college for your child will go a lot smoother if you are well informed, well prepared, and well organized.

The Educational Costs Budget on page 115 will give you a rough idea of what your child's college choices might cost. Consult college catalogs and guidebooks as well as financial aid publications for estimated expenses. *Be certain that the costs you are comparing are current and official.* Chances are good that no two colleges will cost the exact same amount.

If you have absolutely no idea of which colleges will be appropriate choices for your child, you might just plug in figures from the type of school. Don't add in scholarship aid or loans at this point; there is another budget on page 130 for that purpose. For now, we want a straightforward reading of what estimated costs will be.

Photocopy this form if you want to compare additional prices as you go through the more advanced stages of the college search. Also, cluster comparably priced colleges together under one heading.

Some parents are faced with sticker shock when first confronted with college costs. Indeed, for many people, paying for a child's education is second in cost only to the purchase of their homes. Depending on when and where you bought your home, financing a child's education may be even more costly. On the other hand, studies have shown that some parents overestimate the true costs of college tuition and fees.

BUDGET 1: EDUCATIONAL COSTS BUDGET

	Most Expensive	Top Choice	Financial Aid Safety School
School Name			
A. Direct Educational Costs			
Yearly tuition			
Required fees			
B. Books and Supplies			
C. Room and Board			
Living with parents or			
Living on campus or			
Living off campus			
D. Personal Expenses			
Medical			
Transportation:			
If resident student, round trips home			
If commuting student, subway, bus fare, or automobile costs			
Other costs (clothing, lunches if not included under room and board, cell phone, etc.)			
Application fee, travel, and any other additional, one-time expenses related to the admission process			
TOTAL COST = A + B + C + D			

Budget 1 Explained

A. Direct Educational Costs

Tuition costs vary considerably from school to school, and higher costs don't necessarily insure a better educational experience for your child. While most public institutions cost less than private institutions, residency matters. If you are not a resident of the state that the public university is in, your tuition costs may be comparable to those of a private school. In fact, tuition and required fees for out-of-state students at some state universities are higher than at some private colleges.

You may qualify for tuition benefits or discounts if you are a college employee or even live in a college town. Additionally, some schools offer tuition breaks for siblings who attend at the same time or for the children of alumni.

There are some very fine institutions *without* tuition—such as the service academies and Cooper Union. Cooper Union for the Advancement of Science and Art in New York City is, according to its Web site, "the only private, full-scholarship college in the United States dedicated exclusively to preparing students for the professions of architecture, art, and engineering." That's right—it's free! But before you rush off to get an application (yes, there is an application fee), keep in mind that it is super competitive, and for every spot in the freshman class, there are at least 10 applicants.

Northeastern University in Boston offers undergraduates the chance to participate in cooperative ("co-op") education, alternating classroom learning with periods of full-time work at places like Microsoft, Fidelity, *The Boston Globe,* and The Boston Symphony. Typically, opting for co-op adds a fifth year to the college program; graduates benefit greatly by earning money for college expenses and getting an edge in the post-college job market. Forty percent of Northeastern's co-op students work for co-op employers after graduation.

ROTC scholarships make college more affordable for those who wish to join the armed services after graduation. Heather, a non-ROTC student and the only child of a single mom, graduated from a private liberal arts college with $52,000 in loans, and *then* joined the Army. Not only were her loans forgiven when she enlisted in the Army (she has a four-year commitment) but she was given an $8,000 signing bonus.

B. Books and Supplies

While it's safe to assume that a student will spend $750-$1,000 per year on books, depending on your child's major, this figure can range dramatically. For instance, art supplies, uniforms, and special lab equipment may be requirements for some fields of study. Evaluate whether these costs will be one-time investments, or if equipment needs (and costs) will increase.

Some majors lend themselves to taking advantage of paperback and used books. Shakespeare's work hasn't changed in content over the eons, but with the never-ending political and geographic changes in the world, a student could be on the way to academic disaster if second-hand textbooks are out of date.

C. Room and Board

Consider variations in location of the schools (e.g., rents are more expensive in cities, etc.) and options in board plans (e.g., 21 meals a week, lunches, and dinners only, etc.) when penciling in these estimates. While most students don't know where they want to live before enrolling in a college, some are sure that they want to live in a dorm, at home, in an apartment off campus, or in a fraternity or sorority.

If your child will be living at home with you, you will incur some costs (e.g., food and utilities) that you wouldn't if your child was away.

You can get estimates of local rents and fraternity and sorority charges from the college housing office. If renting off campus, consider a month-to-month lease at first, particularly if your child doesn't know anybody or may not be familiar with the area.

D. Personal Expenses

The numbers in this category can vary greatly, depending on geography, extracurricular interests, and your child's ability to stretch—or spend—a dollar. If your child goes to college 2,000 miles from home, airfare will be a big-ticket item in this section. Cities have treasures of museums and concerts, but ticket prices on Broadway can be extravagant on *any* budget, and city life brings with it parking or transportation costs. Thankfully, there are ways to get cheaper tickets, and student discounts are usually available.

If your child is going from a warm climate to a cold one, add in wardrobe costs. A winter coat and good waterproof boots can set you back hundreds of dollars—and that's not counting ski equipment and lift tickets.

A bicycle might be the best form of transportation around campus. Will your child insist on the latest model full-suspension mountain bike or pull the old Raleigh three-speed out of the garage? It's often not a bad idea to get there before making a major purchase such as this to find out what's really needed and to help keep transporting all the stuff to a minimum. Many must-have items (including bikes and computers) can often be bought second hand on or near campus.

Staying in touch via e-mail can contain telephone costs. Having a cell phone with a workable plan and region might be cheaper than having a phone in the room. You might want to have some kind of agreement about who is responsible for what—you may pick up the tab on calls home, but late night calls to girlfriends and boyfriends scattered all over the country should be the responsibility of the student.

If nothing else, if you have read this section in time, you may be able to make some suggestions to relatives for high school graduation presents. Telephone calling cards, a laptop computer, tickets to sporting or cultural events, and restaurant gift certificates are welcomed. A gift certificate at the college bookstore or a cash contribution to a college debit card makes a practical present at any time of year.

Total Costs

While you may be very surprised by the variations in costs among colleges, don't be premature about crossing a college off the list simply because prices are high. It may be that you will qualify for aid at the more expensive college and not at the other, and it may be that the less expensive school is really not a bargain because it doesn't offer your child as many opportunities or advantages.

Topics for Roundtable Family Discussions

- **Is there a certain amount of money that you are willing to commit to a child's education?** If your ability to pay is more than your willingness to pay, you should put your cards on the table as soon as you can in the college admission process. Some families agree to pick up the tab on tuition and room and board, but expect their children to pay for books and personal expenses. This is a good time to work out the ground rules.

- **Are there sources of financial assistance that you should be investigating?** If a grandparent has always said, "I'll be willing to help out when the time comes," this might be the time. Often, grandparents are eager to help out financially—for tax reasons as well as altruistic ones. If grandparents pay tuition directly to a college, this money will *not* be treated as taxable gifts, and the grandparent would still be able to take advantage of making a $10,000 annual gift, reducing his or her taxable estate. Be sure to investigate specific scholarships through your church, club, or employer, too.

- **What sacrifices are you willing and able to make as a family to pay for college?** Vacations, new cars, and home improvements may be luxuries that you won't be able to afford with children in college. If these decisions are discussed and made together, they are usually easier to live with. In addition, if your child has assets such as stocks and bonds, will any or all of them need to be liquidated to pay for school?

- **Expect to borrow.** The number of families borrowing for education continues to rise, and these days most college students and their families borrow from someone or from somewhere. It's important for you to establish an idea of how much debt you are willing to incur. Make sure that your credit rating is healthy. If your family has not experienced any trouble with previous debts, you should be in good shape to borrow again.

- **Don't blackmail your children.** Far too many parents insist that they will foot the bill only if their children attend a school of the parents' choice or study a particular major. Janice unhappily enrolled at her parents' alma mater, and only after being miserable for two years was she able to convince her parents to allow her to transfer.

- **If parents are divorced, be certain that it's clear about who will assume what college expenses.** Paul, a divorced noncustodial father, paid all the bills for his daughter's private college. Now his son is ready to enter college and he's asked his ex-wife to split the cost since he hasn't recovered financially from their older child's bills. She has refused. The father plans to apply for financial aid this time around and may or may not qualify.

II. Applying for Financial Aid

➤ *THE GOOD NEWS:* Federal and state government, educational institutions, and private agencies are committed to making higher education accessible to students regardless of need, and a vast amount of money is available to help those who need it. Billions of dollars are available to assist students pay their college bills. The Taxpayer Relief Act of 1997 has provided the largest investment in higher education since the GI Bill was established in the late 1940s. For details about tax credits for higher education, using Education IRA funds, the HOPE Scholarship, Lifetime Learning credits, and income caps for benefits, go to www.ed.gov/inits/hope/.

➤ *THE BAD NEWS:* You will need to carefully and methodically complete a series of fairly complex forms in order to determine eligibility for these funds. If you've never been organized in your life, this is the time to begin.

Questions & Answers

Q: How do we know if we have a "demonstrated" need for financial aid?

A: In simple terms, financial need is calculated or "demonstrated" by taking the total cost of attendance and subtracting how much you and your family can afford to contribute. The *Expected Family Contribution (EFC)* is calculated by weighing your family's financial assets against financial liabilities. This is done in a standardized "needs analysis" process using what is known in financial aid language as Federal Needs Analysis Methodology. In addition, each college or university has its own philosophy that could make the calculation of your family contribution vary. For example, schools that go strictly by Federal Needs Analysis Methodology ignore home equity, but most private schools will take home equity into account when calculating family contribution. Additionally, aid officers sometimes use their own professional judgment to take special circumstances into account. Colleges often have worksheets, computer programs, and financing and counseling sessions offered for parents to get a ballpark figure for the expected family contribution and to determine the likelihood of getting aid. Many schools have a staff member who is shared by the admission and financial aid offices and will serve as a liaison between the two processes.

Consult the College Board's site at www.collegeboard.com and get up-to-date information about college costs as well as the chance to complete forms that will help you estimate your EFC and calculate estimated loan repayments. Use any pre-award tools as a guide only. Ultimately, financial aid officers spend an inordinate amount of time crunching the numbers you submit. They are well-trained professionals, and the process of institutional needs analysis is complex and specific. Every family's financial situation is different—and not always the way it seems on the surface. You'll need to be patient as you wait for notification of any financial aid award after an admission decision is made.

In order to figure out how much, if any, aid you will qualify for, you will need to fill out more forms than you'd probably like. Generally, to apply for need-based aid, you will need to be prepared to submit:

- **The Free Application for Federal Student Aid (FAFSA).** The FAFSA is a form, available in English and Spanish, required of all students wishing to apply for federal aid. As the title suggests, there is no fee for processing. Since the FAFSA takes into account information on your most recent tax return, you can't file before January 1 of the year in which your child starts college. Families may complete a paper copy of the FAFSA, normally available after December 1 at secondary school guidance offices. An increasing number of families apply online at www.fafsa.ed.gov. If you apply online, errors can be caught and corrected as you complete the form. In addition, online turnaround time is just two to three weeks, compared to a four- to six-week turnaround time for hard copy submission. Students must have a social security number to apply for federal aid.

- **College and university forms.** Some schools have their own forms that need to be completed in addition to the FAFSA. In some cases, it is these forms which initiate an application for financial aid and so it is important that they be submitted on time. These are usually included with the application for admission or may even be available on the college's Web site.

- **Parent and student tax forms.** Keep these records handy and try to file early as signed photocopies will be required as part of the aid application process. If for some reason the appropriate tax forms are not available by the deadline, ask the financial aid office about the possibility of submitting an estimate. Usually, the prior year's information will do but, since the official financial aid award will be based on the most recent tax year, it's better to submit that if possible.

- **CSS/Financial Aid PROFILE.™** This form is required, in addition to the FAFSA, by over 300 colleges and private scholarship organizations. It provides more information than is required by the federal government to estimate aid eligibility. Some colleges will request the PROFILE™ from all applicants, some from first-timers only, and others from only Early Decision or Early Action candidates. There is a modest fee for PROFILE™ users. Get more details and file electronically at www.collegeboard.com/profile, or call the College Board's toll-free number at (800) 788-6888.

- Additionally, you may be required to submit a **Divorced/Separated Parent's Statement** along with both parents' tax returns. Colleges vary on their policies for dealing with noncustodial parents, so investigate. If the noncustodial parent is reluctant to complete forms at the request of a child or ex-spouse, the financial aid office may be willing to intercede and contact that parent directly or to waive the requirement. Don't hesitate to contact the financial aid office for advice in dealing with parents' information.

- A **Business or Farm Supplement**, along with corporate income tax returns, may be required if one or both parents own businesses or farms.

Copies of both the Divorced/Separated Parent's Statement and the Business or Farm Supplement come with the PROFILE™.

After you complete and return the FAFSA for processing, the SAR (Student Aid Report) will be sent to you. (You'll get it faster if you apply online.) It will show your expected family contribution using the federal calculations. This standardized information will also be forwarded to the colleges your child selects. There will be a section for corrections. Remember to follow directions carefully.

While your expected family contribution remains relatively constant wherever your child goes to school (depending on method of calculation), financial need varies depending on educational costs.

For example, assume your family's contribution is calculated at $10,000 and two of the colleges your child is considering are College X, costing $35,000 and College Y, costing $15,000.

Financial Need at College X is equal to:

$35,000 **College Costs**
minus 10,000 **Expected Family Contribution**

$25,000 Financial Need

Financial Need at College Y is equal to:

$15,000 **College Costs**
minus 10,000 **Expected Family Contribution**

$5,000 Financial Need

Consequently, even though College X is more expensive than College Y, your expected family contribution remains constant, and assuming that both College X and College Y award your child aid *to the full extent of need* ($25,000 at College X and $5,000 at College Y), both will be affordable.

While your calculated financial need varies at different schools (for the purposes of awarding institutional monies which comprise the bulk of financial aid awarded by private colleges), so do the colleges' philosophies of awarding aid.

Need-Based Aid

Need-based financial aid is money awarded to students on the basis of demonstrated financial need. Some colleges award aid to the *full extent of need.* That is, your child will be offered $12,000 if that is what she qualifies for on the basis of needs analysis. Other colleges spread their money farther by practicing what is known as *need gapping.* In this case, students are awarded part of what they need so that more students can be offered aid. Asking about the philosophy of awarding aid will prevent surprises when award letters arrive.

In addition, some colleges exercise *preferential packaging.* That is, they will lower the amount of self-help (loans, work-study) and up the amount of gift aid (grants and scholarships that need not be repaid) for students they are trying to recruit. Be certain to analyze what percentage of aid is self-help and what percentage is gift aid when comparing financial aid packages.

Some colleges also practice what some call *front loading.* In this case, they award a very attractive financial aid package to first-year students to entice them to enroll, and then, they either end all aid or reduce aid to a much lower rate after the first year. If your child is offered aid, be certain to ask if you can expect a comparable amount for the entire four years, assuming of course that your financial need remains consistent.

Need-blind admission means that admission decisions are made without any regard to financial need.

Questions & Answers

Q: Do those colleges that are need-blind really treat the rich and the poor the same at decision time?

A: Ideally, yes. *Need-blind* means that admission officers pay absolutely no attention to an applicant's ability to pay when making admission decisions. Admission officers enforcing a *need-blind* admission policy may not know (or care) if an applicant has applied for, or qualifies for, need-based aid. Colleges with vast resources are able to offer financial aid to the full extent of need to everybody who qualifies for admission and who, through the standardized needs analysis, is deemed needy.

Colleges with more modest budgets may spread their money out by *gapping* (not meeting full extent of need) or by offering admission to some students but not offering aid (called "admit/deny"). Some colleges will, with or without confessing, use financial need as criteria for admission when fine-tuning decisions about equally qualified candidates. This is called *need-sensitive* or *need-conscious* admission. Keep in mind that many colleges must use their aid creatively to attract the best students.

Q: **Can applying for aid hurt your chances for admission if you don't qualify for aid?**

A: Not needing aid can be a "hook" in the admission process. (See Chapter 7.) However, there are many good reasons to apply for aid even if you suspect you might not qualify. One, you may qualify after another sibling enters college or if your family financial situation changes for the worse. Some colleges require that students complete a certain number of credits before applying for aid if they did not apply initially. So even though you might not qualify the first time, you might in the future.

Second, you might be surprised and qualify right from the start. Often middle-class families worry that they will deplete an entire nest egg to pay for college. In fact, just 5 to 6 percent of parents' assets are "taxed" for financial aid purposes, compared to up to 35 percent of student assets. Particularly at high priced colleges, many middle-class families are surprised and relieved that they do qualify for aid.

Merit Aid

Merit aid is money awarded for some sort of achievement—academic, artistic, athletic, etc.—and demonstrated financial need is not necessary to qualify. The majority of private and public colleges and universities award some kind of merit aid. Some colleges require an interview, writing sample, or audition as part of the application process for merit awards. Others require no special application. Students need to research scholarship-awarding practices for the schools to which they apply.

The University of Rhode Island offers a number of merit-based Centennial Scholarships ranging up to four-year full tuition awards. Students interested must apply by the Early Action deadline in December and must write an essay to be considered.

In Arizona, The Flinn Scholars Program offers a sought-after award that rewards top high school students who continue their educations in-state at one of Arizona's own universities. The competition is keen with only one in 25 students qualifying for the very generous award.

Merit aid is not given only to brainy students, either. Ellen, an average student, came from a part of the country that is traditionally underrepresented at her college. She was given a break on her dorm costs since she was helping the college cast their marketing net wider.

In addition, there are private scholarship competitions that require essays, science projects, and artwork. There are special scholarships for bowlers, farmers, air traffic controllers, and beauty queens. There's even a scholarship competition available for high school students who attend their proms in outfits made completely from duct tape. Check out www.fastweb.com to do a scholarship search.

III. Tips for Applying for Financial Aid

- **Deadlines may vary dramatically but *whatever* they are, stick to them.** Don't lose the opportunity to qualify for aid simply because you procrastinated. Keep financial aid deadlines on the family calendar, in the kitchen, or in your date book. Some colleges operate on a first-come, first-served basis, particularly those that make rolling decisions, so keep that in mind if your son or daughter is a procrastinator by nature. Carefully investigate what requirements there are for Early Decision or Early Action applications.

- **Keep photocopies/hard copies of all submitted materials marked with dates sent.** That way if anything is lost in the mail, misdirected through cyberspace, misplaced at the college office (yes, they are human), you can replace it right away.

- **Maintain a file for each aid application.** Hold on to all correspondence. Print and file all e-mail messages. Keep a record of phone calls (names and dates, too). Happily, many offices have toll-free numbers and calling hours in the evening and on weekends. While some colleges will send reminders if any piece of the application is missing, many will not. However, more and more colleges are making it possible to log onto their Web sites with a PIN number to determine if admission or financial aid documents have not arrived.

- **Try to file your federal tax forms early, if possible.** The FAFSA and PROFILE™ refer to the 1040 form and, if actual figures are available, the form will be more accurate, and you won't need to update it later. If you cannot file early, you should use your best estimates. For example, the last pay stub for the previous year will show what your total wages were. You should *not* wait to fill out the FAFSA or PROFILE™ for tax forms that will be completed later than the application is due. Financial aid officers can update estimates electronically with actual figures, once available.

- **Follow directions carefully.** If you complete forms by hand, rather than computer, be certain that the writing is neat and clear on the applications and that each question is answered as carefully and completely as possible. The forms give very specific instructions. For your own purposes, underline deadlines and very important points.

- **Use designated space for comments and notes about special circumstances.** If necessary, add an additional letter to the college's own application.

- **Make an appointment to meet with a financial aid officer** to discuss special circumstances. Offices often schedule telephone visits or will correspond via e-mail. Be certain to write down the name of your contact, and stay in touch when you need questions answered. Keep toll-free numbers and Web sites handy.

- **Make certain that your son or daughter's name and social security number (or the ID number assigned by a particular college) is on every form and document.** Be consistent and use formal names, not nicknames. Also, if your last name is different than that of your child, make sure *your* name and relationship is listed clearly on correspondence.

- **If you need to revise information originally submitted to the federal processor, these revisions should be made on the SAR.** The Department of Education will send the SAR to you as soon as a week after you file the FAFSA electronically. If you have a change to make in your initial application, it needs to be made on the SAR. Follow CSS's own correction procedure for making changes on the PROFILE™.

- **Follow-up.** Make sure that you, as a parent, have done your part of the job and check up on your child's responsibilities. Keep in mind that procrastination may jeopardize your chance of receiving aid. Check with the financial aid office and find out if anything is missing from your folder. *Warning: Incomplete folders don't get considered at all at many institutions.*

- **Put plenty of time into the financial aid process.** Students often spend months—and sometimes even years—corresponding with an admission office to get an application filed and completed. Usually, the time spent on the financial aid application is a matter of weeks. Both application processes are important. Keep that in mind and spend adequate time preparing both sets of forms. Consider the time spent as an investment. A director of financial aid remembers, "A parent once told me he paid his son minimum wage to research and apply for scholarships and financial aid in order to reinforce the importance of the financial commitment." If you invest 40 hours in the financial aid process and your child is awarded $15,000 worth of aid, that's a salary of $375 per hour!

- **Don't wait until after you receive an admission decision before applying for financial aid.** Students sometimes think that they won't be admitted so they don't bother to apply for aid or they hope that by not applying for aid they may be enhancing their chances of admission. If you think that your family might need aid, apply *on time.* If you wait until too late in the admission cycle, you may be disqualifying your child only on the basis of timing.

  Remember, apply for aid now, even if you think you won't need it until your child's second or third year of college. Some colleges will not consider an aid application from a student who didn't apply at the time of admission until the student has earned two years worth of credit.

- **Upperclassmen are generally expected to contribute more** in self-help—loan and Federal Work-Study. Also, expected summer contributions rise from freshman year to senior year. Be certain to find out what the expectations will be for your child.

- **Special circumstances such as rental property ownership, inheritance, home refinancing, or remarriage** may affect the way the EFC is calculated. Consult a financial aid officer.

- **If your family applies for financial aid and is not awarded any,** either because your situation was assessed as no-need or because there simply was not enough aid available, investigate the possibility of reapplying and being awarded aid at a later date. If you will never receive aid, you need to accept that fact and make appropriate plans. Don't get yourself in a situation where you can't pay the bill or your child will have to work an exorbitant number of hours a week in addition to going to class. This is a formula for disaster.

- **Remember to apply to a "financial-aid safety school."** Be certain that your son or daughter will have at least one choice for college that you can afford even if you receive little or no financial assistance.

- **Investigate additional sources of aid available to you through your employer, church, fraternal organizations, etc.** Call your company's human resources office for suggestions and keep your eyes and ears open for announcements in the paper and at meetings.

Questions & Answers

Q: I have heard that there are millions of dollars of financial aid that goes unused each year. Is this true? If so, how can we apply?

A: Some scholarships and loans are very specific and can only be awarded to students fulfilling certain criteria. For example, there is a loan forgiveness program for college students in Alaska who remain in the state working as state troopers after graduation. The American Society of Mechanical Engineers Auxiliary, Inc. gives grants and loans to upperclassmen in accredited mechanical engineering programs. In some cases, organizations will award their funds to a non-specific applicant if nobody with the stated qualifications applies, but others stick to their guns and wait for someone to come through the ranks meeting the established criteria. Keep looking in libraries and in the guidance office for opportunities that may be appropriate for your child. A great Web site to browse is www.fastweb.com. (We know we've mentioned it before, but it's a winner.)

Consult the Federal Student Aid Information Center operated by the U.S. Department of Education with questions about their sources of aid. Among its resources is the free brochure, *The Student Guide*, available online, in paper, and in Spanish and English at www.ed.gov. This publication presents an overview of major aid programs available to students along with details about the application process.

Parents who try to beat the system and qualify for aid for which they lack income eligibility are often unsuccessful since so much official documentation is needed. Additionally, a process called verification that randomly checks the applications of students applying for aid, catches inaccuracies. There are stiff penalties for cheaters. If you have any reason to suspect any fraud, waste, or abuse involving federal student aid funds, call (800) MIS-USED, the hotline to the U.S. Department of Education's Inspector General's office.

IV. Financial Aid Packages

If your child receives financial aid, a "package" is awarded. That is, a combination of the two basic kinds of financial aid—gift aid and self-help.

- **Gift aid** is a present—scholarships and grants that never have to be paid back. Sometimes there is a string attached—your child needs to be studying a particular subject or must maintain a certain GPA, etc. A financial aid award letter should spell out all of this information.

- **Self-help** requires some effort from your child and, in the case of some loans, from you. Loans and Federal Work-Study jobs make up varying amounts of a financial aid package, and that mix will be very important to you as you compare costs of one school against another.

Ideally, an offer of financial aid is mailed at about the same time as an offer of admission, and often it arrives in the same envelope. If your financial aid decision is delayed and is not available by May 1 (Candidates Reply Date), request an extension of the deposit deadline so that you can make an informed decision about attendance.

Budget 2, Educational Financing Budget on page 130, will give you a chance to outline the amount and types of aid you might receive from different colleges. This exercise is most helpful *after* you have received financial aid offers, obviously, but if you can project what might be available to you, it can serve as a good rough guide earlier in the process. The various types of aid are described on the pages following the budget, so depending on what stage you're in now, you may just want to flip ahead to read about the programs, and later, come back to this comparative shopper's guide.

BUDGET 2: EDUCATIONAL FINANCING BUDGET

	Top choice	Middle choice	Financial Aid Safety School
School Name	_____	_____	_____
A. Estimated Family Contributions			
Parental support	_____	_____	_____
Federal PLUS Loan (Parent Loan for Undergraduate Students)	_____	_____	_____
Child's savings	_____	_____	_____
Child's earnings	_____	_____	_____
Other family support (grandparents, aunts, uncles, etc.)	_____	_____	_____
B. Federal Assistance			
Federal Pell Grant	_____	_____	_____
Federal Supplemental Educational Opportunity Grants	_____	_____	_____
Federal Stafford Loan Subsidized (need based)	_____	_____	_____
Unsubsidized (non-need based)	_____	_____	_____
Federal Perkins Loan	_____	_____	_____
Federal Supplemental Loans for Students	_____	_____	_____
Federal Work-Study	_____	_____	_____
C. State Assistance			
Scholarships and grants for residents	_____	_____	_____
Loans	_____	_____	_____
Special programs	_____	_____	_____
D. College/University Assistance			
Scholarships and grants	_____	_____	_____
Work aid	_____	_____	_____
Loans	_____	_____	_____
E. Private Organizations			
Loans	_____	_____	_____
Scholarships	_____	_____	_____
F. Other Sources	_____	_____	_____
TOTAL= A + B + C + D + E + F	_____	_____	_____

Budget 2 Explained

A. Estimated Family Contributions

The major responsibility for paying for your education belongs to you and your child. Parents' ability to pay not willingness to pay is what is measured by needs analysis. And since your son or daughter will be the one to benefit from the education, he or she will be expected to contribute a percentage of savings as well as some earnings.

A **Federal PLUS Loan (Parent Loan for Undergraduate Students)** is for parents who want to borrow to help pay for their children's education, and like a Stafford Loan (see below), is made by a lender such as a bank, credit union, savings and loan association, or even a college. Repayment begins 60 days after the money is advanced.

An *independent* student is required to report only his or her income and assets (and spouse's if married) unlike a dependent student, who must report parental assets and income along with his own. If you, as parents, are able to pay but are unwilling to pay, that doesn't make your child independent, at least not according to federal guidelines.

Federal guidelines stipulate that a student is independent if she or he has reached the age of 24. If a student is not 24 but is one of the following, independent status will be granted for purposes of applying for federal aid:

- an orphan or a ward of the court (or a ward of the court until age 18)

- a veteran of the U.S. Armed Forces

- has legal dependent(s) other than a spouse

- married, or a graduate or professional student

These guidelines are accurate as of this writing, but may change. For updated information, or if you think that you have unusual circumstances not listed that warrant classifying your child as independent, consult the financial aid office. In some extraordinary circumstances, a college financial aid administrator may determine that an otherwise dependent student should be treated as an independent student for financial aid.

B. Federal Assistance

In addition to having demonstrated financial need, students have to be U.S. citizens (or eligible non-citizens—e.g., permanent residents), be enrolled and making *satisfactory academic progress* as a regular student working toward a degree in an eligible program, have a high school diploma, General Educational Development (GED) Certificate, or meet other approved state standards, and have a valid Social Security number in order to qualify for federal money. Men have to be registered for the draft.

- A **Federal Pell Grant** is an award from the government that generally serves as a foundation of financial aid to which aid from other federal and non-federal sources may be added. All students who qualify for a Federal Pell Grant are guaranteed receipt of a Federal Pell Grant at any school that participates in the Federal Pell Grant program. *Only the most needy students qualify.*

- A **Federal Supplemental Educational Opportunity Grant (FSEOG)** is an award to help undergraduates with *exceptional* financial need, as determined by the individual schools, with priority given to Federal Pell Grant recipients. FSEOGs are awarded above and beyond Federal Pell Grants, and *there is no guarantee that every eligible student will receive one.*

- **Federal Stafford Loans** are the federal government's major form of self-help and are available through the William D. Ford Federal Direct Loan Program (nicknamed "Direct") and the Federal Family Education Loan (FFELP) Program. The major differences between a Direct and a FFELP Loan are the source of funds, some parts of the application, and the repayment plans. These loans must be paid back, and you can't borrow more than the cost of education at your school minus your family's contribution and any other financial aid you receive. Stafford loans are either "subsidized" or "unsubsidized." A subsidized loan is awarded on the basis of financial need, and the government pays interest on the loan until the student begins repayment. An unsubsidized Stafford loan is awarded to any student regardless of need and the interest is charged to the student from the time the loan is issued until paid in full. Normally, repayment begins six months after a student graduates—or drops below full-time enrollment. Repayment can be stretched to 10 years. Loan forgiveness is available for some graduates who choose to teach in certain underserved schools.

- A **Federal Perkins Loan** is a low-interest loan for students with *exceptional* financial need as determined by the school. These loans are made through a school's financial aid office—your school is your lender. Schools have varying levels of Perkins money and may or may not be able to offer you one. There is loan forgiveness for some health professionals, VISTA and Peace Corp volunteers, and for teachers working in areas deemed disadvantaged.

- A **Federal Supplemental Loan for Students** is for student borrowers and provides additional funds and, like the Federal PLUS Loan, is administered by a bank, credit union, or savings and loan.

- **Federal Work-Study** provides jobs to students who need financial aid, and the pay is at least the current federal minimum wage (and can be higher, depending on the campus and on the skills required for the job). Students are assigned a suggested amount of Federal Work-Study money they can earn in a term. The amount awarded is based on financial need as well as on the availability of resources, and the government funds the program. Having a job is a great way to gain experience and to get plugged into the campus in another way. Jobs range from kitchen duty to conducting scientific research with a faculty member.

The federal government awards approximately 75 percent of all student aid, much of which is in the form of loans. There are yearly limits and overall maximum amounts lent to borrowers. In addition, there are a variety of repayment plans as well as loan consolidation repayment plans.

The programs listed in this section are administered by the U.S. Department of Education. For more information and with specific questions contact:

> Federal Student Aid Information Center
> P.O. Box 84
> Washington, D.C. 20044
> Phone: (800) 4-FED-AID
> Web site: www.ed.gov

C. State Assistance

Loans, scholarships, and special programs are available through individual states, and application procedures vary. Some states, like New York, will not let you take state money out of state. Check into the transferability of your own state scholarship, if you are investigating colleges in states other than your home state. Often, you can be considered for state programs by completing only the FAFSA, but in some cases you will need to submit additional forms. The FAFSA usually needs to be submitted by a certain date in some states or the student forfeits eligibility. Check with your local guidance office to get more information about state agency policies. State higher education financial agencies serve as excellent sources of information about scholarships and financing information.

D. College/University Assistance

A college or university may have its own resources to award to your child in the form of jobs, loans, or scholarships and grants. Some colleges have specific scholarships for children of alumni or merit awards for talent in the arts, in addition to academic and athletic scholarships. These university funds may be awarded in addition to other sources of aid or may be the only sources of aid you receive. Generally, if you apply for financial aid, you will be considered for whatever special funds are available. In some cases, as in a writing competition or a talent scholarship, additional work such as an interview, essay, or a tape may be required. Stick to the deadlines!

E. Private Organizations

Churches, employers, labor organizations, and fraternal groups represent just a few sources of aid for college students. Sometimes called outside scholarships and loans because they don't come from the government or college, these sources are calculated into your total financial aid package. Check out www.fastweb.com to do an exhaustive search.

F. Other Sources

Although the bulk of aid comes from the government, the colleges, and private organizations, you may qualify for other kinds of aid not listed above. Examples include tuition exchange or other employee benefits and live-in positions, in exchange for room and board and a stipend.

Tips for Comparing Financial Aid Packages

- **Find out how outside scholarships (that is, those *not* granted by the college or the government) will be handled.** Will the college financial aid office deduct any or all this entire amount from the loan? From the grant? From both? Colleges vary on this and will be willing to explain their policies to you.

  It's against the law to over-fund a student. That is, if a student's need is calculated at $30,000 and her college awards the full amount of aid and she is also awarded $5,000 from outside scholarships, an adjustment has to be made. Often colleges replace some self-help (loan and work study) with the outside scholarship, which sweetens the composition of the financial aid package by increasing the amount of gift aid in the mix. Although some students complain that they are being penalized for earning outside aid, it's really an advantage because they can reduce their self-help.

- **Don't assume that a less expensive school will necessarily cost you less.** Look very carefully at the amount of aid each place is offering you and compare that to the total cost of attendance to find out what each college will cost you and your family.

- **If there is a discrepancy in the amount of aid you have been awarded at comparably priced colleges, contact the financial aid offices.** It might be that one application asked information that another didn't and so your family contribution was calculated differently. If you are able to supply more information, you may be able to get a more generous award. On the other hand, it might be that one college simply gave you a more generous package. Financial aid officers might be able to match an award from a competitor school, particularly if they are interested in recruiting your child. Be honest with the financial aid officer. Tell him or her what the other college has offered.

  Alan was torn when one college offered his daughter $8,000 in merit aid and her preferred college offered no aid. Alan called the favored college, explained the situation, and it was able to match the merit award. Both dad and daughter were happy with the outcome. If you go out on a limb and bluff to a financial aid officer, you'll get caught, as most colleges will require a copy of the other offer letter of aid to verify the difference. But honest negotiation is worth a try—the worst thing that can happen is that the college will say no.

- **Colleges have different amounts of aid available and distribute aid with different philosophies.** These differences become very clear as you compare awards made by colleges able to meet *total need* with awards made by colleges practicing *need gapping*. In addition, some colleges package their financial aid with merit taken into consideration. That is, they sweeten the pot by lowering loan and upping the grant for students with special appeal.

- **Don't be surprised if you as parents don't agree with your child on the value of the varying awards and the value of the varying educational experiences.** Be patient, be clear, and try to listen to your child to hear what he really wants and needs. Passionate arguments and lots of door slamming can be avoided by trying to communicate reasonably and calmly.

Questions & *Answers*

Q: Does a stepparent have to provide information when a child applies for financial aid?

A: Yes. If a student receives support from a parent—divorced and then remarried—financial information from the stepparent is required on the FAFSA. While the stepparent might not have to pay for college, his or her income and assets will be considered to provide a more realistic picture of the family's financial situation.

Q: Our family owns rental property. How will that be considered when we apply for aid?

A: It depends. If the rental property is a vacation home, the equity will be counted as a parent asset. If the rental property generates income the family needs to live on, colleges may be willing to treat the equity as a business asset, which will not affect the EFC as much.

Q: How reliable are scholarship search services?

A: Unfortunately, scholarship search services don't have a good reputation because there are many fraudulent services trying to take advantage of innocent and trusting families. Because there is so much information available for free on the Web, it's not necessary to pay money to subscribe to a scholarship search service.

It seems that some search organizations are making promises they can't keep. Beware if you are promised a guarantee of a scholarship or a certain amount of aid. Be suspicious if your child is notified that he is a finalist in a contest he never entered. Don't give your credit card number out, especially over the phone, to a scholarship solicitor promising a huge grant in return. If you suspect a scam, contact your state Attorney General's Office or the Federal Trade Commission at www.ftc.gov, or call it toll free at (877) 382-4357.

Your public library, the guidance office, and college financial aid offices offer up-to-date and comprehensive information for you to use to find appropriate scholarships. If you are considering hiring any kind of scholarship search agency, first ask your guidance office or a college financial aid office for an opinion.

Q: My wife and I are responsible for paying health and home insurance for her mother. We cannot, however, claim her mother as a dependent since she receives social security, files her own taxes, and claims herself as a dependent. Will financial aid officers take this into consideration?

A: You should point out these circumstances, and financial aid officers may make an allowance for what you pay or include your wife's mother as a member of your household to increase aid eligibility. Be prepared to document the expenses you pay for relatives not claimed as dependents.

Q: My two youngest children attend private school. Will college financial aid officers consider these tuition obligations when computing aid for our older son?

A: Yes. Generally, college aid officers use a cap (subject to yearly adjustment) for the amount of private school tuition allowed against income.

Q: My husband and I are thinking of refinancing our home. Will taking on more debt at this time mean that we qualify for more financial aid? If so, is there any down side to refinancing?

A: Colleges often count equity in a home among your assets. If debt is increased, equity decreases. However, the value of your home equity translates to the bottom line at a very low rate. If you can refinance at a low interest rate and reduce monthly payments to free up cash to pay college expenses, then there is certainly no disadvantage to you.

Q: When it comes to calculating financial aid, we've heard the terms *institutional methodology* and *federal methodology.* What are the differences?

A: Federal Methodology (FM) is the formula set into law for calculating eligibility for federal aid programs including Federal Pell Grants, Federal Supplemental Educational Opportunity Grants (FSEOG), Federal Direct Stafford/Ford Loans, Federal Perkins Loans, and Federal Work-Study (FWS).

Institutional Methodology (IM) is the formula used by the colleges that provide significant *institutional* dollars to students in the form of need-based grant aid. (In other words, these colleges use their *own* money, in addition to the government's.) The intention is to more fairly allocate those dollars among the student applicants.

Differences between FM and IM exist both in terms of what data is collected and how that data is used in each needs analysis calculation. For example, FM does not include home equity, IM does. FM calculates EFC by dividing equally among all children in college in one family; IM divides EFC among children, often based on the relative cost of each college. IM considers retirement accounts and private elementary and secondary tuition for siblings, FM does not. The financial aid offices will be able to detail more specific differences for you.

Q: I am 63; my wife is 59. Because we are so close to retirement age, will we be eligible to receive more financial aid than younger parents? Are there any other special financial considerations or recommendations for older parents?

A: College financial aid officers may choose to reduce or eliminate home equity from need analysis for parents close to retirement. You must point out on your application that you are close to retirement in hopes that such an allowance will be made. Older parents often think that if they retire, they may be eligible for considerably more financial aid. That really depends. Some pensions are not significantly lower than earnings were, and certain allowances made for expenses incurred by people who work will not be used in the needs analysis equation for retirees.

V. Non-Aid Advice

One director of financial aid remembers a father describing himself as a member of the "disenfranchised middle class," who telephoned when his daughter was denied aid. The financial aid officer politely pointed out that since his annual income was in excess of $250,000 and he owned an expensive house in an exclusive neighborhood, he simply didn't qualify. The financial aid director remembers, "Perception is everything. Perhaps compared to his friends he wasn't wealthy—but he was wealthy enough not to qualify for need-based aid."

➤ **THE GOOD NEWS:** While it is difficult to assume all college expenses, not qualifying for aid might be a hook in the admission process and may give your child a slight edge over an equally qualified aid applicant.

➤ **THE BAD NEWS:** It is tough not to get any help with college bills. Some parents resent the fact that they are footing the whole bill while other families are helped because of financial need or merit.

It is a huge mistake not to apply for aid, if you need it, in order to sway an admission decision. The financial strain that can result is likely to undermine your child's college experience. On the other hand, never assume that applying for aid is a guarantee that you'll get it.

Parents who pay full freight for their children include those who applied for aid but didn't get any (either because they were deemed no need or because there wasn't any to give) as well as those who never filed an aid application.

Payment plans have helped to take some of the sting out of tuition bills by offering 10- or 12-month installments. Many colleges have a wide variety of creative financing plans for tuition payment. Parents are even offered the option of a pre-payment plan. That is, you can pay the full amount covering four years' tuition the first year and be guaranteed no tuition increases. Be certain to read the fine print about what happens if a child transfers out or leaves before graduating. Some colleges offer the option of paying the bill by credit card, and you may be able to earn airline miles or discounts on cars this way.

People are saving less and borrowing more these days, so most parents expect to borrow for their child's education. Unfortunately, college costs have risen much faster than incomes of most parents. As a family, you'll need to decide how much is too much to borrow and in whose names the borrowing will be done. (A PLUS loan, described earlier in this chapter is a popular option for families.)

You can learn more about borrowing for college by consulting the following services:

Academic Management Services, www.amsweb.com; 50 Vision Boulevard, East Providence, Rhode Island 02914; (800) 556-6684 or (401) 431-1490

Student Loan Servicing Alliance, www.slsaservicers.org; c/o Bank of Boston, P.O. Box 1296, Mail Stop 99-26-11, Boston, Massachusetts 02105; (617) 434-8971

SallieMae, www.salliemae.com; Excellent information—particularly on borrowing and repayment—available from this financial services corporation that specializes in funding education.

Loans are also available from banks, credit unions, and generous relatives and friends. Business groups, religious organizations, clubs, and professional associations sometimes have privately funded loan programs often with interest rates below those at banks. Ask financial aid officers for more details about available loan programs.

Some parents borrow against their life insurance policies to pay college bills while others are willing and able to take out second mortgages or home equity loans. If you use an accountant, ask for suggestions that work for your specific financial situation.

Don't forget to tell your child about the good old-fashioned way to get money—by earning it. The majority of college students work for pay in addition to their school work, so even though your child may not qualify for the Federal Work-Study program, life guarding, babysitting, tutoring, waiting tables, etc., are still options. Colleges and universities generally have an office of student employment that will help students find part-time employment, including spot jobs such as helping out during registration, commencement, etc.

Final Warning: Don't forget that *financial aid safety school*—the one you can afford without any outside assistance. For some fortunate families, every college fits the bill, but it may be that *your* child will attend a community college for a year or two, or commute to a local school, and then transfer to a more costly choice.

VI. Additional Resources

Web Sites to Browse

- You can calculate your EFC and find out lots about financial aid and scholarships. (www.petersons.com)

- The U.S. Department of Education Web site includes information in Spanish and English. (www.ed.gov)

- The Department of Education's comprehensive site includes *Funding Your Education,* as well many useful resources and statistics. (www.ed.gov/offices/OSFAP/students)

- Complete the FAFSA online on this site. (www.fafsa.ed.gov)

- The Financial Aid Information Page sponsored by the National Association of Student Financial Aid Administrators includes a college cost projector as well as information about specific situations such as bankruptcy and home schooling. (www.finaid.org)

- The College Board site includes worksheets to estimate family contribution and compare financial aid awards. (www.collegeboard.com)

- The FastWeb Scholarship Service database includes 800,000 private scholarships. This site includes search profiles for aid and admission, as well as applications for download. (www.fastweb.org)

- College parents of America site offers many good tips and also a newsletter about financing. (www.collegeparents.org)

Publications (from Peterson's Thomson Learning)

College Money Handbook: This comprehensive annual guidebook answers the most commonly asked questions and offers an index of hundreds of college financial aid offerings.

Scholarship Almanac: This extensive guide provides an annual compilation of the 500 largest scholarships in the United States.

Scholarships, Grants and Prizes: This guide provides specifics about billions of dollars in aid. Organized by academic and career areas, as well as by area of residence, this is an invaluable resource for students searching for relevant aid.

6

Pushing Papers: The Application Itself

The mechanics of actually applying to college have changed a lot since your day. Remember those crowded cards that never quite fit in the typewriter? Remember that sinking feeling that comes from ferreting through dresser drawers for missing pages?

➤ *THE GOOD NEWS:* Anyone with Internet access can also access applications to the majority of colleges and universities, even at the eleventh hour. Many applications can be downloaded and printed or submitted entirely electronically. Most institutions expect that essays and activities lists will be composed on computers—not painstakingly typed or handwritten on their own unfriendly forms. Moreover, most schools also offer several application options.

➤ *THE BAD NEWS:* More options can mean more confusion.

Because colleges give greatest weight to high school records (with test scores sometimes a close second), it may seem as if your child's fate is already sealed before the application is even examined. Yet, a strong application will often make a difference in an admission decision. "It lets us see the person behind the paperwork and helps us to look beyond the GPA. An excellent application can help overcome an average record," claims a former Swarthmore dean. "Conversely," notes an official at the University of Virginia, "We've denied admission to people with good grades who did a lousy job on the application."

Of course, as parents, your part in all of this is precarious. You can read the pages below and understand what makes a good application. You can share this information with your son or daughter and volunteer to act as a proofreader, a sounding board, or even a secretary. But ultimately, this is your child's job to do, not yours.

I. Different Decision Plans

While some admission jargon seems standard from Seton Hall to Stockton State, when it comes to application options, known as "decision plans," even experts get befuddled.

Most confounding are the early application offerings. "Early Decision" usually means that a student has decided on one first-choice college and, in exchange for submitting all credentials by a deadline that is sooner than the school ordinarily demands, will receive an early reply.

Beware: Such decision plans generally require a statement of commitment in which your child agrees to attend that college and to withdraw all other applications if accepted early. This is different than "Early Action" or "Early Evaluation" alternatives where colleges will offer either tentative or definite admission decisions but the candidate need not commit until May.

Some places offer both an Early Decision and Early Action option. Students who like the school but aren't ready to commit to it should select the latter. Other colleges offer two rounds of Early Decision. Candidates can apply by mid-November and receive notification a month later, or apply in early January and hear in February. In both cases, these decisions are also binding.

You may also encounter the term "Early Admission" used interchangeably with Early Decision. Often, however, Early Admission is a program for high school juniors who decide to forgo their senior year and head straight to college. But these Early Admission candidates typically apply via "Regular Decision," which is still the most common route to college. Students meet a deadline that is generally in the winter and receive an answer by April. Confused yet?

With "Rolling Admission," applications are evaluated as they arrive and decisions mailed shortly thereafter, usually within two months. While this plan often catches the eye of procrastinators, keep in mind that places are filled on a first-come-first-served basis. Note too, that Rolling Admission plans usually have financial aid and/or housing priority deadlines. Try to apply well in advance of these. Latecomers may lose out.

"Open Admission" means that all students who meet minimum requirements (usually a high school diploma) may enroll. This policy is most common at two-year public institutions.

Now you must be confused! Be certain to check with each of your target schools to determine not only what their admission plans are called, but also what guidelines or restrictions apply. It's also fine to ask about decision and notification dates.

*Q*uestions & *A*nswers

Q: Is it harder or easier to get in via an early decision plan?

A: Common sense suggests that early decision applicants are top-notch students—not only more organized but also more qualified than the masses who, months later, will be racing to finish their regular-decision forms. While many admission officers do little to dispel this myth, in truth, the early decision option can be a good bet for more middle-of-the-road candidates as well. To some degree, the bird-in-hand-versus-two-in-the-bush theory is operating here. Even if some of the early birds aren't as strong as the rest of the flock that will follow in the spring, admission folks know they are sure things. "It is somewhat easier to be admitted early decision here," says Lee Stetson, dean of admission at the University of Pennsylvania (where about 40 percent of the class enters under the ED option). "Everybody likes to be loved, and we're no exception at Penn. We want students who really want to attend, not those who are resigned to come."

➤ **THE GOOD NEWS:** Students who are admitted early only have to complete one application and may even avoid retaking standardized tests as seniors. Moreover, those candidates who are deferred (in other words, not accepted early but reevaluated in the spring), have sent a positive message that may pay off. An early-decision application is one way to let a college know that it is your child's first choice.

➤ **THE BAD NEWS:** Early decision plans are not advisable for late-bloomers who didn't get off the mark until junior year, nor for those with poor junior standardized test scores. Colleges will want to see first-semester senior grades and senior scores before committing and, if previous numbers were particularly weak, the early decision candidate may be rejected outright, not deferred, before having a chance to prove himself as a senior.

*Q*uestions & *A*nswers

Q: We've heard that there's such a stampede to apply under the Early Decision plan at some top colleges that those who wait for the regular deadline are squeezed out. But how can we be sure that we get the financial aid we need if our daughter applies to only one school?

A: The Early Decision option is under fire in some circles. Critics claim that it forces children to make choices they're not ready to make, that it cuts admission odds for those who don't jump on the ED bandwagon, and that it favors the affluent who have better access to good counseling. Even many college admission officials concede that ED is more beneficial to the schools themselves than it is to their prospective students. Thus, some colleges have recently made changes to long-standing ED policies, and others currently have them under review (so make sure the information you use is up-to-date).

Early Decision can be especially tricky for those who require financial aid. Applicants receive a tentative aid package at the time of the decision (based on estimates from the previous year's tax forms). However, if aid isn't what you expected (or if you don't qualify at all), you might need to investigate other options, and your child may be forced to refuse the offer of admission, despite the signed commitment form. While your child can still stay in the running at that school, there is no guarantee that he or she will be admitted in the spring.

Students needing financial assistance are often advised to avoid Early Decision plans. They are told that by submitting applications to several schools—not just one— they will have varying aid awards to compare in April. Some colleges, too, don't make their best aid offers to Early Decision candidates whom they assume are certain to enroll anyway. On the other hand, a borderline candidate who needs money may squeak in under the more relaxed Early Decision wire but could be denied outright in the Regular-Decision pool.

Thus, there are no easy answers. In your situation, the best route is probably to encourage your daughter to apply early *only* if she finds a college she truly adores. If she does, then you should contact the financial aid office there before the application deadline and ask for advice.

Keep in mind that your daughter may be admitted with an aid package that isn't sufficient, and you will be faced with a disappointed kid who must turn down a first-choice school. Colleges aren't thrilled when ED applicants change their minds, but they don't blackball them at other schools, either. When done for financial reasons, it's often simply inevitable. However, when done because a candidate's interest wanes, it's not just unfortunate, it's unethical. When applying Early Decision, be as certain as possible that this is really a first-choice school, not the path of least resistance.

II. Which Application Do We Use?

When your child has decided which schools will receive applications and which decision plan is appropriate at each, the next step is to determine the application—or type of application—to use.

In your era, every college published its own official application form. It had to be requested well in advance and kept out of reach of the family dog once it arrived. Today, the paper application still exists, but most colleges also offer at least one electronic alternative.

Your child should select the application that works best for him. Colleges do not ever make decisions based on what form—or format—is used.

➤ **THE GOOD NEWS:** High school students are typically more familiar (and comfortable) with the burgeoning number of application routes available to them than their parents are. If your child seems to be forging ahead without you, by all means, step back. Provide assistance when it's needed (e.g., read those essays, if they're offered), but don't worry if 21st century application lingo sounds like a foreign language, because it's one that you really don't have to learn.

➤ **THE BAD NEWS:** If deadlines are looming and it looks like Junior is dragging his feet, you may need to help streamline the application process. Begin by determining which application options are offered by the schools that made the final cut. This is easily done by checking a college Web page (usually you click on "undergraduate admission" and then on "applying") or by telephoning admission offices. Viewbooks generally include this information as well. Some even include copies of the paper application form.

If your child does not have Internet access or balks at using a computer for any part of the application process (and both are highly unlikely these days) then your job is to make sure that the paper alternatives have been received or requested.

Applying by Computer

When it comes to college applications, computers make sense. It's certainly easier to correct errors electronically than it ever was on Mom's old Smith-Corona. Of course, as with any technological "improvement," there are wrinkles.

➤ **FIRST, THE BAD NEWS:** Online application options are growing at such a rapid rate that the hours you might save by choosing them may be lost, instead, in a quagmire of 'Net-surfing confusion. For example, a number of the Web sites discussed in Chapter 2 (e.g., Petersons, The College Board, Princeton Review) all have their own versions of electronic applications that can be accessed from their sites—but not all colleges accept all formats. You, or your child, may be further confused by hearing terms like "Apply," "ExPAN," "CollegeLink," or "Embark." All of these are outfits that produce electronic applications.

Moreover, some applications can be downloaded, completed, and then submitted entirely electronically. Others can be completed online but must be printed and mailed. Some still, must be printed before they're filled out.

➤ *NOW, THE GOOD NEWS:* You don't have to understand this stuff to use it. If you child wants to include a computer in the application process, your best bet is to go directly to each institution's home page. From there you will almost always find direct links to an electronic application, if such a format is offered. Instructions tend to be crystal clear.

Some students, however, prefer to access applications from a one-stop-shopping site like Peterson's. The advantage here is that these sites enable students to save applications in progress, to keep a file on where they've applied, and to see which applications have not been completed. The disadvantage, as noted above, is that not all of these sites provide application materials for every college. Students who are not meticulous record keepers may lose track of forms they've not finished.

Students who apply electronically will be instructed to pay application fees with a credit card or by sending a check in the mail. Some colleges even offer application fee discounts, or waivers, to those who apply online.

Applying On Paper

For students with limited computer access, or for those who simply prefer the look and feel of paper products, there are still more options than in the past. In addition to acquiring paper applications during college visits, by mail, in viewbooks, etc., many can be downloaded from Web sites and then printed. The result is that they look an awful lot like the good old-fashioned forms from Mom or Dad's day, but your child can easily reprint a copy when mistakes are made.

Hint: Students who can't—or won't—use the Internet at all may find it helpful to photocopy an entire paper application to use as a rough draft before beginning it.

*Q*uestions & *A*nswers

Q: Why won't colleges make life simpler by accepting the same application?

A: Some do. For example, the handy Common Application can be completed once, then photocopied and sent to any of the more than 200 colleges nationwide that have agreed to honor it in order to minimize the efforts of their overtaxed applicants. It can also be accessed and completed online. The list of subscribing colleges and universities and the application itself are available at www.commonapp.org, in most high school guidance offices, or by calling (800) 253-7746. Many of the subscriber colleges offer links to the Common Application directly from their Web pages. (*Hint:*

Nearly three-dozen member schools slash or drop application fees for online applicants.)

The Common Application can also be completed on a computer disk, and some high school guidance offices provide disks for free. Otherwise they can be ordered for a small fee by calling the toll-free number above. Some colleges will require an additional brief supplement (and occasionally an extra essay), so if your child is using the Common Application, it is important to notify admission offices and ask if other forms are necessary. Supplement specifics—and often the forms themselves—are usually found on college Web sites as well.

When a student is applying Early Decision or to a special program or department, colleges should be alerted, and you should ask if any additional steps need to be taken.

If your child is applying to several schools in a state system or to colleges that share other bonds, you may lighten the application load by asking admission officials if a multi-user application is available.

Hint: Before your child completes a single application, make a list of which target colleges accept which formats and/or forms. Look for overlap. With a little bit of advance planning, such consolidation may help save time and effort.

Q: Do admission officials accord the Common Application the same respect that they give their own?

A: Despite some rumors to the contrary, colleges subscribing to the Common Application pledge to give it equal weight, and they do. (Some, including Harvard, use it exclusively.) In fact, the Common Application offers five very broad essay-question options, and officials often find the results are a breath of fresh air after spending an evening with 106 other dissertations on some esoteric subject that their own Board of Admission cooked up.

Any multi-user format that a target college accepts will be equally welcome as that school's own form. However, when sending paper applications or printouts, be sure to photocopy them neatly and clearly. Colleges don't appreciate getting an illegible, seventh-generation photocopy.

If you're still worried that bypassing an institution's own application will make your son or daughter seem like a less-than-serious applicant, here's a final bit of advice: Don't let the Common Application (or other generic alternative) be the only thing in your child's file. Include some indication of special interest in each institution. While a trip to campus and an interview are certainly the best bets in that department, they're not always possible. Even a brief note asking for specific information suggests to admission officials that your child has a genuine interest in their school and isn't merely mailing in a photocopied form as an afterthought.

III. General Application Tips

Whether your child is applying electronically or on paper—or using a combination of both—there are a few suggestions that he or she should heed:

- **Complete All Required Forms**

Some institutions have a different form (or a supplement to a standard form) for separate schools within a university (e.g., music, education). Read instructions carefully to be certain that your child has all required components. Some colleges also use different forms for international students and non-permanent residents of the U.S. (If you think your child may have completed the wrong application, don't panic; just call the admission office. They may require that the right one be substituted, but they will probably just let it slide.)

Some schools have a two-part process. Part I is a brief form requesting basic biographical data. When your child returns it to the admission office, Part II will be put in the mail. Some students using paper applications find this lag time annoying. (**Hint:** Colleges using this two-part format often have both parts on the Web at once.)

- **Know That Appearances Count**

"I am quite influenced by the neatness of an application," maintains one Duquesne University admissions official. "Sloppiness makes me wonder how concerned an applicant is with creating a good impression."

"It makes me ask, 'are they seriously interested or are we just a backup?'" concurs a Denison University dean. An application's appearance is, indeed, bound to make at least a subconscious impression. "Sloppiness never helped anyone get accepted," quips a top official at the University of Virginia.

On the other hand, don't be too much of a neat freak, either. One mother recalls a last-minute rush to replace an application because her daughter had gotten a small ink smear on one corner. Each form, in fact, is handled by so many admission staff members that officials realize that fingerprints, wrinkles, and even coffee stains are more likely to be their fault than yours.

Ordinarily, applicants who use paper forms are asked to type or print. Your child should elect whichever can be done most neatly. If printing, use ink. Essays should not be written by hand unless given specific instructions to do so. (See "The Almighty Essay" later in this chapter.)

- **Spelling and Grammar Count, Too**

"In borderline cases, good spelling is especially important," insists an admission counselor at Ohio State University. "It tells us both about the quality of a candidate's education and about the amount of time and care put into the application." Even those counselors who offer amnesty for smudges, scratch-outs, and poor penmanship are likely to be less forgiving when it comes to spelling. One official from Beloit College in Wisconsin calls himself "a stickler for spelling" and cringes when recalling the hapless prospect who misspelled the college's name.

Words commonly misspelled on applications include: business, medicine, psychology, architecture, archaeology/archeology, foreign, interest, profession, counselor, and received. Capitalization is often omitted from English, French, and other proper nouns. Apostrophes are erroneously used to make plurals or omitted from contractions and possessives.

Grammar, too, can influence an admission decision. "When students use poor grammar on an application, we have to wonder if they are capable of college-level written expression," says an official from Duquesne.

If you don't trust your talents as a proofreader, urge your child to make rough drafts and check grammar or spelling uncertainties with a school counselor, teacher, or other expert before electronic applications are zapped into cyberspace or permanent marks are made on paper application forms.

• The Deadline Isn't Always The Bottom Line

➤ *THE GOOD NEWS:* Observe application deadlines as closely as possible and never be late with financial aid materials. Yet don't rule out a college because of a missed deadline. Most schools are more lenient than you might think.

➤ *THE BAD NEWS:* There is no such thing as a standard deadline. They're all over the calendar.

Many schools accept applications days, and even weeks, after they are due. If your child is behind schedule with paperwork or discovers a new college at the last minute, it's likely that there will be some leeway with closing dates.

Not even Harvard will throw away an application that's a day or two delayed, but an explanatory note is always helpful. Whenever possible, if you need an extension, request it *in advance* of the deadline. Make a record of the staff member you spoke with. For long extensions (two weeks or more), follow up your phone calls with a note (or e-mail) asking for a *written* acknowledgment of your extension. Keep in mind that an application is a complex affair, composed of many parts. If possible, submit at least the initial section on time—usually it's a quickie that asks for name, address, high school (and fee!)—making the college aware of your child's intent to apply. The essay, recommendations, and so on can be sent later.

Electronic applications are good options for latecomers, and some colleges accept materials by fax, too—but many won't. Always ask. Express mail companies make a bundle on eleventh-hour applicants but, in most cases, if an application arrives only two or three days late, the tardiness will be ignored altogether. However, it's a risk you really don't want to take when a brief phone call may assure you extra time. One admission officer remembers a beautiful bouquet of balloons that arrived with a very late application and a note of apology. She kept the balloons but refused the tardy application.

To complicate life further, there are deadlines and there are *deadlines*. Financial aid deadlines may be months before the application due date. Some universities have different deadlines for different departments And remember, as you read above, latecomers at "Rolling Admission" colleges may miss out not only on financial aid but also on housing—and sometimes on acceptance altogether.

- **Always Ask If Sooner Is Better**

This is a key point. At many colleges, no application folders are reviewed until the due date has passed. Thus, the candidate who "completes" (admission jargon for finishing all application components) weeks in advance has no advantage over one who meets the deadline by only hours (although early applicants have more time to track down missing records). However, some colleges give priority to applicants who apply early.

Schools without Rolling Admission usually notify all of their candidates at once. Don't expect that just because your child applied well before the deadline, you'll hear sooner.

Questions & *Answers*

Q: **Must all parts of an application be submitted together?**

A: Most applications are composed of separate forms, cards, and other components. It's impossible for all to be sent at once because some parts, such as confidential recommendations and transcripts, must come directly from others. Your child may want to submit initial forms early and dawdle on an essay. That's okay, too. Just make sure that everything sent includes your child's full name, school, address and, if available, social security number.

Q: How do we know if an application has arrived safely?

A: You'll find that some colleges include postcards in their application package that you self-address and which they will mail back when your child's application is received. Other colleges automatically send out a confirmation when forms arrive. Students who apply electronically may receive an e-mail notice that all systems are go. Your child may be assigned a PIN number that will provide access to application-status information—and possibly to admission decisions later on.

If you don't get any sort of notification, feel free to telephone. *It is the applicant's responsibility to follow up and make sure that all components— including transcripts and recommendations—have arrived.*

One university admission official tells a sad story about a candidate who didn't call until after admission decisions had been made and she hadn't received one. She angrily blamed the office of admission for the oversight until she discovered her application—check and all—in her father's desk drawer.

Above all, make copies. Online applications are a cinch to print before they're submitted electronically, and the inconvenience of photocopying everything you send out through the mail is nothing compared to the nightmare of rewriting even one application.

IV. Tips for Tackling Specific Application Sections

All applications are not created equal. Each is just different enough from the next to keep candidates on their toes, but most are similar enough, too, to allow some universal truths. For instance . . .

Fill in the Blanks

- Don't leave blanks blank. If a question isn't relevant, your child should say so by writing "N/A" (the standard abbreviation for "Not Applicable") or by using a dash.

- Family employment and education answers should be clear to those outside the family. Never abbreviate company names and/or colleges unless nationally known. (And your kids shouldn't worry if you didn't graduate from fancy colleges or if you didn't go to college at all. In fact, being "first generation" can often work in their favor.) On the other hand, this is not a time for modesty either. Some students ride into competitive colleges on the coattails of VIP parents. If you or your spouse is the editor-in-chief of a major newspaper, your child should clearly say so and not just write "journalist" on the form.

- Don't ignore the race/ethnic background question. By law, answers are optional, but a minority background is usually a plus and never a liability. A child who identifies at all with a racial or ethnic minority group should check the appropriate box. It is not necessary to have been born in a foreign country or have both parents belong to the group. Students from racially mixed backgrounds can check more than one box or explain in the "other" category.

- If English is not your child's first language and/or not spoken at home, make sure this is indicated on the application. Some forms will ask directly. Otherwise, your child should attach a brief separate statement explaining his language history or use an asterisk (*) in an appropriate spot on the form itself (such as in the racial/ethnic group section or next to the verbal SAT or ACT score). Find out also if a TOEFL exam is required or useful. (See Chapter 3.)

- Say "see attached" as needed. If the form does not provide adequate space to list extracurricular activities, job experience, etc., it is fine to include a separate page or résumé. (See "Special Extras" below.) This is preferable to trying to jam too much information into too little space, but make sure that each additional page includes your child's name and a clear heading.

- Find out if "major" choices are binding before committing. Answer questions about academic preferences thoughtfully and thoroughly.

Most applications ask your child for an intended major. This helps colleges to see what departments are most (or least) popular among high school students, to facilitate sending brochures or follow-up letters from faculty, and to ascertain that applicants are not planning on studying something that isn't even offered at that college (it happens!). While many students are undecided and say so, it's more impressive to list a range of potential interests. As discussed in Chapter 2, be aware of binding commitments (most often found at universities with pre-professional programs such as pharmacy, agriculture, business, etc. and rarely at liberal arts schools) and determine in advance if, once admitted, switches are possible.

➤ *THE GOOD NEWS:* Sometimes, selecting an undersubscribed field can work in your child's favor. For instance, while many liberal arts institutions have more than their share of aspiring biologists, psychologists, and historians, it can be tougher to attract astronomers or Renaissance music majors. Admission officials who see one of those subjects listed on your child's application may snap to attention. Thus, an applicant wavering between a common choice and a less prevalent one (e.g., English and classics, at many institutions) should be sure to select both.

➤ *THE BAD NEWS:* It's hard to know what each college's priorities are in a given year, even with departmental enrollment statistics smack in front of you. Moreover, according to Katharine Fretwell, director of admission at Amherst College, simply *choosing* an under-enrolled area isn't enough to win favor. Instead, she explains, admission officials are likely to scour each folder for evidence of course selection, research experience, club participation, or other indicators that the passion is genuine. "Past participation and declared ambition together are usually the best predictors of future performance and participation," Fretwell maintains.

If your child wants to cite a prospective field in which he or she has had no apparent experience, a brief note of explanation might be helpful. For example, "My school has a limited curriculum, and my family has a limited budget, so I have yet to explore the study of German language. However, Thomas Mann and Hermann Hesse are two of my favorite authors, and I hope to some day read their writing in its original form."

Thus, your child certainly shouldn't rummage through a school's "Majors by Popularity" index and select the one at the bottom in order to improve the chances of admission. Above all, she shouldn't be like one unfortunate aspirant who gave admission officials a chuckle. When asked for her "Probable Area of Study," she responded, "In my room or in the library."

Be Cute But Cautious

Some candidates can pull off cutesy gimmicks while, for others, they fall flat. Such attention-getters (like the Pomona applicant who wrote her entire application in alternating blue and orange, the college's colors) *do* make admission officers sit up and take notice, and even those who grimace and say, "Oh, please, spare me" are apt to remember such an audacious applicant and maybe admire her inventiveness. Outrageousness is most effective if:

   a) it's appropriate to your child's personality;

   b) your child is a strong candidate to begin with (or a long-shot with nothing to lose) and;

   c) your child can come up with an idea that is pretty clever. (No hints here. It ought to be original.)

Special Extras: Consider a Résumé

A growing number of applications now arrive at admission offices complete with elaborate student résumés that would humble Leonardo da Vinci. Not only is it easier to say "see attached" than it is to repeat activity information on each college form, but some students today do too much to put their best foot forward in the limited space provided. However, sometimes the official form is fine.

Whether your child uses a separate sheet or the application itself, it's important to be sure that activities—and your child's role in them—are clear. In particular, leadership positions should be stated, and if your child started a club and didn't merely join it, then say so.

Maya tried to condense her life into seven lines, but it just wouldn't fit. She wasn't a team captain. In fact, she hadn't even played a sport since sixth grade. She wasn't a class officer either, but she was the only student in her entire school to be selected for the mayor's task force on crime. She co-chaired the subcommittee on youth affairs with a city councilor and helped design a pilot project that served as a model throughout the state. Add to that three science fair awards, eight years of flute lessons, and an after-school job. Wisely, Maya typed "See résumé enclosed" on each application and then submitted separate sheets.

When your child has been busy throughout high school or engaged in uncommon enterprises, there won't be room to list everything on an application form, and you won't want to list everything on a résumé, either. Be selective. Focus on those activities that have been most significant or long-term. If your daughter collected donations for the new playground one afternoon in ninth grade, it's not fodder for colleges. A year of varsity volleyball—however uneventful—is.

Including too much can actually backfire. Colleges will question a student's commitment and priorities. They'll envision your Calvin careening down a corridor, sticking his head in every door while 16 clubs meet simultaneously—and with his chemistry notes lying in his locker. They'll also be skeptical when activities look like application window-dressing that didn't get going until the start of senior year.

More Résumé Tips

- **Don't worry if your software isn't state-of-the-art.** Colleges don't care how many megabytes go into producing résumés, as long as they're neat and easy to read. Make sure your child's name, social security number (or address), and school are at the top of every page.

- **Explain everything that isn't obvious.** Avoid cryptic titles or acronyms. Even programs or organizations that are widely recognized like Girls' State or SADD should never be abbreviated and ought to be followed by a short explanation. (e.g., Instead of listing "AFS/UK" say "American Field Service summer family home stay program participant, in the United Kingdom.") Adding an explanatory sentence or two after each entry can really help admission officials understand your child's pursuits.

  Similarly, just like on a professional résumé, work experience also requires a short description. Some students hold positions of real responsibility. Simply listing, "Clerk; Luigi's" doesn't tell admission officials that this applicant supervises six other workers and is in charge of opening and closing a busy grocery store every weekend.

- **Include the amount of time involved.** Did Jared volunteer at the soup kitchen for an hour a week, an hour a month, or an hour, period?

- **Turn a résumé from ho-hum to ho-ho.** One hospital candy striper, for example, listed her job title as "Jello Queen." A cheerleading captain admitted that she loved her squad but "the Laker Girls aren't looking over their shoulders at us." A Key Club officer confided that, "The only thing we do at our meetings is plan more meetings." While, of course, your child shouldn't transform an entire high school career into a four-year joke, a little humor reminds admission professionals that, as similar as activity lists can sound, there are very different individuals behind them.

- **Use asterisks or similar symbols to identify those activities your child has found most important and those that will be continued in college.** Application forms will sometimes ask students to list the most important activities first.

- **Make sure that important honors, extra-special commitment, or unique ventures stand out in some way.** Admission officers don't always understand that certain achievements (serving on the headmaster search committee; winning the poetry slam) are big deals in your neck of the woods. What makes an achievement especially unusual? Did Tom snare that spot in the state marching band after only one year of drum lessons? Be sure to say so.

  Sometimes the essay or personal statement is an appropriate place to expand on outstanding or atypical accomplishments. In some cases, a supplemental essay—even a short one—is suggested. (See the section on essays later in this chapter.)

Short Subjects

➤ *THE GOOD NEWS:* Many applications don't have them. They cut right to the chase scene and go straight for the essay without a warm-up.

➤ *THE BAD NEWS:* These are the questions from hell—those brief one-paragraph puzzlers that are a cross between a fill-in-the-blank and an authentic essay (and the worst of both worlds).

Most students who encounter short answer questions spend too little time on them. They're saving their creative juices for the essay to follow. As a result, admission officers don't expect to be interested or amused by these items, and are pleasantly surprised—and impressed—if they find otherwise. So why not encourage your child to offer short answers that will stand out in a crowd?

Here are two typical short answer questions followed by three responses: *Exceptional, Acceptable,* and *Awful.* Note that the best answers take liberties with orthodox style and let the writer's personality shine through.

- ***Which of your extracurricular activities is most important to you and why?***

Exceptional: You can't miss us. We're the ones with the ink stains on our shirtsleeves, the ever-furrowed brows. Yes, we're the newspaper staff, the folks who live on too little sleep and too much coffee so we can get that tabloid on the lunchroom tables every Tuesday. I guess it's in my blood. I need to know what's going on around me, and I even harbor hope that I can challenge or change it through my writing.

Acceptable: I am most interested in my involvement with the school newspaper. I like to write, to try to present information in unique or unusual ways, and to stay in touch with what's going on in my immediate surroundings.

Awful: Newspaper. I like *writting.*

- ***How have your academic experiences in high school contributed to your intellectual development?***

Exceptional: "Physics!" My classmates covered their ears as I shrieked. "I can't believe I'm taking physics." I'd never been a "science person," and now here I was in a room full of calculators. The other thing I couldn't believe was how closely physics was connected to a subject that had always intrigued me—philosophy. My physics teacher introduced me to the ties between seemingly discrete academic disciplines, and it fueled my enthusiasm to study both in college.

Acceptable: I have come to appreciate the ways in which different subjects are connected to each other. For example, I reluctantly took physics my senior year and found that it includes issues that touch on another new area of interest: philosophy.

Awful: I learned that a lot of different subjects are really connected.

Other Tips for Short Subjects

- *Practice makes perfect.* Urge a child using paper forms to perfect answers elsewhere before printing or typing on the application.

- *A separate sheet is acceptable.* When using paper applications, it is permissible to say "see attached" beneath short-answer questions and type both the question and reply on a separate sheet. Proper labeling (including your child's name, in case the sheet gets detached) is imperative. Each answer should be about the same length as the space allotted on the original form.

V. The Almighty Essay

The irony of college application essays is this: students are informed, and rightfully so, that a good essay can gain admission for an otherwise average applicant; a bad one may scratch a contender from the list. Entire books are devoted to telling teenagers how to create compositions that will "work." As a result, applicants are so intimidated by the thought of such a make-or-break endeavor that some procrastinate until the last possible minute and then dash off a stack of mediocre efforts.

Admission officers use essays not only to assess a candidate's writing, spelling, and vocabulary skills, but also to get a look—sometimes their *only* look—at the personality behind the prose, at a prospect's interests, sense of humor, values, and goals. For this reason, college essay topics usually emphasize the personal—not merely academic—side of their authors. Yes, some colleges still ask applicants to unravel obtuse quotations from eminent alumni, but those who pose such questions often offer other options as well. More typical of today's topics are those that simply say: "Tell us something about yourself that we might not learn from the rest of your application."

Other typical topics include:

- With which literary character do you most readily identify? What traits do you share? (Fordham)

- Recall an occasion when you took a risk that you now know was the right thing to do. (University of Pennsylvania)

- Describe what you would consider to be the perfect adventure. (Hollins)

- You have answered many questions on this form, all asked by someone else. If you were in a position to ask a provocative and revealing question of college applicants, what would that question be? (Dartmouth)

- Discuss something *(anything)* you just wish you understood better than you now do. (As tempted as you may be, don't choose "the college admissions process.") (Princeton)

Some colleges demand several short essays; many allow applicants to select one of three or four topics. However, given the very open-ended nature of these questions, it's tough for most teenagers to decide how to best respond. Reassure your child that there are never right or wrong answers, nor are there trick questions. Any response that is well supported and well written is the correct one.

Beware of Overworked Topics

Strictly speaking, a good essay can be written about anything, and college officials certainly appreciate unique and imaginative entries. However, when informally polled, many such officials agreed that there are some subjects that crop up over and over and which rarely spawn essays that are creative and memorable. These subjects include:

- Winning (or losing) the "big game"

- The orchestra's annual concert

- Boyfriend or girlfriend problems

- My dear departed dog

- Religious epiphanies

- Anything that suggests that the applicant doesn't see the world beyond the boundaries of the high school (e.g., the pressures of prom-planning)

- Oversimplified solutions to world problems ("People need to realize that people are people wherever you go and have to try to understand one another.")

"We realize that these issues are important to our applicants," one admission counselor observes, "but only the most able writer is likely to be able to turn such commonly chosen topics into a strong personal statement." And speaking of taboo topics that should only be attempted with great caution, an Ivy League admission official proclaims that she's "just amazed by how stupid some students are when it comes to picking essay subjects. One year I read two essays on throwing up, one on constipation, and one on nose picking. We realize that they're trying to find a topic that will stand out, but they've got to remember that this essay will be read by a committee that may include the dean of admission, the dean of students, and faculty members."

Aim for Originality

So what are good essay subjects? Again, anything goes—the more original the better (let sound judgment prevail when it comes to the bodily functions)—but admission professionals seem to always warm up to those which include:

- Overcoming adversity (e.g., recovering from a serious illness; struggling with family substance abuse; living with a disabled sibling)

- Insight into an uncommon lifestyle, experience, or achievement (growing up on a commune; being raised by a grandparent; attending school in Saudi Arabia; climbing a challenging mountain)

- Information about an unusual hobby (building Victorian dollhouses; raising goats; collecting political campaign buttons)

- Lessons learned from literature

A Crash Course in Essay Writing

While, perhaps, great writers are born, not made, and even months of preparation won't transform your child from Hem N. Haw to Hemingway, there is some essay advice worth heeding. Begin by reading the two examples below. Both were written by the same author and address the topic: "*If you could have dinner with anyone, living, dead, or fictional, whom would you choose, and why?*"

Essay #1

There are many, many people who would make interesting dinner partners, and for a number of reasons. If I had to pick only one person, living or dead, I would choose my Aunt Rae. Unfortunately, she's the latter, having died when I was just eleven and, actually she was my great, great aunt—the sister of my father's grandmother, if you can follow that. Aunt Rae was always important to me because she instilled in me my love of reading and, especially, my appreciation of literature by and about women.

I first met Aunt Rae when I was eight. It was October of fourth grade, and my teacher, Mrs. Millan, was encouraging her pupils to read by offering us a gold star each time we finished a biography from the classroom bookshelf. I proudly told my "new" aunt that I had already completed seven books. She asked about whom I had read and was surprised (and a bit perturbed) that all of these subjects were male. She urged me to borrow her books about Helen Keller and Jane Addams, and I was quickly mesmerized.

Soon, Sunday afternoons with Aunt Rae became a regular routine, and I plowed through her extensive collection of biographies, each detailing the fascinating life of a different woman, from Juliet Ward Howe to Florence Nightingale; from Harriet Beecher Stowe to Harriet Tubman. Afterwards, we would share tea and strange cookies she called "madeleines."

Aunt Rae, like the heroines in her books, had had an interesting life herself. She was a native of England and flew supply planes in World War II. She married an American man who died during a Navy mission in the Pacific, so she left her homeland and came here, taking the reins of her late-husband's hardware supply business.

I wish I could say that all of my time with Aunt Rae was special but, like many youngsters, I grew impatient with her prodding and with her insistence that I share her passion for literature and history and other adult affairs. It is only now, as I look back on what she taught me and inspired in me, and as I look ahead to my goal of one day becoming a writer myself, that I most appreciate my Aunt Rae, and miss her, and long to see her again, even if only for one brief dinner.

Essay #2

MY DINNER WITH AUNT RAE

"Ah. You remembered the madeleines. I knew you would." She brought a delicate biscuit to her lips and sighed. "Milk and honey is much overrated, I'm afraid." Everything was indeed in order. For weeks I had planned this reunion, careful with each detail. Most important, though, were the madeleines—the shell-shaped French tea cakes that used to be part of every meeting with my Aunt Rae. In those days, of course, I was no more than eight or nine at the time. I secretly longed for more familiar fare—butterscotch brownies perhaps, or lemon squares. But Aunt Rae had never treated me like a child, even then, and that was part of her allure.

"You look like you've seen a ghost," she announced as she reached for another biscuit. Certainly, I hadn't known what to expect—a white-sheeted Casper like a schoolboy on Halloween? The ephemeral Elvira of *Blithe Spirit* that I'd struggled to perfect as a sophomore? Aunt Rae chuckled heartily, and a decade melted away. In fact, she looked exactly as I had recalled her so many times: the sturdy shoes and cotton shirtwaist dress; the sand and silver hair drawn up in an earnest bun. I was suddenly grateful that my mother had kept me from the hospice in those final weeks.

Technically speaking, she had been my great, great aunt—my father's grandmother's sister. I suppose this would not make her a close relative by some calculations but, to me, she was all-important. Born in England, Aunt Rae had piloted a supply plane in World War II and, when her American sailor husband was lost in the Sea of Japan, had installed herself in Savannah to oversee his family hardware business. I found her life as unfathomable and as enthralling as the faded photograph of the long-gone spouse on the mantle piece.

"Now, tell me again why I'm here," she implored. "What they said wasn't entirely clear...up there." She cast her eyes toward the ceiling. "It's an essay, Aunt Rae," I explained. "For college, I get to choose someone to have dinner with—famous or fictional; living or dead. I picked you."

"Well, my dear. I must say I'm flattered," she replied. "Were Helen Keller or Jane Addams unavailable?" Aunt Rae surely never missed a trick. She was harking back to our earliest encounter—the one that had precipitated so many others. I had just begun fourth grade. My teacher, Mrs. Millan, was awarding us gold stars for each biography we finished from the classroom shelf. Eric Eisenberg and I were neck and neck. Already seven stars apiece. When Aunt Rae met me for the first time, I was winding up *Wyatt Earp, U.S. Marshal.* She questioned me on other titles I'd completed. "Why, they're all men! " she proclaimed when I was through my recitation. Although I hadn't given it much thought before, she was right. Nowhere on Mrs. Millan's shelf was there even a single female's story. But Aunt Rae had had her own collection, and before that weekend was over, I had befriended both Helen Keller and Jane Addams. The following Sunday, she introduced me to Harriet Beecher Stowe then to Sacajawea. Always a contented reader, under Aunt Rae's tutelage, I became an insatiable one.

For most of that year, my Sundays were spent in Aunt Rae's cluttered library. Afterwards, there would be madeleines and tea. Eric Eisenberg got left in the dust as I clamored for more insight into a myriad of women's lives. Yet, those afternoons with Aunt Rae were never easy. She was an exacting mentor and had no patience for my childish complaints or whims. For my birthdays she gave me hand-blown glass from Venice, papyrus from Sicily—never games or toys. She spurred me to read Jane Austen while my friends were touting *Nancy Drew.* I could recite the Brontë sisters by name, but not the Brady Bunch. My visits slipped to once a month—and then to every other—but books still routinely arrived in the mail, and I consumed each one with fervor.

"So, why me?" again Aunt Rae insisted. "Have you run out of literary recommendations? Do I still need to tell you what to read?" "Actually, no," I answered, more shyly than is my usual nature. "It's not reading that's the issue here. Now, it's my turn to write." And so, I admitted to my great, great aunt my dream of becoming an author. I told her of my project on Susan B. Anthony that had made such a stir at school ("the best work I've ever seen," my junior humanities teacher had maintained) and of the workshop on Maya Angelou that I had run for preteen girls last summer at the YWCA. "I want to write a biography, a full-length one," I confided. "Nobody renowned; just somebody special." I took the last madeleine from the plate. "I want my subject to be *you.*"

The cookie surprised me with its sweetness. It was richer than I had remembered; far more interesting than a brownie or a lemon square. It was an acquired taste, I decided—not unlike Aunt Rae, herself.

The two essays tell the same story. The first is solid, but the second has more spark. With both, the applicant is admissible but, while #1 is hardly memorable, #2 might be enough to prompt a positive decision from an otherwise ambivalent admission board.

Even if you hardly consider yourself a literary critic, you can offer valuable editorial assistance—and the tips that follow— to your child:

- **A title is a nice touch, especially if it's catchy.** The title of Essay #2 is a clever pun, an allusion to a well-known and rather intellectual film, *My Dinner with Andre.* In only four words, and before the essay has really begun, this applicant has shown off her witty and sophisticated side.

- **The introduction is crucial.** If your child does only one thing right in the essay, this should be it. Never let the reader doze off at the first sentence. Note that the start of Essay #1 is a real snoozer. How many others must begin almost identically? Essay #2, however, immediately engages. Curiosity is piqued. Just who is this Aunt Rae, and what about these madeleines and milk and honey?

- **Good writers take risks with style.** Observe how Essay #2 plays with intentionally incomplete sentences ("Already seven stars apiece") and with phrases set off by dashes and parentheses.

- **Vocabulary should be varied and interesting.** Teenagers tend to use the same boring words (like "varied" and "interesting") over and over and over. Check for repetition. Suggest more colorful alternatives. On the other hand, don't encourage your child to use words he is not comfortable or familiar with. He should use a thesaurus for suggestions, but the writing shouldn't sound as if he swallowed one.

- **Humor is a big plus, especially when one considers those beleaguered admission officers plodding through piles of applications as the clock ticks past midnight.** Just because an essay will be taken seriously doesn't mean it has to be a serious essay. Essay #2 uses touches of humor judiciously. (e.g., "You look like you've seen a ghost;" "Were Helen Keller or Jane Addams unavailable?") Nonetheless, if a kid has never been Rosie O'Donnell or Eddie Murphy, this isn't the time to start.

- **Sentimentality can be an asset if used sparingly.** Both essays end on a note that is slightly sentimental but not maudlin or melodramatic.

- **Show off an academic side.** Your child does have one? Essay # 2 hints at the author's familiarity with writers Jane Austen, the Brontë sisters, and Maya Angelou, as well as with historical figures like Susan B. Anthony.

- **Be revealing.** Essay #2 craftily tells us much about this applicant. We certainly learn that she's an excellent writer, one who uses subtlety well. (We see, for example, from references to ghosts and "up there" that Aunt Rae is deceased.) Moreover, we also learn that this author is an actor (she had the lead in *Blithe Spirit*); an avid reader; a strong student ("the best work I've ever seen"); and a community leader (the summer workshop at the YWCA). We even find out that she's not especially timid ("more shyly than is my usual nature"). Clearly, the admission officials who read this essay will get some genuine insight into the person behind it.

- **Finish strong.** While not as critical as the introduction, an essay should end with a bang, not a whimper. The reader should have no doubt that it's over and shouldn't be left scampering around the floor searching for a nonexistent second page.

  Essay #2 successfully uses the full-circle style of writing. The concluding paragraph neatly brings the reader back to the madeleines in the first sentence and explains their significance as a symbol of Aunt Rae's nature.

- **Check and recheck spelling and grammar.** Computerized check systems are valuable tools, but most don't pick up the types of common errors that most of us make (using "on" when we mean "one;" "that" for "than," etc.). Even parents who don't trust their own spelling skills can recognize a "form" that should be a "from."

- **Neatness counts.** Remember that a separate, well-labeled sheet of paper can substitute for the form provided, especially if your child (or you) has blighted the initial document beyond recognition.

- **Unless directed otherwise, aim for one to two typed pages.** When instructions do set length restrictions, there is usually leeway to go somewhat shorter or longer. Read directions closely. There's a difference between the ones that request " ...about one page" and those that say "... should not exceed one page."

- **Use a computer or typewriter for the essay section, unless instructed otherwise.** Brown University, for example, requests handwritten essays. "We think it helps to personalize the application process," explains a Brown official, "but we don't have handwriting analysts hidden in the basement as some applicants may fear."

- **Sleep on it.** Most students wait until the bitter end to tackle the essay. Urge your child to let it mellow and then review it, days later, with a fresh perspective.

- **Get a second opinion.** It's not cheating for your child to ask an advisor, teacher, etc. to review an essay after it's written. Key questions to ask are: Is it grammatically correct? Is it clear? Does it answer the question being asked? Is the introduction inviting? Will it stand out in a crowd? As parents, you should be available to offer suggestions but shouldn't *insist* that you see an essay at all. Remember, this is a personal statement, and teenagers are somehow more comfortable bearing all to a total stranger than to Mom or Dad. You know how that is.

- **The toughest topic isn't worth tackling.** Some applicants believe that, if given several choices, they will earn extra brownie points for choosing what appears to be the hardest one. In fact, sophisticated essays can spring from simple subjects, and essay topic offerings are never a test of an applicant's ambition. Among our career favorites, for instance, was one written about a laundry mishap, another about playing in an awful high school band, and a third entitled, "Why I shop at Wal-Mart."

- **Consolidate.** Help your child "recycle" essays. Although admission officials don't appreciate submissions that are clearly answering another college's question, not their own, there is often enough similarity among topics that an essay can be used again at least once, with few or even no revisions. (However, be sure that you edit out any references to Oberlin on the Carleton essay.)

Gather all applications together before your child begins to complete any, and then determine topic overlaps. For instance, both sample essays above could be recycled to respond to questions such as *Who is your hero or heroine?*; *Who has had a great influence on you?*; *What is an important interest of yours?*; *What is your career goal?*; or any open-ended query that says *Choose your own topic*; *Make up your own question*, or *Tell us about yourself*.

Of course, those who use the Common Application and other multi-recipient options are able to share one statement among several schools—a good reason to select generic formats when possible.

The fewer essays your child has to crank out, the easier it will be to produce strong contenders. Or...

- **Bail Out.** Some colleges don't require any essay at all. Others will list it as optional. If your child seems to be a fairly strong applicant and balks at submitting a nonrequisite essay, don't gather gray hairs protesting. However, more middle-of-the-road candidates—or those with special circumstances to explain—should include at least a brief personal statement.

Questions & Answers

Q: We've heard rumors about applicants who cheat on applications. They don't write their own essays or they invent extracurricular achievements. How do colleges guard against dishonesty?

A: Very carefully and not always successfully. When a student with abysmal test scores and average grades submits an essay that Robert Benchley would be proud to claim, officials are suspicious. They'll scrutinize recommendations for signs of literary achievement and, perhaps, call a guidance counselor for further information. But, when good students write especially polished essays, admission people have no choice but to give the benefit of the doubt. As for embellishing "extras," heaven help the student who gets caught. It does happen, but rarely. If Johnny lists "Class President" on his application, and the counselor only mentions his leadership as a bathroom monitor, most astute officials will pick up on it. Students have been denied acceptance for making false statements. It's hard, however, to spot exaggeration. The once-a-month hospital volunteer can list a once-a-week commitment, and no one is apt to be the wiser. Like many things in life, it's a question of personal ethics and responsibility.

VI. Recommendations

Most colleges require a recommendation from your child's guidance counselor, as well as from one or more teachers. Private schools often pride themselves on presenting long, informative, anecdotal counselor "recs," while some overworked public school counselors submit those which say little more than "Melinda is a hard-working and personable young woman who will succeed at the college of her choice." While admission officers won't discriminate against students whose school references are brief and vague, strong and personal recommendations certainly give a clear-cut picture of the candidate. If your child does attend a school where counselor loads are large, provide the guidance staff with a résumé (even a very informal one) and a summary of achievements, interests, and goals. Stress qualities that you want colleges to see (e.g., community service involvement, team leadership, willingness to seek academic assistance, etc.) As you read in Chapter 2, you may also wish to include personal information that may help to explain bad grades or other problems. This will make appreciative counselors more able to write a revealing recommendation.

Never feel that you are bothering teachers by asking for references. This is part of their job and most are actually flattered to be asked (and asked and asked). Don't feel, either, that you have to spread the wealth. If Joelle has done her best work in Ms. Smiley's class, then, by all means, let Ms. Smiley write all of Joelle's recommendations. (But be fair; give her the whole stack of forms at once so she can reuse her well-turned phrases.) Be sure, also, to give teachers plenty of time before deadlines and to provide stamped, addressed envelopes.

Along with those envelopes, your child might want to compile and provide a brief list of his or her finest moments under each chosen teacher's tutelage. For instance, if Mrs. Reifsnyder wrote, "I laughed and cried all the way through," on Erika's English essay last April, Erika may remember it for the rest of her life; her teacher might need a reminder. This list shouldn't include laudatory phrases ("I'm brilliant, hardworking, and humble") but it's helpful to suggest a few specifics ("You read my Tartuffe translation to the entire class.") Some kids, of course, may shudder at the very thought of this, so don't push it, but assure those who are on the fence that teachers will value the hints.

Select teachers for whom your child has done good work (and that doesn't always mean "A" work. A "C-" in advanced chemistry may have been the result of enormous determination and effort). It's also preferable to choose those who have taught your child a major subject in the junior or senior year. Sometimes the teacher who knows a student best is a club advisor or coach (who may not have had your child in class at all). Activity advisors may be asked to write supplemental letters (see below), but should not replace academic references.

Supporting Materials and Optional Information

Some candidates are convinced that even the most enormous application just doesn't tell the whole story. In such cases, consider providing additional supporting material that may be a plus at decision time.

Admission offices often receive such extras. Most commonly they include slides of artwork; tapes (video or audio) of music or theater performances; samples of poetry, fiction, or other written work; newspaper clippings about past achievements; recommendations from family friends, employers, coaches, alumni, etc.

Many a modern parent has been traumatized by tales of other parents who engage professional production companies to present *Junior's Life as Colleges Want to See It,* via thirty or so minutes of carefully selected celluloid. How heavily do admission counselors weigh these additions? Should you indeed be humbled by those who have the time, talent, (or money) to get such addenda all together? Our suggestions follow:

Arts (visual, music, theater, dance)

Specialized schools/programs usually require slides, tapes, etc. as an integral part of an application. When not required, however, these are often overlooked by busy admission counselors. If you believe that your child's artistic abilities are exceptional, ask admission offices if they automatically forward all submissions to faculty evaluators. If the answer is no, consider sending copies of slides or tapes directly to appropriate faculty members. (Use course catalogs and/or Web sites for guidance.) Make sure that tapes are of good quality and clearly labeled with the candidate's name and a brief description of content. Don't count on getting the material back (although if you enclose a prepaid addressed envelope, you might). Include a cover letter where your child expresses wishes to study under this chosen mentor. Follow up by telephone or e-mail in a couple weeks. A professor who is truly impressed is usually willing to call the admission office to put in a good word, and this can definitely help your child's candidacy.

Writing Samples

When verbal SAT scores are low or English course grades are only average, an additional writing sample, such as an English class essay or history term paper, can be beneficial. Send just one. Some schools, like Wheaton College in Massachusetts, actually require all applicants to submit a graded writing sample. "We want to see both what a candidate considers good work and what a school considers good work," explains a Wheaton admission official. "If a paper is weak and the grade is good, it tells us that this applicant comes from a place where expectations are not high." Whether requisite or not, including an "A" paper (with the grade and comments on it) is an A+ idea. If the work is truly excellent, admission officers will be impressed. If it's not, they will be more likely to put poor test scores or a not-so-hot application essay in perspective.

When an application touts your child's passion as a poet or a budding novelist, an ecology columnist or a theater critic, then an example is in order.

Writing samples should be sent to the office of admission, along with the application. (Committed creative writers can also consider contacting faculty members, as in "Arts" above.)

...And More Essays

Some students have special situations that warrant explaining in an extra essay. Did your family only recently immigrate to America? Has your child been diagnosed with a learning disability or hospitalized for several months? Are parental problems to blame for a semester of "C"s? Any significant experience, from attending six schools in seven years to trying out for the Olympic diving team, can be fuel for a supplementary personal statement. (See also "Unsolicited Letters" below.) Sometimes these statements need be only a few sentences where your child explains transcript irregularities like:

> "After finishing British Literature as a junior, I knew I wouldn't survive my senior year without taking Ms. Stone's Shakespeare seminar. I didn't want to miss out on the Advanced Placement English class either, but the schedule conflicts that resulted meant that calculus got lost in the shuffle."

But admission officials are wary of those who doth protest too much, so advise your child to avoid a whiny tone. ("My French teacher was really awful, and she didn't like me, and neither did my calculus teacher, so my bad grades were really just due to those personality conflicts...")

You or your child may also have to make a judgment call about how much you want to reveal about personal issues. For instance, if your son suffered from a clinical depression, and his grades suffered along with him, it probably makes sense to tell admission officials about the situation and, especially, about how it is being treated. On the other hand, if your daughter is struggling with an eating disorder but still managing to pull down straight "A"s, should you tell all in an application? And what about the applicant who was arrested for shoplifting in his senior year?

Colleges aren't supposed to make decisions based on such personal matters, but sometimes they do anyway. Some admission officials find an applicant's efforts to overcome personal problems especially admirable, but others may be reluctant to accept candidates who are going to bring serious problems with them to campus. It's usually to your child's advantage to tell admission offices about ongoing health or psychological problems, so that he or she won't be heading to a place that can't handle them. However, if the crisis is clearly behind you, this becomes another one of those moral dilemmas that you're going to have to decide for yourselves.

Newspaper Clippings

These should be included with an application only if the applicant is the author or featured subject, and the clipping is recent (within two years). (Older articles are okay when the achievement being touted is truly amazing or unique.) Two clippings usually suffice.

Gotta Getta Gimmick?

In the race for space on selective campuses, some students resort to including a variety of unexpected extras in their application packages. Lee Coffin, dean of admissions at Connecticut College, concedes that a "No" decision became a "Yes" when the admission office received an extraordinary animated video that an applicant had drawn and produced himself. "We all sat down and watched the tape together," Coffin recounts, "and agreed to admit this candidate after all, on the strength of his creative genius...and then he turned *us* down!"

Even less talented prospects have successfully cashed in on ideas that are longer on novelty than on artistry, such as the Bard College hopeful who enclosed two photographed self-portraits. One, which showed a grinning candidate, was captioned, "This is me, if I'm accepted." The other depicted a frowning counterpart labeled, "This is me, if I'm denied."

The majority of applicants, however, *don't* go in for gimmicks. Even those who do may find that they don't necessarily work; they just never hurt. And they are, for sure, a way to garner at least fifteen minutes of fame in an admission office.

Unsolicited Letters

Supplemental letters that are most helpful to admission staff show an important side of an applicant that other credentials have not. These may come from physicians, counselors, clergy, and others who can shed light on a medical, psychological, or family situation that may have affected your child, or from a club advisor or employer who recognizes your child's special non-academic strengths. (See also "...And More Essays" above.)

Some parents beat the bushes to drum up support from other, often distant corners. Is your uncle an alumnus? The next-door neighbor a trustee? Your sister's boss the former dean? Is anyone in any way linked to you also linked to your child's target schools? Admission officers *sometimes* give credence to such endorsements, especially if the author is a big-time V.I.P., either at that college itself or in the world at large. And don't worry if your connection turns out to be a *persona non grata* at a target school—it won't reflect badly on your child.

Don't worry, too, if you have no such rabbits to pull out of your hat—most other candidates won't either—and keep in mind that there's an old saying in admission circles: "The thicker the folder, the thicker the kid."

Parent Letters

Some schools, like Smith, have finally wised up to the fact that if anyone can offer a close-up look at a candidate, it's you—the parents. Indeed, whether a college invites it or not, a short letter of support from an applicant's mother or father can add a dimension that no other form will provide. Some parents are hindered by their own writer's block or by fears that poor grammar or spelling may hurt their child's chances. In fact, some of the most poignant and effective parent letters have come from those whose inexperience—but sincerity—shines through.

Parent letters are bound to offer platitudes like "responsible," "hard-working," and "good-natured," but be sure to also include anecdotes or examples that illustrate your child's special traits, as in the letter below. This may also be the time to explain serious medical problems or other personal issues, if any, that have affected your family and your child.

Dear Board of Admission:

It's been a long while since I've written anything besides a grocery list, and just thinking about the task ahead makes me appreciate what Jessica and her friends have to go through all the time. Please bear with me while I tackle this challenge of sharing the most important person in the world to me with strangers.

Jessica is an only child. We lost her little sister at birth. Because of this, it might have been easy to spoil her, but she has never allowed it. For instance, in eighth grade, when a less fortunate friend signed up for a paper route to finance gymnastics lessons, Jess insisted on getting one, too and, from that day on, has paid all of her own gymnastics fees.

As you can see from Jessica's application, she has been so successful with her gymnastics that she now competes on a statewide level. Yet, despite the cost of costumes, travel, and classes, she has never gone back on her decision to pay her own way. Since delivering newspapers didn't put a dent in mounting expenses, Jess found her first "real" job at a nearby nursing home where she helps with morning meal service. Her application probably tells you that, too. What it won't tell you, though, is that she gets up at 5 a.m., three days a week, and rides her bike a mile to work and then two miles to school at 8. Often, on weekends or in the evening, she returns to the home again, this time as a visitor. "There are so many patients there who have nobody," she tells me, "and I can't spend time with them while I'm working."

For most of Jessica's school years, she has also been a top student. She was selected for advanced math and science as a freshman, took accelerated chemistry as a junior (usually a senior class) and was one of three who helped implement an Advanced Placement American History course last year. I hope you will focus on that, and not on the bad semester she had as a sophomore. That fall, my father was diagnosed with cancer and moved into our house. Jess quickly volunteered her room to "Pop-pop" and slept on the couch in the basement den. It wasn't relocation that hurt her grades, but the enormous stress that all of us were under which ended with my father's death at home. I think that as a result of this experience, Jess learned an enormous amount about the importance of family and about strength and hope and faith. But I'm not sure how much French and geometry she learned during those months.

I could go on and on with examples that point out this wonderful young woman's determination, her optimism, and her generosity. But better yet, discover this for yourselves by offering her a place in your freshman class.

Sincerely yours,

Yvonne P.

Financial Aid Forms

Financing a college education is such a tricky topic that it rates a chapter all its own. (See Chapter 5.) Remember, always take financial aid deadlines and requirements seriously.

Application Fee (or Waiver)

Ordinarily, an application will not be processed and your child will not formally be considered an applicant until an application fee is received (though some colleges have no fee to apply or waive them for online applications). Typical fees range from about $25 to $60, a pittance compared to the tuition bills to follow, but still a problem for those with limited resources. Fortunately, most institutions grant fee waivers to needy candidates. However, the process of obtaining one will vary from school to school. Some colleges include fee waiver information, or even a short form, with application materials. Generally, a fee waiver is granted if, along with the application, your child sends a statement or form from the guidance department (or a social worker, clergy member, etc.) confirming financial need.

You won't be penalized for requesting a waiver, but keep in mind that they're designed for genuine hardship cases, not for those whose credit cards are overused or who don't want to pay to apply to safety schools. (Once financial aid forms are in, colleges may check to see if the waiver was really needed. If not, you will be billed for the application fee and your integrity might be questioned.)

Questions & Answers

Q: I fear that admission officers won't get to know my daughter, the real Elizabeth, from reading her application.

A: Admission staff probably will spend less than 30 minutes reviewing your child's credentials. Don't expect them to know—and love—her as much as you do after 17 or 18 years. Even the best applications don't tell everything about the candidates who submit them, but here's a quick and easy exercise that you and your daughter can try:

Write down 20 words that describe Elizabeth (e.g., "daughter," "swimmer," "friend," "book lover," etc.). The first six or eight usually come pretty easily; it's the last 10 or so that are tough but often more revealing ("dreamer," "procrastinator," "perfectionist," etc.) Parents and children should do this exercise separately and compare notes.

When Elizabeth finishes the application, take stock of which characteristics have been revealed. Have any important ones been left out? ("diplomat?" "gourmet cook?" "class wit?") If so, how can they be included?

This game is also a good one to play as you are making college matches. For example, a risk-taker might want to consider unusual colleges or those far from home. A procrastinator might not do well at a place without enough personal attention and structure.

Now What?

The applications are finally in and the waiting process has begun. So what are admission officials up to while *you're* waiting?

CHAPTER 7

How Admission Decisions Are Made

➤ **THE GOOD NEWS:** Admission decisions aren't made by tossing applications down the stairwell and accepting those students whose folders reach the bottom step. The process is fair and thorough, and admission professionals take this part of their job very seriously.

➤ **THE BAD NEWS:** So many factors go into these decisions that the results can sometimes seem unpredictable and maybe even off-the-mark.

How are decisions made? Who makes them? What counts and what doesn't? What parents *really* want to know is, *"What looks good on a college application?"* The subtext here is, "How can my child get into not just *any* college, but those popular and picky places where all the applicants seem to be National Merit finalists? What will give my kid a competitive edge?

First, all application materials are collected in a folder. Every scrap of paper which bears your child's name—from supplemental essays to phone message slips and thank you notes—is likely to end up there. Then, each folder is read carefully. (**WARNING:** Incomplete folders stay on the shelf.)

At small schools, the entire admission staff may evaluate each applicant (and at great length); at larger ones, a single official may be the sole judge (and some prescreening might be done by a computer). At many places, decisions are made by more than one person, including admission officials and often faculty representatives and other administrators. The committee where your child lands may be determined alphabetically, geographically, departmentally (e.g., school of business applicants), or by the date an application is completed. The individual who interviewed your child, visited your local high school, or spoke so reassuringly to you on the phone may—or may not—be among the arbiters. Typically, committee members examine each folder independently (and commonly assign it an overall rating) before the committee meets to make decisions.

I. Transcripts

In evaluating each candidate, the high school transcript is almost always the most important component. (Exception: specialized schools in areas like art, music, and drama look more carefully at portfolios or audition tapes.) As you read in Chapter 2, included in nearly every candidate's application folder is a school profile which details the curriculum available at that high school, explains the grading system, and sometimes even lists median grades for each class. Admission officers are skilled at understanding the discrepancies among schools and the ways that grades are awarded, recorded, etc. They know, for example, that at some schools, only those who walk on water will earn "A"s, while at others, anyone who hands in the homework is an honors student. They read between the lines of transcripts and school profiles to ascertain a school's strength. (e.g., What percentage of graduates go on to four-year colleges and where? What advanced classes are offered?) They recognize that good students at challenging, competitive high schools (public or private) may have lower grades and class ranks than their counterparts at easier ones (and that some students may not be ranked—or even *graded*—at all). Admission staff are also seeing a growing number of candidates who have been home-schooled and submit detailed narratives in lieu of transcripts.

What are officials looking for? Parents and students may underestimate the importance of secondary school course choices. Decisions made as early as junior high might have affected what classes a child was eligible to take later on and thus, how a college application will be evaluated, especially by the most selective institutions. Minimum high school graduation requirements vary, but most are less stringent than those expected at the more competitive colleges. Colleges normally have *recommended* secondary school programs, not *imperative* ones.

Commonly, high schools grant diplomas to those who have completed a curriculum comparable to this:

English: 4 (full-year courses or equivalent)
Social Studies/History: 2
Mathematics: 2
Science: 2 (usually plus physical education, health, and often keyboarding and electives)

While these minimum requirements are sufficient to allow admission to many not-so-selective schools, the more competitive institutions expect a program that looks more like this:

English: 4
Social Studies/History: 3
Mathematics: 3
Science: at least 2, preferably 3
Foreign Language: 3 years of 1 language or at least 2 years of 2

Such suggested preparation will vary from college to college and from school to school within a university. Even different branches within the same university system may have different recommendations.

Predictably, schools with a technology emphasis look more closely at math and science backgrounds. Most entering MIT students have taken calculus before enrolling. If it's not offered at their high schools, they find it elsewhere. Similarly, Rensselaer Polytechnic Institute in Troy, New York, strongly encourages applicants to take physics and chemistry in secondary school, as well as calculus or, at the very least, pre-calculus.

Here is an example of a strong four-year academic program:

English: 4 or more
Social Studies/History: 3 or 4
Mathematics: 4 years through calculus (or at least through pre-calculus)
Science: at least 3 (with 2 or more lab sciences).
Foreign Language: 4 of at least one language

Questions & *Answers*

Q: My daughter's high school is on a block system. How will college admission officers evaluate her transcript?

A: With so many high schools operating on a block system (where students take fewer, longer classes each term), this is not big news anymore. Admission officials realize that they have to make decisions before they see final grades (or *any* grades in some cases) in some important senior subjects. However, it's essential that they know which classes are planned. For example, if your daughter submits a first-semester transcript that includes English, foreign language, and social studies/history, but expects to start calculus and physics in January, it should be made clear on her application.

Similarly, if your child's school uses a block system, make certain that this is made clear to admission officials so they'll realize that what may look like a single semester of a subject was really the equivalent of a full-year course.

Admission officers expect to see a minimum of 5 solids or major subjects per term, plus at least one elective or minor subject (e.g., band, art—a "major" in some schools, yearbook, etc.). At schools on block or trimester systems or at some independent schools, fewer solids per term will be the norm. No matter how high your child is aiming, he or she will be well served by pursuing a secondary school program that exceeds the basic requirements.

The most competitive colleges also expect that applicants will select the most challenging courses available. If there is a tracking system at your child's school, where students are grouped by ability, the transcript should indicate if classes have been at the highest level (e.g., Honors, Enriched, Level 1) or at a lower one (Standard, Level 2).

While such names vary from school to school, one coast-to-coast constant is the Advanced Placement designation. Schools that list Advanced Placement classes (usually for juniors and seniors, or just for seniors) are participating in a program offered by The College Entrance Examination Board based in Princeton, New Jersey, that enables high school students to take classes which may lead to college credit. Some secondary schools offer Advanced Placement courses in over a dozen subjects; others offer far fewer (or none at all). More information on this program will appear in Chapter 9.

International Baccalaureate (IB) programs are increasingly available in secondary schools in the U.S. and abroad. Initially designed for those who might be heading to non-American universities, this system is gaining stateside popularity among high schools interested in providing a widely acclaimed and challenging curriculum for strong students who can also gain college credit through IB participation and testing. (See Chapter 9.)

Ordinarily, Advanced Placement and IB classes, if offered, are the top-level courses taught in high schools and are well respected by all college officials. Because of their universal recognition, they jump off a transcript and put a spring in admission counselors' steps.

Questions & Answers

Q: Are "B"s in honors or Advanced Placement classes better than "A"s in less demanding ones?

A: "B"s in first-string classes *are* more impressive than "A"s in easier ones. Even an *occasional* "C" won't rule out a career at highly selective college (but tip-top applicants often have all or mostly "A"s in tip-top classes. We're not trying to ruin your day, we just want you to know what your son or daughter may be up against.). Yet, while the most competitive colleges do prefer the most competitive courses, there is room for fluctuation, and a second-level class in one or two weaker areas may work better for your child.

When computing class ranks, most high schools now use a weighted system where extra points are allotted for higher level classes, so the "B+" student in honors courses is likely to be ranked above the straight "A" student in the second tier. Colleges, too, are careful to note those high schools that do not use weighted ranks and take this into consideration when evaluating and comparing candidates. So, if your child attends such a school (and it's a good idea to ask), he won't be penalized for taking a tough load.

Admission professionals know that many high schools don't have Advanced Placement or IB programs and that some don't even have advanced or accelerated classes. Your child will be evaluated in light of what opportunities were available.

Q: My son wants to take part in a dual enrollment program at our local community college. How do admission officers view this?

A: Dual enrollment programs allow students to take some courses on a college campus for credit while they remain enrolled in high school classes. Admission officials are always pleased when students take advantage of challenging opportunities. However, while they will credit your son with making a wise choice, their institution may not necessarily award college credit for his work.

You may have grown up in the sixties, when there weren't as many opportunities to take Advanced Placement or IB classes or to head to a local college for high school credit. But what you might remember from your era is that some schools abandoned courses like Biology II for those with a more "relevant" ring, like *The Ecology of the Okefenokee*. And while, in some schools, such selections still live on, their jazzy titles may be misleading. A tough and very serious class with a funny name may appear to admission officials to be what some dub "fluffy," "flimsy," or "lightweight. Fear not. Older admission officers understand this and even smile with appreciation or sigh with nostalgia when English turns up on such transcripts as *Utopias and Dream Worlds,* or science as *Were Wilbur and Orville Right?*

It may be up to you to point out the difficulties of benign-sounding offerings. Sometimes good guidance counselors will alert colleges to killer classes that masquerade as filler classes, but if Angie's "A" in astrology was her finest hour, let admission officers know—via parent letter or supplementary essay, etc.—just what it took to land it.

More common are cases like Cassandra's. She took a heavy schedule through her junior year and worked hard to knock off graduation requirements in order to "enjoy" her first senior term. She chose long-awaited electives like ceramics and photography in place of math and science. Her top-choice college viewed her transcript with disdain. Many families dwell on the importance of 11th grade without realizing that 12th grade courses are just as crucial.

Although the overall GPA is important, colleges realize that it is calculated on the basis of all four high school years. Class ranks are typically cumulative (based on three- or four-year records). Admission officials tend to be believers in what they dub the "rising record," and may be willing to forgive freshman (and even sophomore) foibles when a student has shown impressive improvement as a junior and senior—the two years that get scrutinized most closely. They may be likewise willing to overlook one awful grade (or an entire catastrophic semester) if followed by a strong rebound (and remember, this is also where an explanatory letter or essay can help).

Colleges are also impressed by students who have sought enrichment opportunities outside of their school, both during the academic year or in the summer. Make sure that these are noted on the application.

Questions & Answers

Q: Don't admission officers from highly selective colleges prefer private school applicants?

A: Colleges, even the choosiest ones, do *not* prefer *either* private school or public school candidates. Since most students attend public high schools, the vast majority at *all* colleges are public school graduates. Diversity is now the clarion call, and that means drawing students from all sorts of backgrounds.

Parents sometimes believe that paying for private school is like buying an insurance policy that promises that their child will be admitted to a name college. However, while admission officers recognize that the top independent schools are excellent proving grounds for top colleges, they are also aware that there are some crummy private schools and many outstanding public ones. (Also, there are crummy students at outstanding schools and outstanding students at crummy schools!) Being a preppie can also backfire. Imagine what it's like to be one of 46 in a senior class to apply to Princeton or among 57 to aim for Brown. Of course, if you're at the head of such a list, the odds are with you, but those down the line a bit might have had a better shot from Sheboygan!

Q: My child switched high schools, and the move has meant some transcript irregularities. Will admission officials figure it all out?

A: Be certain that each college will receive a transcript (or several) that covers your child's entire high school career. This may be the perfect time to add an extra statement explaining why moves were made, and what impact they had on course choices. (e.g., "Velma missed biology" or "Louie took math courses out of sequence") Parents who anticipate relocation should look ahead, where possible, and check into curricular differences at the transfer school.

II. Test Results

All of Chapter 3 is devoted to standardized tests and explains in detail how colleges use them. Test scores are intentionally listed in this chapter *after* transcripts to emphasize that they are less important, but they are also used *in conjunction* with transcripts. For example, Annie scarcely squeaked by when her first-choice college made its decisions. She had terrific test scores (1,400 SATs) but her record had more than its share of "C"s. Kirsten, on the other hand, would never have been admitted to her favorite college on her sorry scores alone, but admission officials were impressed with her "A" average and interesting choice of activities. In general, admission officials prefer students like Kirsten who have demonstrated their ability to perform well in school.

Additional considerations that admission officers keep in mind when reviewing test scores include:

- Is the testing pattern consistent? Did a student clearly have an off day?

- Are scores compatible with academic achievement. If not, why not?

- Are there strengths in one area (e.g., language, math, etc.) while others are weaker?

- Were tests taken under special conditions (e.g., extended time)? Does the student have a diagnosed disability?

- Does the student come from a disadvantaged background?

- Is English spoken at home?

- Were SAT II tests taken close to course completion or a year or more later? If language test scores were low, how many years of study has this student had?

III. Essays/Personal Statements

Chapter 6 covers the ins and outs of essays. Remember, a great essay can really make an admission official sit up and take notice. However, subjectivity prevails here. Some readers are biased toward content; some toward writing style and mechanics. One applicant submitted an ambitious essay that compared the works of three Eastern European writers. Two of her evaluators were impressed by her literary sophistication and the insight of her analysis; a third couldn't get beyond the errors in spelling and sentence structure.

IV. Recommendations

Quality and depth vary tremendously. Colleges don't penalize students when the recommendation is not well written or offers only superficial information. However, a clear and comprehensive letter of recommendation can make a difference. Specifics that admission professionals seek from recommendations include:

- Comparisons to others in the class; to those whom the teacher or counselor has worked with in past years; or with students who have enrolled at the college in question ("In twenty years of teaching, I have encountered few students as determined as Evan" or "Jamie reminds me of Susannah Leone whose test scores were equally dismal but who went on to graduate with honors from your college.")

- Information about grading and/or competition ("Mr. Jones rarely gives above a 'B'" or "This year's Advanced Placement English class was the most able this school has ever seen" or "Julie's 'C+' was the third highest grade in a class of 30.")

- Illustrative examples or anecdotes ("Jennifer is the swim team captain and a state record holder in the backstroke. However, her sensitivity is another special strength. She stays late after every practice to help a far weaker swimmer, to keep her from being cut from the team.")

- Personal information ("Ian struggled with his mother's drinking and finally caused an 'intervention' which led to her enrollment in a treatment program.")

- Other personal traits or study habits (e.g., maturity, response to criticism, acceptance by peers, timely completion of assignments, willingness to go beyond what is expected, participation in class discussions)

The law entitles students to see completed recommendations. However, reference forms include a clause that most students sign to waive this right. This enables counselors and teachers to be candid, which is what admission officials prefer. (Recommendations normally do become part of a student's permanent file.)

V. Extracurricular Activities

➤ **THE GOOD NEWS:** Colleges aren't terribly picky about how your child spends non-class time, as long as it's doing something meaningful. It isn't necessary to have a long list of activities, either. Commitment, some level of accomplishment, initiative, and leadership are far more important.

➤ **THE BAD NEWS:** With so many high school students doing so much; with so many programs and organizations, teams and clubs and causes, it's hard to predict what will make a splash anymore. However, some activities do stand out more than others, and proper presentation can help admission officers look more closely at Davina's debate awards or Roger's rock-climbing.

When evaluating an applicant's extras, these are considerations that crop up during committee meetings:

- How much time does this student devote to an activity? How significant is the contribution? Admission professionals often favor depth over breadth. Phillip, for instance, attends most weekly chess club meetings. Coral, on the other hand, organized a chess clinic and tournament at a nearby junior high. It was such a success that she ran a second one at a homeless shelter, persuading local merchants to donate prizes.

- "Evidence of leadership" is a phrase that comes up often at admission committee meetings, and it can be what separates an accepted student from one who ends up on the wait list. There's a world of difference between the student who *joined* the Geography Club and the one who *founded* it. The more selective a college is, the more carefully this leadership role is examined. Some colleges are impressed by French Club presidents and yearbook business managers, while it takes a *student council* president or *editor-in-chief* to make a mark at others.

- Some balance is best. While there may not be as much talk of "well-roundedness" these days as there was back when Dobie Gillis and Ricky Nelson (and maybe you) went to college, varied ventures appeal to admission officers. The student who participates in the Science Club, the Drama Club, and is also on the tennis team usually stands out more than the one who only chooses athletics as extras. The good, yet not exceptional, player should also have other, different activities on the roster. Similarly, a balance of school-related activities (clubs, teams, choirs, etc.) and those which take place elsewhere (volunteering, scouting, church groups, community theater, etc.) suggests that your child's horizons extend beyond the schoolyard.

- Volunteerism is very important, and the key here is real hands-on *involvement.* Admission people are usually able to differentiate between the candidate who spends every Saturday tutoring at a storefront literacy center and the classmate who spent an hour on the Students Against Styrofoam Dance Decoration Committee.

- Specialists are exceptional. As Lee Coffin, dean of admissions at Connecticut College, points out, "The ideal of the well-rounded student is important, but so is the well-rounded *class.* So, within a class of 450 students, we have those who aren't the least bit well-rounded but will bring something unique to the community." A few collegiate candidates will up their stock in admission officers' eyes by being extraordinarily talented in some area or with a truly off-the-wall interest or experience. This may be the prima ballerina who dances six hours a day, pirouetting all the way to Prague with a national company, or the downhill skier, just one run away from a gold medal. Admission annals, too, are filled with stories about adolescent entrepreneurs who started home-baked cookie companies or computer software services and prodigies who published their own novels or built fighter jets in the garage.

Colleges appreciate uncommon undertakings: hand-bell ringers and Morris Dancers, magicians, skydivers, or dog trainers. Says one admission official, "It's exciting to see unusual activities on an application—not always the student council, the newspaper, or the yearbook."

A final note: You recognize how much effort went into planning the Booster Club barbecue; how tough it was to sacrifice a season of soccer for a semester in Sweden; how many lines your son had to learn for *King Lear.* But admission officers have heard it all before. Be sure that your child presents extracurricular activities and accomplishments well, and *differentiates* between meaningful and minimal contributions. (See Chapter 6 for résumé-writing suggestions.)

VI. Interviews

Interview evaluations often confirm the impression made by other credentials in a folder. However, as you read earlier, an interview may also help a committee to see another side of a student, to understand why certain choices were made, to appreciate the extent of a commitment. Interview write-ups may even contain comments like "TAKE HER!!!" or "a solid student but I'd hate to have to room with him." In some cases, even a favorably impressed interviewer who isn't on a candidate's committee may go out of the way to lobby those who are for a "yes" verdict.

But remember, sometimes interviews are not weighed heavily in the decision-making process.

VII. "Hooks"

A hook, in admission parlance, is any additional advantage that makes a candidate attractive to a particular college. This will vary from school to school and from year to year. Some candidates may try to hide their hooks, preferring to be admitted on only merit (parents tend to discourage this) while others will fight furiously to exploit even the most inconsequential connections. Such hooks may include athletic ability, minority status, veteran status, alumni connections, special talent (e.g., art, music, theater, writing, etc.), underrepresented socioeconomic background (e.g., first-generation college), geography, gender, VIP status, ability to pay full tuition, or miscellaneous institutional needs.

Having a hook can give a candidate a higher rating from the get-go or can pull an application from the deny pile and put it into the admit (or wait list) stack. Hooks come into play most often when judging equally qualified candidates. For example, if a college has to select one of two students who look the same on paper, and one is the daughter of an alumnus and the other is not, the daughter is probably going to get in over the non-connected student. However, no matter how well connected or how gifted a student is *outside* of the classroom, if he doesn't have the grades or the ability, he won't—or shouldn't—be admitted. And, if he does get admitted for special reasons, those connections won't guarantee that he will succeed. One college even had to turn down its own president's son!

The hooks below are the ones discussed most often—and most passionately—in admission committee meetings:

Alumni Connections

While you shouldn't assume that your child is a shoo-in just because *you* went to the target school, you can assume that the folder will be reviewed very carefully and, if denied for any reason, the decision will be painful for the college.

Smith, a college with an extensive alumnae admission effort, takes about 70 percent of its alumnae-connected applicants, as compared with only about 50 percent of its regular pool. If there is a particularly well-connected marginal applicant, the folder gets extra special attention.

Athletes

➤ **THE GOOD NEWS:** Playing a sport can be an excellent way to give your child a boost at decision-making time. A superstar can earn a full scholarship; a less exceptional enthusiast can still up the odds of an acceptance.

➤ **THE BAD NEWS:** Some students (and parents) overestimate the weight that athletic ability carries in the admission process—and they overestimate their ability period. Dave Shelbourne, a football coach and guidance counselor in Indiana, affirms that the "absolute first thing that I am asked by college recruiters is 'What about his grades?' 'Who are your best players who qualify academically?' When I worked in admissions at Wabash College, lots of parents weren't objective about their children's academic and athletic talent."

Some college coaches have a lot of clout in the admission office; others have far less. While many coaches will give a realistic assessment of how much a child's athletic prowess will count at decision time, never forget that it's the office of admission that gets the final say. See Chapter 9, "Special Situations," for more information on athletes and admission.

Students of Color

Colleges normally give students the option of describing themselves as members of these groups: American Indian or Alaskan Native; Black or African-American; Mexican-American or Chicano; Puerto Rican; Other Hispanic-American or Latin American; Asian American or Pacific Islander; or multiracial.

Colleges aggressively recruit students from underrepresented minority populations, and financial aid opportunities are great. Some even set aside funds to pay travel expenses for these students to visit campus. Most admission offices have a counselor who is in charge of this effort, and this person can serve as a good source of information as well as an advocate in the process. While all admission counselors work together to attract a diverse student body, one may be charged with reading all folders of minority students—or at least have a major say in who gets admitted.

If your child has checked one of the categories above, he or she will probably get special consideration by admission committees—just how much consideration depends on the institution in question and your child's racial, ethnic, and socioeconomic background. For example, Spelman College in Atlanta is a predominantly Black college for women that is eager to encourage Latina applicants.

Some families, especially Asians, are concerned that they have become an overrepresented minority on many campuses and that their cultural background may actually work against them. This is not true. What is true, however, is that while they are never discriminated against, they may lose their hook. They have essentially melted into the American melting pot. When a minority student (or any student) is from a disadvantaged family or community, credentials such as test scores, writing samples, and course selection are evaluated with that in mind.

Talent in the Arts

Being a painter or a poet, a musician, dancer, and so on, can really make an application stand out. A conservatory or art school will carefully examine each applicant's ability. For instance, Rhode Island School of Design requires a portfolio, in addition to three drawings (a bicycle, an interior or exterior environment, and a subject of the applicant's choice). Instructions are specific about what to draw, what size the paper must be, and how it should be folded, so students need to follow directions carefully.

In contrast, more generalized institutions may use such strengths to counterbalance weaker areas but don't necessarily have tapes, slides, or other submissions reviewed by professionals in the arts. But consider your child's artistic ability a hook only when it is exceptional (and not just by your standards!).

Geography

At a public college or university, being an in-state resident is obviously a hook. However, at many institutions, coming from an underrepresented region can also be an advantage. Southeastern colleges love to see North Dakota and Montana zip codes on applications, while southwestern schools welcome candidates from Vermont and Maine.

Parents, however, often worry when it seems as if too many of their child's classmates are aiming for the same colleges. They wonder if admission offices set quotas and ask how their child's decision might be affected when stronger cohorts have also applied.

Some high schools are known as "feeder schools" for certain colleges which means that many students typically apply and many, too, may be accepted. In such cases, your guidance counselor is familiar with the college in question and can help predict how your child will stack up. On the other hand, the more competitive colleges often want to cast a net broadly and include many different high schools in each entering class. In such cases, it may be a liability if your child is not as impressive a candidate as the others from her school—although just what impresses a college will vary. Decisions can likewise depend on which program within an institution your child desires. She may be turned down from the School of Engineering while her less able beau will be accepted by the School of Education.

Gerry Carnes, long-time guidance counselor at Brockton High School in Massachusetts, which graduates over 600 seniors a year, is no stranger to this dilemma. "If a student from BHS is applying to nearby Bridgewater State College, being one of 20 applicants is not a hindrance. However, if a student is one of only three or four applying to Brown, then having multiple applications from Brockton High could be a factor in who gets in. But students shouldn't shy away from applying—even someone who is #10 in a class where #5 is also a candidate. Depending on major and extracurricular activities, the college would not necessarily take the student with the higher rank."

The Invisible Hook—Institutional Needs

One reason that an applicant is admitted to a particular college while a similar-seeming (or even less able) applicant is not can be due to a fuzzy factor known as "institutional needs." These needs, explains Amherst College's Katharine Fretwell, are likely to vary from college to college, and—even within a single school—from year to year. One season, says Fretwell, an institution may be after more women, Midwesterners, or hockey goalies; the next time around it could be scientists or string musicians. "Applicants do not have control over these needs and are rarely aware of them," she notes. "And, according to outside observers (candidates, their counselors, parents, or class-mates), the influence of these priorities may create some mysterious admission decisions."

Questions & *Answers*

Q: We've heard that some colleges admit students largely (or even entirely) based on an admission formula. Is this true and, if so, how often does it happen and how does it work? Who benefits most—or least—from this approach?

A: According to CollegeConfidential.com counselor Dave Berry, many large public universities get inundated with applications every year, and thus class rank, GPA, and standardized test scores determine a student's fate, not character, extracurricular commitments, writing skills, etc. "Stated too simply," he explains, "they just enter the numbers into a computer and let the software do the selecting." (An important exception, notes Berry, are the more competitive honors programs *within* a large university, where broader factors are considered.) Go-getters with the right statistics clearly benefit most from a formulaic approach, he maintains. Underachievers, late-bloomers, or even good students with unbalanced strengths may lose out.

Smaller schools, says Berry, rarely go on numbers alone and tend to be more willing to take risks on those whose potential seems to surpass past performance, and some large institutions frown on formulas as well.

"It's probably a bad rule of thumb," admits Berry, "but a guideline I've always carried around is that, if a college application doesn't require an essay (or at least ask for some shorter open-ended responses), students can probably expect to be competing with a numbers-oriented applicant database. The best way to find out whether an institution uses admission formulas is, of course, to ask."

VIII. Thumbs Up or Thumbs Down?

If you were a fly on the wall while an admission committee was meeting, this is what you would likely hear:

Readers begin by sharing the ratings they have given an applicant independently. Commonly, there is consensus. If not, the bickering begins, as one committee member exclaims, "Look how well she plays the harp!" while another is pointing to a 390 math SAT.

At the most competitive colleges, candidates are not even discussed in committee unless they are firing on all cylinders, and excellent grades and scores must be a given. Then, explains Patricia Wei of Yale, "In committee, we say, 'This is a good student. Now what is *special*?' A lot of times we call an applicant 'solid.' It translates into 'fine, but nothing distinctive.' At other colleges where I've worked, 'solid' meant admissible, but here it's the kiss of death."

The goal is to assign an overall rating that every reader can live with. Contrary to what you might suspect, committees often give numerical or letter grades, rather than voting *In* or *Out*; *Accept* or *Reject*. For example, where an "A" to "F" scale is used, while readers may realize that "A" and "B" applicants are likely to be admitted and that "C" applicants stand a good chance as well, they won't know for sure until all folders have been rated and compared as a group. Since competition and space availability are not constant from year to year, cut-off points likewise vary. It's a serious and sensitive undertaking, but hardly an exact science.

Decisions are more clear cut at the top and bottom of the pool. The toughest to make are about those students who fall in the middle. Here is where hooks—and each college's particular needs and priorities—really come into play. Moreover, colleges don't always go by the book when finalizing choices. There is room to make adjustments for "wild cards"— those candidates who, on the basis of statistics or in the light of tight competition, might be far from the top of the pile, yet have that special something that really knocked the socks off the readers.

There are also other fine-tuning issues such as shaping the overall composition of the class. Says Dean Lee Stetson of the University of Pennsylvania, "Eighty-five percent of those who apply would thrive here, but we have to choose among them. We're not looking for only the best numbers, but also for those who will make each freshman class the most interesting, the most 'yeasty,' the most representative of the broad-based society we live in ...and there is some element of crap shoot in the whole process."

Each institution must determine how many offers of admission to make in order to yield the desired number of entering students. For example, while one college must accept 1,000 candidates so that 500 will enroll, another may need to make only 750 offers to net the same total. In any case, colleges always admit more students than they expect to actually enroll.

Although colleges are pretty good at making such estimates based on experience, it's impossible to always be right on the mark. Thus, your child may receive a letter of acceptance, a letter denying admission, or one that explains that he or she has been put on a wait list. (For wait list advice, see Chapter 8.) Other specific admit decisions can include:

- admission to the institution but not to the program of choice within it (programs, majors, and departments also use wait lists)

- admission without housing and/or financial aid

- conditional acceptance such as "contingent on receipt of SAT II scores" or "on completion of summer physics course"

- admission to a later term (e.g., acceptance for second semester)

While most decisions are announced in a form letter, special personal deny letters may be sent to offer counsel or to soften the blow. For instance, an applicant from a disadvantaged background may be encouraged to re-apply after strengthening the academic record elsewhere.

Lest you think that admission officers are hardened and cold-hearted adjudicators, impervious to the feelings of applicants and their families, consider the words of William H. Peck, a former college admission dean and current director of college counseling at Santa Catalina School in California, "Remember that however disappointed you may be about an adverse decision on your child, the admission staff has experienced even more disappointments—those legions of wonderful students who looked at the college and never applied; who applied but were regretfully denied; who were admitted but chose to go elsewhere. We call them 'admissions' offices instead of 'rejections' offices for a reason—admitting students is, after all, the real goal and is a pleasure; denying them is a necessary element of the process, but an unpleasant task."

CHAPTER 8

We're In,
We're Out, What Now?

After all the letters are mailed—the ones that say yes, which may be thick with forms to return, or the thin ones with only an apologetic no—there are shouts of joy and, unfortunately, tears of disappointment. In addition, although there may be good news from the admission office, there may be bad news from the financial aid office. Or, a student may be admitted to her dream university, but not to the program she wanted. Whatever the news, at least there's closure (and that's a relief)—well, for everybody except those on the wait list. More about that later.

➤ *THE GOOD NEWS:* Most students get into a college they like, feel pretty good about their choice, and head off with a bit more excitement than anxiety. In fact, according to a recent study, nearly 70 percent of students go to their first choice college and more than 21 percent attend their second choice. That means 9 out of 10 students land at one of their top choices.

➤ *THE BAD NEWS:* Some students are bitterly disappointed by admission decisions. Often, it's the first time they've experienced a major rejection—and it hurts.

First and foremost, it's important to remember that the college admission decision process does not make any kind of value judgment about how good, strong, special, or successful your child or your family is. Sometimes the nicest kids aren't the highest achievers in schools, and sometimes the most ornery ones—and the real challenges for parents—are the superstars in class and make out very well in the college admission game. Remember that success in life is defined lots of ways—and getting into—or not getting into—one of the *hot* colleges is not going to make (or break) your child's hope for a happy and successful future.

In part, because this generation of parents knows more about college than their own parents, and because they feel pressured to provide more and better opportunities to their children, there is a lot more hysteria surrounding the admission process than necessary. Remind your child to "keep things in perspective," counsels Bill Peck at Santa Catalina School. "If I don't get into my first choice college, and this is the worst disappointment I suffer in my life, then I am indeed fortunate." Most students are sensible and realize that a "reach" college was just that. As a parent, you may have to help your child work through the disappointment if the reach college was also the first-choice college. Whatever school your child attends should become the first-choice school. And please don't imply that your feelings of love for—and approval of—your child have anything to do with college decisions or choices.

Current research shows that the students who become successful in life tend to be well motivated, self-confident, and ambitious. The ability of a student coupled with the opportunity to develop that ability seem to have more to do with how well a student does in the real world than what specific college he or she attended. The match between a student and a school is much more important than the perceived prestige of an institution or the price tag.

Having said that, it's time to consider the very practical issues that need to be handled after the thick and thin letters are mailed from admission offices.

I. Deposits

When your child is admitted to a school, that's when you get the upper hand and colleges have to wait for *your* decision. Candidates' Reply Date is May 1, and your child has the right to wait until that date to let the colleges know if it's thumbs up or thumbs down, even though some places may put pressure on students to respond earlier. A *nonrefundable* tuition and room deposit of several hundred dollars is usually required. Most colleges have the bulk of their decision letters in the mail by the beginning of April.

Try to attend the open houses and similar functions planned for parents and students. Colleges often invite admitted students for one last tour of the campus and might offer overnights, classes, meals, etc. This can be especially helpful if your child has never visited a particular campus or is having a really hard time deciding between two. Some competitor colleges even consult with each other when setting dates for open houses, so that students admitted to more than one place can plan to spread their visits around. (see "'Crunch-Time Visits" in Chapter 4)

If you need an extension of the deposit deadline, contact the admission office. If your financial aid offer is not final or you have a persuasive reason to get a few more days to decide ("We're out of the country until May 7," etc.) call and ask for an extension. Generally, if a student is waiting to hear from another college, an extension won't be granted.

Questions & Answers

Q: If we pay a deposit by May 1 and later our son is taken off the wait list at his first-choice college, what happens?

A: If your child is accepted off a wait list *after* May 1, another deposit will be required for the admitting college, and the deposit paid to the original college will be forfeited. After colleges hear from all admitted candidates on May 1, they can make a decision about whether to take students off the wait list. If your child gets into one college off a wait list and decides to attend, be certain that he notifies the original college of his intentions in writing.

If the deposit poses a tremendous financial burden, ask the admission office if a payment plan can be worked out. Some financial aid offices will waive the deposit in the cases of families with extraordinary financial need. For other families, it's just impossible to get together several hundred dollars by May 1. Colleges may be willing to accept partial payment by the deadline and then set up extended deadlines for the remainder. Example: $100 by May 1, and $50 every week afterward until total is received.

Don't "double deposit." It's not ethical to pay tuition deposits to two or more colleges. Students sometimes are tempted to do this if they can't make up their minds about which college is a more appropriate choice. May 1 is the time to fish or cut bait. Your child will be taking a space away from another student and just protracting the decision process if you don't stick to that deadline.

II. Wait Lists

➤ *THE GOOD NEWS:* Your child didn't get rejected.

➤ *THE BAD NEWS:* Your child didn't get in, either—at least not yet.

Somewhere between the despair of rejection and the elation of acceptance is the uncertainty of the wait list. The college remains interested in your child, but isn't ready to make a final decision. After May 1 (or sometimes before), when the college knows what kind of yield (i.e., the percentage of students admitted who pay their deposits) there is on the class, a decision will be made about who, if anybody, comes off the wait list.

Follow instructions about what to do about staying on the wait list. If a card needs to be returned, an e-mail needs to be written, or a phone call needs to be made to indicate interest in remaining on the wait list, have your child do so promptly. Updated transcripts or additional information about awards won or accomplishments not mentioned in the application should be submitted for review.

Some colleges rank order the wait list, while others don't. Your child may get his number included on the wait list decision letter, which is better news for number 3 than number 333. At many schools, ranking doesn't take place until students respond to the offer. A phone call may be able to give your child a sense of how high—or low—he is. Also, a college may tell you how many applicants they usually take off the list. Don't be surprised if they fudge and tell you that the number varies from year to year. It probably does.

Many colleges plan to use their wait lists every year. Others are more erratic—some years they take a lot off, some years just a few or none.

Almost every parent of a wait-listed student calling an admission office asks how many students were taken off the list last year. A better question might be, "Over the past three or four years, how many students were taken?" Popularity of colleges changes, and enrollment trends and policies vary. It's not good news to find that a school hasn't used a wait list much in the past several years.

There may not be financial aid available for those on the wait list. Just ask to find out if there might be—or has been in the past—any money set aside for wait-list candidates. In all probability, they won't know until they have heard from other candidates. Colleges float more aid than they expect to have accepted by entering students, but variations in the yield influence availability of aid for wait-listed students. Not needing aid may end up being a hook for students from the wait list.

Hooks help determine who gets off the wait list. All sorts of lobbying goes on for wait-listed candidates, and the mix of the class is considered when choosing students off the list. For example, if the yield in the class of minority students is low, that will make a minority student on the wait list even more appealing. If there aren't enough alumni children, kids from the West, males or females—whatever—that may be considered by admission staff when looking at the list.

Questions & Answers

Q: Is it helpful to try to be creative or try to make yourself stand out in any way to get noticed on the wait list?

A: A student takes a risk when going out on a limb by trying to be zany, particularly if that's not a natural style. However, at wait-list stage, a little creativity or risk-taking can pay off.

Yale's Patricia Wei remembers, "A wait-listed student sent me a package, and in it was a sneaker, elaborately decorated, that included her name and the year she hoped to graduate from Yale. With the shoe came a note saying, 'My foot is in the door—the rest is up to you.'" She got in. Of course, the sneaker wasn't the only reason she was tipped in off the wait list, but in this case it didn't hurt.

The vast majority of students, however, do nothing more than send in their wait list response cards and perhaps call once or twice for updates and advice. Plenty of them get good news; don't assume that doing more is better.

If your child had an especially good interview in the admission office, had been recruited by a coach, or corresponded with a faculty member, this is the time for him to get back in touch and politely ask that person to put in a good word. There is no need to think of a place on a wait list as simply another form of rejection. Consider it an honor to still be in the competition, and get to work. A letter or e-mail, a phone call, or an updated transcript can make a difference. A student should let the college know how interested he is. If it's his first choice, be sure the admission office knows that, too.

Occasionally, students taken off the wait list are offered admission for mid-year (January) rather than fall entrance. If this option sounds appealing, be sure to find out if credit will be awarded for courses taken elsewhere in the fall (continuing education courses, community college courses, etc.), if there is a good orientation program at mid-year, or if registration for appropriate freshmen level classes will be difficult in January—especially in the case of year-long classes (elementary languages, introductory sciences, etc.).

III. Not Getting In Anywhere

➤ *THE GOOD NEWS:* Your child was excited about all the colleges he applied to.

➤ *THE BAD NEWS:* He didn't get into any of them.

Sadly, this does happen to students every year. In the case of very selective colleges, more students are denied each year than admitted, even though the bulk of the applicant pool is capable of doing the work. **Hint:** Personalize the application process, but depersonalize the decision process.

Not getting into a college doesn't mean that your child is not bright, or is incapable of academic success or even unworthy of higher education. What it *does* mean is that the colleges selected may be very competitive, or that space was limited, or that the college believes your child is not ready right now. Lots of wonderful, successful adults were once rejected from a college or two.

*Q*uestions & *A*nswers

Q: Can we appeal a deny decision?

A: Sometimes a college will review the folder of a denied applicant if some additional information has become available since the time decisions were made. Call and ask the admission office. Better still, have your child call and ask. Occasionally, if additional information submitted is persuasive, a deny decision may be overturned or a conditional acceptance might be offered. Don't get your hopes up, though, as this rarely happens.

Investigate Other Options

Realistically, in most cases it's best to accept the decisions and go on to investigate other options. Matthew, a gifted high school senior, had talent in track and music, and his SATs were the envy of all his friends. He assumed every one of the highly selective colleges he liked would want him too, so he passed up the chance to go to optional interviews, didn't spend much time on his essays, and generally blew off the seriousness of the application process. In April, he was crushed when he received two wait-list letters and three denies.

The pile of thin letters from the admissions offices served as a wake-up call, and Matthew had no choice but to make an application in May of his senior year (this time with more effort) to a less selective college with a Rolling Admission policy. Not only was he admitted, but also he was awarded a very generous financial aid package. He liked the place when he got there—and didn't feel the need to transfer as he thought he might when he was originally admitted.

There is a place for just about anybody who is ready for college. If your child doesn't get in anywhere, consider a college with a later filing deadline or with an open admission policy (everybody gets in) such as a community college. (Don't be surprised if housing or financial aid is not available at this point.) Your child may consider trading up by transferring elsewhere after a year or two. Community colleges are great places for a formerly unmotivated high school student to pour it on academically.

Talk to an Admission Officer

Always ask an admission officer about chances of admission at a later date. Most institutions will not admit an applicant they've denied until new (and improved) academic credentials are available.

Often, there is no way a student will *ever* be admitted, and it's wise to ask the admission officer if chances for reapplication are good, slim, or nonexistent. If you child is stubborn or willful, you're probably used to him not accepting "no" for an answer. Unfortunately, a child can be hurt by his own inability to be objective and reasonable and can get his college career off to a bad start by not being realistic.

On the other hand, some students know what they are talking about when they ask that a deny decision be reconsidered. Henry Mackal was denied admission to the University of Rhode Island and then admitted on a probational basis after he convinced the university's president that he could do the work. The risk paid off—he graduated with a degree in engineering four years later, and after amassing a fortune, he donated lots of money to the university and they named the field house after him.

Consider a PG (Postgraduate) Year or Time Off

Ask your child's guidance counselor for suggestions and contact the transfer counselor at your local community college for additional options. The reasons for disappointing news will guide you in making a sensible choice. Is your child ready for school? Does she need to look at less competitive choices? Does she need to work on any personal problems before she can concentrate on schoolwork?

"Time off should be more than space between high school and college," according to Jacqueline Murphy, director of admissions at Saint Michael's College in Vermont. "It should be productive. Even if you are working, if college is the ultimate goal, a course or two will help admission people see improvement in your school work."

For some good ways to find valuable year-off opportunities, see also "Deferring Admission to College" and "Attending a PG Year at a Secondary School" in Chapter 9.

IV. Not Wanting to Go Where Accepted

➤ *THE GOOD NEWS:* Your child got several letters of acceptance from colleges.

➤ *THE BAD NEWS:* She doesn't want to go to any of them—anymore.

If your child doesn't want to go to a college because she thinks it will not be challenging enough, try to get more information about the availability of an honors program or any kind of enriched curriculum options. Some students apply to safety schools never planning to attend. However, they may end up happy as a clam there, and this *last* college choice may soon become the number-one choice. Or, a student may be able to use the back-up school as a springboard to a better choice. As a parent, you can help your child look at the bright side of the story. After all, there must have been *something* your child found appealing enough to inspire an application.

A student shouldn't apply to a college that she doesn't like, but for lots of reasons that happens all the time. Some colleges are hot in a high school— tons of students apply to them and so your daughter did, too, without really figuring out if the college was right for her. Many times, students wish they had applied to different types of schools—and are envious of their friends who took the risks and got in.

It may be that she simply has cold feet about leaving home and high school. Take her for a visit to campus, if possible, to examine the areas she doubts. She may not realize what's available. Have her review the pros-and-cons list made during the exploration process. Call the admission office and ask for the names of alumni and current students from your area and urge your child to contact them to get the scoop on what the campus is really like.

The choices basically boil down to the following options. Your child can:

- "put up and shut up" about the colleges that have accepted her; choose the least offensive of all of them, and hopefully become more enthusiastic after getting on campus

- make late applications to other colleges with rolling deadlines or vacancies; (Options will be limited and financial aid and housing may not be available, but those might be sacrifices your child and you are willing to make.)

Each May, annual surveys of vacancies at two- and four-year colleges and universities are available. If your guidance office doesn't have it, contact the National Association for College Admission Counseling (NACAC), 1631 Prince Street, Alexandria, VA 22314-2818; (800) 822-6285; Web site: www.nacac.com.

- attend a prep school as a PG (postgraduate) or take a year off and reapply to more palatable choices; and

- broaden the college search for next year and check out such books as *Cool Colleges for the Hyper-Intelligent, Self-Directed, Late-Blooming, and Just Plain Different* by Donald Asher (Ten Speed Press).

Generally, before any major decision is made, there is some amount of doubt. Remember what it was like before you got married? Even the happiest couples admit that they wondered if this really was the right person, the right time, the right match. Of course, if you are divorced, you also know how miserable one can be after making a wrong choice. So be sympathetic and try to help your child determine how serious the doubts are and how best to allay them.

Summer orientation or a cheerful letter from a future roommate or information about fall sports can get a reluctant pre-freshman geared up for a less-than-enthusiastic college choice.

Another option for your child to consider is taking some time off from school. Classes in the "School of Hard Knocks" can often motivate an underachiever and light a fire under a lethargic student. In addition, adult students are flooding college classrooms, and they enter with a sharper sense of purpose than they would have had right out of high school.

V. Campus Security

Next to financing and finding the right match, parents asked most often about campus security.

➤ *THE GOOD NEWS:* Federal regulations legislate that campus crime statistics be available to the public. A comprehensive report, listing the incidents of crimes, should be posted somewhere central on campus for you to review. If you don't see it, ask at the admission or security office or check out the Web site of the U.S. Department of Education Office of Postsecondary Education Campus Security at www.ope.ed.gov/security/.

➤ *THE BAD NEWS:* Awful things can happen on college campuses, especially when students drink and act irresponsibly, believing they are invincible. (Sound familiar?) You've probably read about some of the most horrendous incidents in the newspapers. You worry, understandably, that your worst fears might be realized as your child leaves the nest and won't have you around to monitor locks and enforce curfews.

Campus security reports indicate that issues that keep public safety officers busy on campuses range from motor vehicle violations and dorm lock outs to alcohol and drug infractions, restraining orders, harassing phone calls, date rapes, and dealing with local characters who prowl the campus. If your child tends to get into mischief now, there's at least a good chance he might still be getting into mischief in college.

➤ *MORE GOOD NEWS:* Violent crime is not a problem on most college campuses.

Theft is the biggest issue at most schools. Cell phones, unlocked bikes and laptops get stolen. Leather jackets disappear, CDs walk away, and expensive toiletries evaporate. Beyond cautioning your child to lock the room, bike, or car, and to be really careful with special items, one of the best things to do is check what kind of coverage your homeowner's insurance policy offers for loss of items belonging to a child away at college. Also, find out how safe computers, TVs, and other expensive items are in dorm rooms over term breaks. If the dorms aren't secure and home is far away, is there adequate, secure storage provided on campus?

When looking at a campus, check the door locks. Are there locks on inside as well as outside doors? Are there working locks on windows? If a visitor comes to a dorm, is he let in without proper identification? Who is in charge of the daily activities within residence halls? Is there a monitor or a head resident available at all times to keep an eye on what is going on?

Ask what kind of security force is on campus. Is it on-site? Does it have police powers? Have budget-tightening measures curtailed any staff or services? How involved is the security force in preventing crimes? Is it actively involved in the orientation process? Is there ongoing education? Are students instructed about personal safety and their responsibility to their dorm mates? Are students kept informed about rashes of thefts or seasonal prowlers? Are sketches of suspicious people posted in the cafeterias or in the dorms for students to be on the lookout for flashers, burglars, and stalkers?

If you are aware of a well-publicized crime that has taken place on a campus, don't assume the campus isn't safe. Ask the security office about it. What happened? What did security do about it? What is security doing to educate students and prevent it from happening again?

Find out if there is an escort service for students at night, especially in schools located in urban areas. Is transportation provided at night from the library to dorms or to commuter parking lots? Car theft can be more of a problem in urban areas, too. If your child is going to bring a car to campus, what kind of overnight parking is available? Is a car really needed? Should you invest in a car security system? If your child is going to be driving at night to a part-time job or class, perhaps a cell phone might be a good graduation gift.

Buy a copy of the local paper when visiting a campus. What stories are published about crimes? Are there murders listed on every page or is the theft of a mountain bike given front-page coverage? If the area the college is in is very different than the area of your home, be certain that your child understands the differences. What might be okay at school might not be okay at home—and vice versa.

Investigate the college's alcohol and drug policies. Unfortunately, alcohol abuse and misuse are major problems on most college campuses, and car accidents, date rapes, and fights happen too often when students are under the influence. Continue to talk with your child about drinking responsibly.

Dorms and fraternity houses have burned to the ground and students' lives have been lost because somebody fell asleep with a candle lit or left a burning cigarette in a trash can or misused an electrical appliance.

While you don't want to be a nagging, hovering parent, you *do* want your child to come home from college safely—so be sure to calmly and reasonably discuss safety habits. Also, find out the school's policy before you send microwave ovens, refrigerators, etc. Prohibitions are often for safety reasons—not due to concerns about utility costs or theft.

VI. Planning to Transfer

➤ *THE GOOD NEWS:* Lots of students transfer.

➤ *THE BAD NEWS:* Lots of students transfer.

You probably thought that once your child got accepted to college and decided to go (and you figured out how to pay for it) that everything would be all set for four years. That's not always the case.

Almost a million students transfer each year from one college to another. There is no need for students to stick it out at a college where they don't fit in, aren't happy, or can't study what they want to study. On campuses from coast to coast, transfer students repeatedly turn out to be top scholars and leaders, faculty favorites, and graduation-award winners. High tuition and fees also spur many students to build a transfer deliberately into their college career. They attend a community college for two years, save money, develop academic strength, focus on a career path, and then transfer. Others trade up. That is, after not being admitted to their dream school the first time around, they work on polishing academic skills and reapply for admission after a year or two of college level work. Many colleges and universities don't require standardized tests as part of the transfer application, and that can open up new opportunities to some students.

Some parents are not wildly enthusiastic when their child mentions making a move. They worry when their children don't stick to things—or wonder if they will be penalized credit-wise, or lose out on financial aid or housing. Keep in mind that transferring is not quitting or failing—it's changing—and colleges and universities are more welcoming and more accommodating to transfers than ever before. Wise enrollment management officials at colleges rely on transfers to keep beds and classrooms full. Policies on financial aid and housing are more liberal than in the past, and at many colleges, transfers tend to be among the most satisfied graduates.

With so many college students transferring—and with even more considering it—there is a decent chance that you might at least discuss with your son or daughter the possibility of a switch.

9

Special Situations

When it comes to college admissions, there are special situations that may require additional planning, preparation, and paperwork. The following seven relatively common—but still special—situations are grouped together in this chapter and presented alphabetically:

- **Advanced standing:** Advanced Placement (AP), International Baccalaureate (IB), and other pre-college credit

- **Athletes:** Playing college sports at any level

- **Deferring admission to college:** Postponing entrance to college for a year after high school graduation

- **Early enrollment at college:** Entering college before completing high school

- **International students:** Entering U.S. colleges from foreign countries

- **PG (postgraduate) year at a secondary school:** Prepping for a year after high school graduation

- **Students with disabilities and special needs:** Learning, physical, and psychological disabilities

I. Advanced Standing

Advanced Placement (AP)

The AP program, sponsored by the College Board, offers 35 college-level courses and exams to high school students. Approximately 3,000 colleges in more than 50 countries use the exam results for evaluation and placement. Over 90 percent of the colleges in the United States use satisfactory grades on AP exams for placement and/or credit.

Standardized exams, which include multiple-choice and essay questions—in addition to portfolio evaluations in studio art—are administered in a wide variety of fields of study each May. Exams are graded on a 5 (extremely well qualified to receive college credit or advanced placement) to 1 (no recommendation to receive college credit or advanced placement) point scale. While the cut-off for acceptable scores is generally 3, many colleges—especially the highly selective ones—will only accept scores of 4 and 5 (and this may vary within the college depending on the student's major as well as other considerations). Check each college's policy in the catalog, since some are much more restrictive than others.

While most AP courses are taken senior year, not all are. Consequently, since AP exams are administered each May, students should take the AP exam the same year that the AP course is taken. For instance, if AP Biology is taught in 10th grade, the exam should be taken sophomore spring. That way, the subject is still fresh in students' minds. In addition, an AP exam may be repeated so your child can have another shot at the same exam junior or senior year.

Students pay under $100 to take each test, which is a pretty good deal when you calculate how many hundreds—or thousands—of dollars you might save if scores are acceptable for college credit. The College Board reports that more than 1,400 institutions will grant *a year's worth* of advanced standing to students with adequate AP scores. So, if your child is interested in one of *those* schools and wants to accelerate in college and graduate in less than four years by applying AP credit toward degree requirements, that could save you a considerable amount in tuition and room and board fees. Don't push things, though. Many students don't want to—and are not required to—graduate early, even if they have extra credits. If your child doesn't want to push ahead and finish up a degree sooner, he or she might be able to take more advanced classes, fulfill core requirements, take a lighter load or switch majors by having AP credit on the record.

College admission officers like it when students challenge themselves academically, so having AP courses on a transcript indicates that a student wants to stretch. However, if your local high school doesn't offer AP courses, don't feel that your child will be penalized in the admission process. Remember, colleges evaluate what is available to the student and how the student took advantage of what was offered—if AP wasn't an option, that's not the student's fault.

For more information on AP, contact your guidance office: Advanced Placement Program, The College Board, 45 Columbus Avenue, New York, NY 10023-6992; (212) 713-8066; Web site: http://apcentral.collegeboard.com.

International Baccalaureate (IB)

The International Baccalaureate (IB) is a two-year academic curriculum available in English, French, and Spanish designed for students ages 16-19 and developed to meet the requirements of a variety of educational systems throughout the world. Founded in the mid-1960s, the IB has over 1,200 member schools in 110 countries ranging from Australia to Vietnam, and nearly 400 high schools in the U.S. and almost 100 in Canada currently offer this option to their students.

Exams are administered and graded, and if a student earns the IB diploma, many colleges and universities will grant credit and/or advanced standing. *I*B students take six exams—three at the *higher* level and three at the *standard* level. Typically, college credit is awarded for *higher-level* exams only. (Some institutions may award credit for standard exams.) The best grade a student can earn is 7 and, while normally results of 5 and above are necessary for college credit, many institutions will award some credit for lower scores, especially in languages.

As with AP exams, colleges have their own specific policies regarding acceptable scores on the IB and placement rules. Some universities award higher-level scores of 5 through 7 *varying* amounts of credit, and in some instances standard level scores of 5 or better are also considered. Consult each college for individual practices.

Standards and policies vary and if you are interested in more information as well as a comprehensive listing of IB educational programs in the United States, contact International Baccalaureate North America, 475 Riverside Drive, Suite 1600, New York, NY, 100016-3903; (212) 696-4464; Web site: www.IBO.org.

Questions & Answers

Q: Is it better to have IB or AP credit?

A: Since both provide good, solid academic challenges, and since college credit can be awarded for both programs, one is not necessarily better than the other. With AP courses, students get to pick and choose what they're good at and what they enjoy most—sort of like ordering a la carte from a menu. On the other hand, the IB is comparable to ordering a complete meal from a menu and, while there are some choices within the meal (Spanish instead of French, for example), no course in the meal can be skipped. To earn an IB diploma, students must take the full curriculum including subjects that may not be their favorites or their strong points. Your child's school might also allow students to take some IB courses without sitting for the certificate or diploma. Either way, both IB and AP offer great academic challenges to high school students, and college credit may be awarded for appropriate scores.

Other Types of Pre-College Credit

Other than AP or IB credit, colleges have a variety of policies governing what credit—if any—will be awarded for work completed before matriculation at the freshman level.

While some colleges will not award any college credit to entering freshmen (except for AP and IB), some are quite generous. Many tend not to award credit for college courses taken in high school that count toward high school graduation requirements. Opportunities for high school students to take courses for credit at local colleges have increased, and colleges vary dramatically on how they view the credit earned.

➤ *THE GOOD NEWS:* While college credit might not be awarded, your child may be able to place out of a class on the basis of the information covered in the college-level course. In addition, if your child is able to take an AP exam that parallels the college course content and scores well enough, credit may be granted.

➤ *THE BAD NEWS:* If your child takes a class at a local college during senior year or a summer course at a community college, he or she may—or may not—be awarded credit when enrolling in college.

Consult current college catalogs for particulars and ask your child's guidance counselor for advice about specific courses. While not all students wish to accelerate and graduate early, most hate to be bored and, if they have mastered subjects in high school, they can go to deeper levels in college. Save the course syllabi, papers, and exams for any college-level courses completed in high school. They may come in handy when your child is seeking university credit or determining appropriate departmental placement.

Other types of credit accepted at some colleges include College Board's CLEP (College Level Examination Program), online and correspondence courses, and— in some unusual cases—"life experience." CLEP is a credit-by-exam program that includes a wide range of introductory college subjects, from English composition and literature to business. The Department of Defense's DANTES Subject Standardized Tests offer distance-learning options for people in the armed services. Normally, adult students returning to the classroom choose these options, but if your child has any of these credits, for one reason or another, consult individual colleges for their policies. Don't be surprised if credit is denied.

Normally, the more selective the college, the more stringent the rules will be that govern transfer of outside courses for entering freshmen. Naturally, a college wants entering freshmen to take full advantage of courses offered there and so, understandably, there are restrictions on what comes in from the outside.

II. Athletes

For some students, one of the key considerations when selecting target colleges will be "Can I play a sport (or even more than one) here?" Knowing that your child intends to continue to compete at the college level will help you narrow the field as you make appropriate matches.

➤ *THE GOOD NEWS:* Student athletes reap many benefits at college. Not only might they get a break in the admission process, but also they become part of a cohesive special interest group as soon as they enroll. They get to travel, meet lots of people, stay in shape, and—in the case of an extraordinary athlete—earn partial or full scholarships.

➤ *THE BAD NEWS:* Choosing a college *may* become even more complicated than it is for non-athletes.

By the time young athletes reach the college-exploration stage, most realize that there is a big difference between landing a spot on a National Collegiate Athletic Association (NCAA) Division I team and on a Division III squad. (Division II falls, predictably, somewhere in the middle.) The likelihood of being recruited or selected for a team varies not only from division to division, but also from conference to conference, school to school, and sport to sport. There are differences, too, between competitiveness for female athletes and male athletes—again, depending on the college and the sport.

Title IX of the Educational Amendments of 1972 bans sex discrimination and legislates equal opportunities for women, including in sports. However, it's still up to parents and students to determine if men's and women's teams garner the same respect and enthusiasm in a particular college community.

Division I and II institutions are permitted to give athletic scholarships, although not all do. The Ivy League schools, for instance, offer Division I athletic programs but provide no funds for athletes without financial need. Division III colleges are not allowed to offer aid based on athletic ability.

The mistakes most commonly made by student athletes and their parents are:

- assuming that talent in a sport at the high school level is almost sure to translate to a college scholarship;

- misjudging a student's athletic ability; (Typically, parents and teenagers inflate a high school athlete's potential as a *college* athlete, although there are also those with college-level athletic potential who *under*estimate their skills.)

- confusing interest by a coach as a guarantee of admission; and

- confusing interest by a coach as a guarantee of playing time (or even of making the team) if admitted.

A good place to get information and solid advice on the ins and outs of eligibility and distinctions among recruiting rules in Division I, II, and III schools is the *NCAA Guide for the College-Bound Student-Athlete*. You can find it online at www.ncaa.org or possibly at your local high school. A copy can also be ordered by calling (800) 638-3731.

If a student plans to play a sport at the Division I or II levels as a freshman, it is necessary to register and be certified by the NCAA Initial-Eligibility Clearinghouse. Call (319) 337-1492 to obtain registration materials. There is a nominal application fee. Eligibility information, including academic and testing regulations, is explained in detail on the NCAA Web site. You will see that there are minimum standardized-test scores and core curriculum requirements that each athlete must meet (a good reason to plan ahead, if possible).

If your child is interested in playing a sport in college, it's a good idea to contact the coach early in the search process. High school coaches often have collegiate contacts and are happy to make the first call. As early as the initial inquiry, your child might be asked to provide information detailing athletic accomplishments. Later, a videotape and statistics might be requested.

In the case of truly outstanding athletes, college coaches will be chomping at the bit to contact *them* but must abide by stringent NCAA regulations. For instance, letters from coaches (and even from faculty members or students) aren't permitted until September 1 of the beginning of an athlete's junior year in high school. Additional guidelines govern the initiation of telephone calls and campus visits. Check out www.ncaa.org/cbsa for specifics in each division.

Top prospects in line for scholarship funds may be expected to sign a "National Letter of Intent." The National Letter of Intent program is administered by the Collegiate Commissioners Association (CCA) and boasts over 500 participating institutions in more than 50 leagues. This letter serves as certification that a student intends to enroll at a designated institution in the fall. It is designed to protect students from unfair or misleading recruitment practices, but it also assures coaches and athletic directors that sought-after star players will show up for practice as promised. Students who sign such a letter must abide by numerous rules, and there are stringent penalties for those who do not. For more information about these and about Letter of Intent timetables, visit www.national-letter.org.

While many students are eager to continue a favorite sport in college, far fewer will be signing letters of intent or collecting athletic scholarship offers. Many fine high school athletes happily opt for club, intramural, or spectator sports in college. If your child is a more typical athlete rather than a star (think local cable versus network coverage), consider the following:

- **Just because your child is recruited by a coach, don't assume admission is a given.** Generally, there is an admission officer who serves as a liaison with the athletic department and, while decision-making may be collaborative, remember that admission people admit applicants—not coaches, not athletic directors, and not sports writers.

- **A coach's interest, at any level, is not a promise of playing time, either.** Coaches, at all levels, encourage more athletes than can ever fit on the bench. However, if your child is awarded a scholarship in a Division I or II program, it is certainly an indication that he or she is slated for playing time—at least eventually.

If your child is talented enough to play at *any* level—and even qualifies for an athletic scholarship—there are still decisions to be made. Would your child be happier as a perpetual practice player at a Division I school or as a four-year starter in Division III? Remember that your child is a student first and an athlete second when making college choices. Ask about graduation rates of athletes. Ask, too, what happens to the scholarship if your child is injured or cut. What is the coach's philosophy (and track record) on injuries? How do athletes manage absences from class when the team travels? What kind of tutoring might be available? Are faculty members supportive?

Smith College Director of Athletics Lynn Oberbillig, who has also coached at the Division I level, offers these additional tips:

- It is not too early to start looking for the right team in ninth or tenth grade.

- Take some time to watch college teams play to better assess your child's abilities.

- Watch a college team practice; it gives you the best idea of how a coach relates to the team.

- Beware of the coach who "negative recruits" against other schools.

Finally, the *NCAA Guide for the College-Bound Student-Athlete* includes a helpful section on "What to Ask" about college athletic programs. (It's at www.ncaa.org/cbsa/whattoask.html.) While perhaps designed for top recruits, there are many suggestions (e.g., "Describe the other players competing at the same position" or "How would you best describe your coaching style?") that *any* aspiring athlete (or athlete's parents) might find helpful.

III. Deferring Admission

Many students ask colleges for a break for a year before enrolling. They are not ready to go straight from high school to college for a variety of reasons. Some study abroad for the year *after* high school, some travel, some work, and others wish to pursue art or a sport or another skill full-time without the distractions of the academic year. Other students choose this time to take care of a health problem or to work on personal or family problems.

If your child plans to stop out of school for a year, encourage him to apply to colleges during senior year rather than waiting until the year off to do so. It's easier to get application materials together while enrolled in high school, and—particularly if the year off is spent abroad or in a remote area in this country—the mail service may not guarantee meeting deadlines. Also, if he has a change of heart and decides *not* to take that time off, there will be the option of enrolling at college.

Generally, to defer admission, an accepted student needs to put his or her reasons in writing to the dean of admission and submit a deposit by the *published deadline* to reserve a place in the following year's freshman class. Colleges vary on their policies about what is an appropriate reason—the major source of disagreement seems to center around credit for academic programs completed during the year off. For example, some colleges will not allow a student to enroll in another degree-granting program and will not give college credit for any work completed during the year off. In this case, if a student does enroll elsewhere during the year off, he might need to reapply as a transfer.

Some colleges and universities will discourage—or just won't allow—a one-semester or one-quarter deferral. Orientation can be difficult in the middle of the year. There may not be on-campus housing or financial aid available, and enrolling in mid-year may prohibit your son or daughter from taking some required, yearlong courses, which might be prerequisites for higher-level courses. Elementary language and sciences are often especially difficult to enter in mid-stream.

Don't be surprised if your child's goals and college plans change during the year off. Kevin deferred admission to Colby College in Maine to have knee surgery for an injury sustained while playing football. During his rehabilitation, he became very interested in physical therapy. Since Colby didn't have a program, he reapplied to colleges during his year off and entered the University of Vermont where he could study PT. Colleges expect to lose some of the students who defer and, while they are disappointed, nobody is totally stunned by that turn of events.

Be certain to check with the financial aid office and find out what impact—if any—taking a year off will have. If your child has been offered financial assistance, ask if it will it be guaranteed the next year. How will you have to update the aid application? If a student earns any money during the year off, how will that affect eligibility for aid? How much of his earnings will be expected by the college to go toward costs? (Geraldine, a bright and ambitious young woman, took a year off to do some fashion modeling and earned enough money to pay for her college tuition.) Will deferring admission affect any one-time merit award or housing?

There are hundreds—thousands even—of opportunities for high school students during their interim year ranging from the familiar AFS (American Field Studies) Intercultural Programs to Habitat for Humanity to serving as an English tutor abroad. Many charge tuition and a few come with a stipend. Some have financial aid available and some offer room and board as payment. All offer students chances to mature and learn.

Students can work before, during, and after college in the national AmeriCorps program, which provides educational awards in return for community service. If students complete the entire term of service, they may be awarded loan forgiveness or educational payment awards. For more information, contact (800) 942-2677; www.americorps.org.

If your child wants to take time off but doesn't know what to do, ask around about good programs, and look for guidebooks and brochures in the guidance office or library. Don't limit your options to the formal, organized programs, either. Almost any student can benefit greatly from a year in the "School of Life." Remember, working long hours at a minimum-wage job might be just the thing to motivate a lackluster student. He may be chomping at the bit to return to the classroom as soon as he realizes how many more employment options he'll have with a college degree.

Some parents worry that the child who takes time off will never go back. While some *do* drop out of the academic world for a while, most who take time off with a purpose or plan return to school with a new vigor and focus, and they become better college students than they would have been without the pause that refreshes.

"Rather than taking time off, make sure it's time spent *on* doing something meaningful and useful that will enhance their experiences in college later. There's no reason to throw good money down the drain at college when the time isn't right," advises John Boshoven, counselor at Community High School in Ann Arbor, Michigan.

For other year-off ideas, check out:

- The Center for Interim Programs (www.interimprograms.com)
- Taking Time Off (www.takingtimeoff.com)
- Time Out Associates (www.timeoutassociates.com)

IV. Early Enrollment, Early Entrance

A relatively small, but steady, number of high school students find that they have exhausted academic and extracurricular options at their high schools well before they are ready to graduate.

So, since they feel that they will be spinning their academic wheels until graduation, they leave high school—with or without a diploma—and enroll at college, usually after the junior year. Admission people take extra care in evaluating early admission candidates to make certain that they are *socially mature*—as well as *academically ready*—for higher education. To determine how ready an applicant is, the admission office may request a personal interview (even if it's not required for other applicants) or ask for an additional writing statement detailing reasons for wanting to enroll early.

Consult your child's guidance counselor to discuss whether or not Early Enrollment is a reasonable option. Carlene Riccelli, college advisor at Amherst Regional High School in Massachusetts, is careful to make sure her students have exhausted the high school curriculum and have taken full advantage of the opportunities available before leaving early. Since Amherst Regional offers the option of taking college courses at the nearby University of Massachusetts, as well as at Amherst College, only three or four opt to leave early out of a class of 350. "Frequently, I hear reasons that are *not* legitimate for early admission. 'All my friends have graduated' or 'I don't want to live with my parents anymore' are examples."

Social adjustment to college life is often more of a challenge for students who are quite a bit younger than others. A precocious 15-year-old might be smart enough to tutor her 21-year-old classmates in organic chemistry, but might find herself very lonely when roommates are selected and party invitations go out.

Rather than severing ties completely with the high school, some students opt for a compromise and try for a dual enrollment program. For example, some community colleges have developed programs for high school seniors who may elect to attend full-time in lieu of the senior year in high school or part-time while attending high school. The students benefit by expanding their academic choices, and community colleges benefit by having highly motivated students seeking enrichment in their classrooms.

Simon's Rock College of Bard in Great Barrington, Massachusetts, is the only early college in the country, and students enroll after completing the sophomore or junior year in high school.

➤ *THE GOOD NEWS:* There are plenty of good options available to high school students who feel underwhelmed by their school's offerings.

➤ *THE BAD NEWS:* Colleges treat the options differently. For instance, if your child enrolls in a dual program with a community college while still taking courses at the high school, some colleges may consider your child a transfer student and some a freshman applicant. It can add a touch of confusion to the admission process, so your best bet is to consult with colleges first about the options your child is considering.

If your family is interested in financial aid, be warned that in order to qualify for federal funds, students need to:

- have a high school diploma or earn a GED certificate (General Educational Development—a standardized test taken by those who haven't graduated from high school);

- pass an independently administered test approved by the U.S. Department of Education (i.e., PSAT, SAT, ACT, Army Entrance Exam, etc.);

- complete a program treated as home school or private school under state law; or

- meet other standards your state establishes that are approved by the U.S. Department of Education.

Even if your child applies to and is admitted to college at the end of junior year, he can always defer admission if he needs extra time before leaving home.

V. International Students

➤ *THE GOOD NEWS:* International students are welcomed to U.S. colleges in large numbers and, not only do they enjoy academic challenges at American institutions, but they grow culturally by experiencing life in a country different than their own.

➤ *THE BAD NEWS:* Students must be U.S. citizens (or eligible non-citizens such as permanent residents) to qualify for federal financial aid. Consequently, funding from colleges and universities—as well as from outside sources—is limited, and competition for scholarships is often brutal.

Admission officers travel all over the world to recruit top international students, and studying in a country other than a homeland has never been more popular. While many of the questions are the same for domestic and international students, some are different.

- When a student writes for information, he should be sure to mention if he is not a citizen of the United States so that an appropriate application and specific information about available aid (if any) and requirements will be mailed.

- Adhere to deadlines and, if possible, follow up by phone, fax, or e-mail about the receipt of credentials. The mail in different parts of the world is painfully slow and unreliable, so it's advisable to post mail to admission offices one month ahead of the deadline or apply online. Be sure to include your e-mail address and/or fax number on the application. Many colleges send decisions electronically or by telegram and follow up with a letter. If your child hasn't heard from a college by the expected time, call—but be sure to check time differences first. In addition, although international calls are expensive, you might be spending your money well by calling to make certain that an application has been received and completed by the deadline.

- Many colleges will waive the application fee if it causes a burden—read application instructions for details. Some may ask that a school official verify the financial necessity of a waiver; some may simply take your child's word for the fact that she can't get money out of her country.

- International students whose language of instruction is not English are required to demonstrate English proficiency. Options include submitting scores from TOEFL (Test of English as a Foreign Language), College Board's ELPT (English Language Proficiency Test™), or completing an AP course and exam in International English Language, APIEL. Consult individual colleges for their requirements and recommendations. (TOEFL is explained in detail in Chapter 3.)

- Some international students choose to take an intensive summer course in English right before enrolling to brush up on skills, especially conversational English. Colleges *may* offer a conditional acceptance, requiring such a program. Ask each school's international-student advisor to recommend high-quality and appropriate programs.

- The I-20 form (Certificate of Eligibility) is issued once your child has decided to enroll at a college, and this enables him to apply for a student visa at a U.S. Embassy or consulate in your home country. Your child also needs to get a passport. The college or university admitting your child will correspond with you regarding details for obtaining the student visa.

It's especially important that international students make a comfortable match for themselves, since college will be a home away from home. Some international students, because of finances, aren't able to go home in the summers, and a large number don't go home for holidays. The office of international students or the dean's office can help make suggestions about housing during holidays and summer. Also, there will probably be an international student association that will serve as social and cultural support for your child while abroad.

Often, international students are surprised by how informal students are here and how relaxed the relationship is between students and faculty. The international student office may have a guidebook and/or an orientation program that will help familiarize your child with social mores and customs. Sometimes, slang and money are the biggest adjustments. With McDonald's serving all over the world now, U.S. food is not as foreign anymore but many students have to adjust to some new flavors and smells.

If climate is totally different, consider having your child buy clothes after arriving on campus to find out what styles are appropriate. Tag sales (sales of used materials usually on lawns of private homes) as well as used clothing stores will have many bargains.

VI. Attending a PG (Postgraduate) Year at a Secondary School

A very sensible option for many students not ready for college right after high school graduation is spending a PG year at one of the many independent secondary schools in the United States and Canada offering this option. While some students take an extra year of high school just to polish academic skills and reapply to colleges that rejected or wait listed them, others use it as a year to sharpen athletic prowess and not "waste" a year of eligibility playing a sport at a college that doesn't interest them while they try for admission to a high-power school.

➤ *THE GOOD NEWS:* Prepping for a year can polish up academic skills, help a student mature socially, broaden horizons for college choices, and give a student a chance to retake standardize tests.

➤ *THE BAD NEWS:* Depending on what the student hopes to accomplish in a year, it could be little more than a waste of time and money.

Sometimes parents hope that their children will turn around in a PG year and become the students that they never have been. While that is the case sometimes, in other cases, pushy parents with unrealistic expectations send their kids off to a PG year hoping for a miracle in the classroom that never materializes.

Alex applied—and was admitted to—several colleges his senior year, but he didn't feel ready to go. His cousins—all male athletes—each did a PG year at Phillips Exeter Academy in New Hampshire, and he followed their lead. He deferred admission, enrolled at Exeter, and did very well. Ultimately, he enrolled at the same college he would have attended after high school, but after a PG year felt more solid academically and more settled socially.

Tryna, on the other hand, a wonderful young woman but not a terrific student, went off to a PG year kicking and screaming, at the insistence of her parents. School is not her strength, and she hated every minute of the experience. Although she was admitted to a junior college at the end of her PG year, she probably would have been accepted there right out of high school, too, and— if she had it to do over again—she wouldn't. Tryna could have saved her parents an awful lot of money (and herself some heartache), if she had skipped the PG year.

A PG year is a time for enrichment. Courses are taken above and beyond high school graduation requirements, weak areas can be focused on, strong areas can be polished, SATs and ACTs can be retaken, writing skills can be sharpened, and—in the case of boarding students—dorm-living survival skills can be developed. Some students are very young at the end of high school, and one additional year at the secondary level might make a difference between an okay freshman year and a great freshman year. To get the most out of a PG experience, a student needs to be well motivated.

Athletics often motivate students to try a PG year. Paul, a strong hockey player at a large public high school, was encouraged by all the college coaches who recruited him to consider a PG year, especially since he would be just 17 when he graduated from high school. "They counseled me that, after a year at a prep school, I would be bigger physically, more mature emotionally and mentally, and better prepared for the academic rigors of college," he remembers. "I covered my bases and applied to the PG program at Choate as well as to several colleges." Although admitted to a few colleges (but not his top choice), he decided to go to Choate. "The college counselor at Choate advised me to apply to Bowdoin, but since they rejected me previously, I was bitter and didn't want to. However, since there was no fee charged to reapply, I figured that I had nothing to lose and tried again." Happily, he was admitted, enrolled, and became captain of the Bowdoin hockey team.

You can look into PG years at the same time you are looking at colleges, but don't worry if you consider this option after mid-April of twelfth grade since many independent schools continue to accept applications for PGs throughout the summer. Check a guidebook, such as *The Handbook of Private Schools* by Porter Sargents, Inc., to get names of some prep schools with a postgraduate option.

VII. Students with Disabilities and Special Health Needs

According to statistics from the American Council on Education, the percentage of first-time, full-time college freshmen reporting disabilities has increased significantly since the late 1970s. In particular, the number of those reporting learning disabilities has climbed markedly.

Law prohibits colleges from discriminating against a student with a disability. Section 504 of the Rehabilitation Act of 1973 requires that postsecondary institutions receiving federal funds provide *reasonable* accommodations to students with disabilities. In addition, the Americans with Disabilities Act (ADA) of 1990 provides guidelines to all public and private schools. Reasonable accommodations may include accessible classrooms, extended time to complete exams, note takers, permitting computer use to write exams or papers, books on tapes, and a quiet space without distractions for exams.

While in high school, your child may have received services under the Individuals with Disabilities Education Act (IDEA), the special education legislation that guarantees free, appropriate, education *through age 22 or high school graduation, whichever comes first*. The rules are different in higher education, and colleges vary dramatically in the amount of resources—financial and human—they are willing and able to commit to students with disabilities. Consequently, what might be available to your child at one college may not be at another.

To obtain support services at the college level, students must self-identify and provide official, accurate and current documentation describing the nature of the disability. Ask colleges for their documentation guidelines and give these to the evaluator. This sort of documentation can be very expensive, and colleges are not required to provide or pay for testing. Consider having your child evaluated by the public school system before graduating, since colleges often require documentation that is not more than two years old. As long as they haven't graduated from high school, even students enrolled in private schools may be eligible for an evaluation through the public school system.

Depending on the extent of your child's disability, you will have to add more look-sees to your list when considering different campus options. Every disability is different—and whether your child's is learning, physical, or psychological—you need to spend time as a family deciding exactly how much support will be needed at the college level. Any specialist you have worked with (physical therapist, speech pathologist, social worker, etc.), as well as your child's guidance counselor, can offer helpful suggestions.

Consult an Independent Living Center (ILC) close to the college you're considering to get information about self-advocacy, benefit eligibility, local offerings and opportunities. For a national directory of centers, consult the Web site of Independent Living Research Utilization at www.ilru.org. You'll find information about the housing market, equipment loan programs, personal assistant services, and peer counseling.

When corresponding with a college about visiting the campus, contact the office that deals with students with disabilities. The office of admission can point you in the right direction. Most colleges and universities have an Office of

Disability Support Services, which might also be called Disability Resource Center or Office of Special Student Services, etc. You not only want to find out how accessible and accommodating the campus is technically, but you also want to get a feel for how sensitive they are about making housing assignments, what kind of special academic support is available (readers, interpreters, tutors, etc.), and generally what the feel of campus is for a student with a disability. You want your child to fit in, as well as get the support needed to make his college experience the best it can be. It's helpful if your child can meet with a student with a comparable disability and, by doing so, get the inside scoop on accessibility.

An overnight visit is a must if your child plans to board. Even though the gym is listed as wheelchair accessible, is there a lift in the pool? What kind of climate is there in the dorms? Does the campus community accept and integrate people who are different? Is there any extra charge for special services? Will you or your child get assistance in hiring a personal care attendant? How many other students have similar disabilities? What kind of medical care is available?

Colleges and universities are not required to change their curriculum requirements for students with learning disabilities once they are admitted. So, if your child has a learning disability that makes mastering math impossible, you may want to avoid a school that requires calculus for graduation. Colleges are more apt to consider a substitution than a waiver. For example, a student with a learning disability might be allowed to substitute a course in literature, culture, or history of a country to fulfill a foreign language requirement. You might ask for examples of substitutions or waivers offered in recent past. Offices dealing with students with disabilities can provide a tremendous amount of information to prospective students and help them determine if they will fit in on campus

Parents of students with disabilities often are more involved with the education of their children than other parents. This is a good time to do some heavy-duty thinking and talking about how independent your child is. If he is going to live away from home, how skillful is he in taking care of business such as laundry, arranging for transportation, and sticking up for himself? Will he take the initiative to attend helpful sessions sponsored by Disability Services on time management and note taking? If not, who at the college might serve as a good mentor or role model?

Your child will need to be able to accurately describe his disability and service needs. Your child will be a better self-advocate knowing how to articulate his situation accurately and clearly. Be sure he's reviewed the documentation submitted to the college. Discuss what has worked well in the past, and ask what he thinks he needs in the future.

Some students, for a variety of reasons, are reluctant to admit that they have a disability or are shy about asking for special treatment. While it's not possible to expect your child to have an overnight personality change, perhaps you (or somebody else he trusts) can convince him that what he's asking for is *fair*—not necessarily *special*—treatment. Students at the college with a similar disability might be your best bet.

Consider a college such as Gallaudet University, which deals exclusively with deaf students, or Landmark College, specializing in working with students with learning disabilities. Gallaudet is an internationally renowned school located in Washington, D.C. "Gallaudet is unique in its mission to educate deaf and hard of hearing students. Students come to us from a variety of secondary educational backgrounds—including those from residential deaf school settings, mainstream programs, and oral-based programs, as well as those who attended school without structured communication support," says Deborah E. DeStefano, director of admissions.

Founded in 1983, Landmark College in Putney, Vermont, is the nation's only accredited college exclusively serving students with dyslexia, specific learning disabilities, or Attention Deficit Hyperactivity Disorder (ADHD). Credit courses lead to an associate degree in general studies, and a noncredit curriculum gets students ready to enter or return to degree-granting undergraduate programs. "At Landmark College, students acquire academic skills and strategies that ensure success in college, graduate school, and professional schools, and in the work world," maintains Leatrice Johnson, dean of admission.

Some colleges and universities offer pre-college summer programs ranging in length from a week to a month for high school juniors and seniors with learning disabilities. These programs help prepare students for the issues they will face in college. Consult HEATH, the national clearinghouse on postsecondary education for individuals with disabilities at www.heath.gwu.edu for a list of programs across the country.

Investigate how the college will help students get oriented and how they will be plugged into any special activities after enrollment. Colleges have newsletters, student organizations, planned activities, and advisors to help students fit in after enrollment. Navigate the Web sites to get some information on what is available.

Self-reporting a disability of any sort can help *explain* rather than *excuse* some parts of an application. A student with a serious—but unmentioned—sight impairment completed her application by hand and it was a mess. Before knowing she was nearly blind, evaluators thought she was sloppy and careless. After a guidance counselor mentioned her disability, those same evaluators thought she was spunky and remarkable to do as good a job as she had done. It was still illegible—which isn't the best first impression to make—but nevertheless, it was authentic.

A bright, young man with a learning disability and the younger sibling of three high-powered, high-testing college graduates did not want special treatment because of his learning disability. He chose not to take extended time SATs and, consequently, his scores were—predictably—low. Hoping to continue to hide his secret, he applied only to colleges that did not require standardized tests, which limited his choices considerably. Had he taken SATs with extended time or documented his learning disability, an admission office would have had more valuable information to go on to interpret his testing pattern. Further, he could take advantage of the support services available to him and probably have a more productive college career.

If your child has a physical disability that could make a traditional campus visit difficult, encourage him to let the admission office know before arriving on campus. Arrangements can be made to insure that the visit is as productive and comfortable as possible. One young woman, a person of small stature, arrived at the admission office of a large, urban campus planning to go on a tour. She wasn't expecting a group tour and felt that the busy city streets and huge campus would be impossible for her to negotiate on foot. Had she called ahead, a personal guide could have led the tour at her own pace, or arrangements for a driver could have been made.

Special accommodations such as extended time, large print test booklets, or accessible testing sites can be made for students with disabilities when they take standardized tests. (See Chapter 3.)

Resources

"How to Choose a College: Guide for the Student with a Disability." A joint project of the Association on Higher Education and Disability and The Heath Resource Center, this brochure provides an excellent outline of the college selection process. To order a copy, contact HEATH or AHEAD at the addresses listed below:

The George Washington University HEATH Resource Center
2121 K Street, NW
Suite 220
Washington, D.C. 20037
Phone: (800) 544-3284 (Voice/TTY)
        (202) 973-0904 (Voice/TTY)
        (202) 973-0908 (fax)
E-mail: askheath@gwu.edu

AHEAD
Association on Higher Education and Disability
P.O. Box 21192
Columbus, Ohio 4322
Web site: www.ahead.org

National Council on Independent Living
1916 Wilson Boulevard
Suite 209
Arlington, VA 22201
Phone: (703) 525-3406 (Voice)
        (703) 525-4153 (TTY)
E-mail: ncil@ncil.org

Peterson's Colleges with Programs for Students with Learning Disabilities or Attention Deficit Disorders, edited by Charles T. Mangrum II and Stephen S. Strichart.
Peterson's/Thomson Learning
Phone: (800) 338-3282
Web site: www.petersons.com

CHAPTER 10

Words of Wisdom: Advice from Parents

While our sons and daughters learn the best lessons by doing things (including making mistakes) on their own, another good (and safer) way to learn is through the experience of others. Below you'll find friendly advice from parents—most of whom work in education as admission professionals, guidance counselors, and financial aid officers. We asked for candor when collecting these quotes and promised to protect the innocent by using first names only.

If it makes you feel any better, the admission professionals who are also parents of college-bound children are not immune to the concerns that plague civilian parents going through this process.

Are We Having Fun Yet?

Jackie B., a college professor and the survivor of the admission process with her oldest child admits, "Getting my son to write the essays and complete the admission and financial aid applications was a hand-wringing experience. After our hand wringing was completed, we moved to the heart-pounding stage as we approached the mailbox each day with high hopes. My son got the news he hoped for so it was all worth it."

"The search process is wonderfully haphazard and unpredictable, and students can make very good choices for what seem (to their parents) like all the wrong reasons. Having narrowed the field to two top choices, our daughter applied Early Decision to the one in the mountains as opposed to the one on the prairie I was certain suited her better. In fact, it was an excellent choice. Our second child, worn out by the exhaustive search we'd undertaken with our first, refused to visit any colleges at all. He confined himself to reading college catalogs and to e-mailing instructors and current students with questions," remembers a college-professor mom who is now braced for the search for graduate schools.

Linda, a super organized, college employee with terrific sons lamented, "What I thought was going to be a new and exciting experience for our family turned out to be two long, tedious, dragged-out, stressful years. For each of our three sons, everything was done at the last minute and decisions were made at the very last date acceptable. (This is especially true for our oldest son.) We couldn't even discuss schools during their junior years. The boys were too busy with sports, practices, and friends. When they did get a day or weekend off, they slept late and became couch potatoes. Checking out schools was the last thing they wanted to do. It was only in the fall of senior year that they started even *thinking* of colleges, never mind visiting them. Thank God for the guidance counselors who kept us on track to meet those haunting deadlines. I tell friends going through the same thing to hang in there, because everything will work out. But be prepared for this laissez-faire attitude."

Boys vs. Girls

Susan, a college counselor at an all girls' high school observes, "What surprised me working with my son was the different reaction he had from the girls I have counseled professionally. When he got rejections, he threw them in the garbage. 'If they don't want me, I don't want them,' was his response. No angst like the girls who take rejection personally."

"Boys and girls both worry about the process and the outcome, but boys worry more quietly," observes a seasoned guidance counselor and dad of both a son and daughter.

Chill

Jackie M., a mother of two and director of admission, muses, "Over the years, I have observed a lot of examples of how I don't want to behave as a parent. So many parents seem to be stuck on the same 10 schools that are the 'right' ones. In fact, there are many great schools; the admission process goes smoother when parents focus less on what college their children are *getting into* and more on what their children will get *out of* college. The pressure that some parents put on their children is very unhealthy. I wish that some parents would step away a bit and let their children follow their own passions and interests."

Counting Your Blessings

"I am trying not to take anything for granted and trying not to blow the importance of a college choice out of proportion," admits Kay, the mother of two college-bound children and a seasoned college counselor. "My friend's son unexpectedly needed an operation on his brain during the college search. The family shifted its focus from his SATs to wondering whether he would graduate from high school. Another friend is trying to decide whether her son should go to college or go to rehab. Believe it or not, rehab is a lot more expensive than the colleges they're considering."

Dealing with Disappointment

"Model how to handle disappointment by sharing your own disappointments with your children, explaining how you got through them. If they never hear about your disappointments, they might think it unusual or strange to have them; they might feel even more isolated with their hurts. Be a good listener, offer plenty of hugs, and remind them of the good things to be thankful for—and keep them talking!" suggests a seasoned high school counselor and father of three.

"In a perfect world, college admission decisions for each student should be illustrated on a bell curve," suggests a mom of two who has worked at secondary schools for 20 years. "It's not unpredictable that a student will get rejected from reach schools, admitted to one or two safeties, and do pretty well with the majority, which should fall in the middle. If a student gets in everywhere he applied, he probably didn't stretch enough. If he gets denied too many places, he probably didn't pick enough of a range of schools."

Dress Code, Anyone?

"After working out whether the two colleges that had admitted him could each offer a rich experience in the areas he thought he might major in, my son's decision rested on a single question. 'Can I wear my pants (the awful, grungy, ragged-bottomed ones with the wedges he sewed in himself) at Carleton?' (He was sure he could wear them at Oberlin.) When the answer (from a trusted source—a classmate visiting her brother at Carleton) was yes, he made his choice," remembers Sharon, an English professor.

Dumped at the College Fair

Therese, a college representative who distributed admission materials at fairs for over 15 years, remembers, "I was looking forward to attending my first college fair as a mom with my junior daughter. I printed up address labels and told my admission friends from other colleges to look for me on the other side of the table. As I got ready to leave the house, my daughter announced that she had too much homework and wouldn't be joining me at the fair. However, she had promised a classmate that I would drive her. So I ended up going with somebody else's daughter who ditched me as soon as we entered the gym. I ran into a colleague (also dumped by her child) and we walked around together and talked to our buddies and licked our wounds. Talk about the cobbler's children without shoes."

Embarrassing Questions

Navigating the college search as a father rather than a dean necessitated a shift in gears for Jerry. "I have always told the parents and students I've met in my professional life that there is no such thing as a silly or stupid question. When we pulled into the parking lot of the first college my own daughter was visiting, she begged, 'Dad, please don't ask any embarrassing questions!' I asked her to provide me with a list of those, but I did not receive any specifics. I was however, very careful in my inquiries, especially on the student tour!"

Emotional Turmoil

Cora-Jean, a single mother of three, reflects, "What was most surprising to me was the emotional turmoil I experienced around letting go and seeing my daughter go off, essentially on her own. I was immensely proud and shared her enthusiasm about this 'rite of passage,' but I wasn't prepared for the sadness. I didn't understand that it was going to be a passage for me, too. I suddenly had a strong sense that I was all out of opportunity to 'fix' things."

Essays

A long-time college employee complains, "Trying to get my son to sit down and write a simple essay was impossible. He wouldn't take the time and said, 'I don't know what to write,' even though he was given multiple choices on the application. I knew that he could write because of the comments written by teachers on his papers in high school. What worked was telling him that the content was more important than the length of the essay. That seemed to take some pressure off and, before he knew it, he had constructed a decent essay. I think it's important for students to write their own essays. It's good preparation for what's to come in college. They really need to learn how to think for themselves."

Family Politics

"In a duel, one of the duelers always gets shot. Pick your battles carefully, and let your child win once in a while. Also, set realistic consequences on which you'll always follow though," says a school counselor who has been there with his daughter.

Barbara, a school nurse sadly recalls, "As a high school senior, I was bribed to attend a school my mother and grandmother wanted me to attend and received gifts all during my stay. I had decided that I would never do that to my child. I do not agree with my daughter's college choice (actually it was my last choice for her), but I will be here to support her because I feel if she is not comfortable and happy, she will not succeed in life."

Issues

"Unfortunately, before a realistic and successful college search and success at college can occur, your child might have to deal with other big issues. Taking untreated depression or alcohol abuse to college is lighting the fuse on the bomb," advises a high school counselor.

Matches

"Some parents equate their children's happiness and/or chances for success too strongly with a college's place on the pecking order or its overall prestige," observes Michael, the father of two recent college graduates. "Those who get beyond that seem genuinely interested in the 'right match'—the school where a student will be challenged but not overwhelmed and will grow in both knowledge and self-esteem."

After going through the process with both his son and daughter, Spencer advises, "Helping your son or daughter select the right school is like buying a new coat. The more you try on the easier it is to know which one is just right for you."

Merit Aid

Dave, a guidance counselor whose sons both attended private colleges on merit scholarships advises, "Start doing your homework about colleges and their academic and merit-aid programs early, and as you narrow down the choices, make a personal contact and/or visit with the admission office. Having a support person on the college campus is a real plus when it comes to staying abreast of individual scholarship requirements and deadlines."

Sue, a mom and financial aid officer regrets, "I wish I had done a little more about making Kate more responsible for understanding her bill, her financial aid, and her obligations. She pretty much understood her obligations regarding working in the summers to earn her own book and spending money, but she didn't have a clue about her bill, how it was paid, and what her loans were. I gave her the information, but I should have been a little more forceful in making sure she understood."

Meredith, a financial aid director and a mother of a college senior explains, "Families should have honest discussions with their children about family finances and how educational costs figure into the larger picture. This is probably a very new type of discussion to have with a child, but an important one. Often children who don't understand feel resentful or guilty. This conversation should cover long-term consequences of this important decision such as whether a particular institution may be 'worth it.' It is imperative to have a frank discussion about whether loans taken will be paid by the parent or child. Teenagers are most interested only in the next few years. However, loan burden, if any, may determine type or place of employment for many years after college graduation.

It is extremely hard for a parent to tell a child that the financial aid offer from their first-choice institution is not enough in your view. Expectations of what families see as their 'demonstrated need' and what institutions identify as need often are not the same. Take the time to educate yourself as best as possible on how the aid process works at those institutions to which your child applies, and on the average aid award offered families. If possible, give your child some flexibility in terms of whether he or she would accept the additional loan burden necessary to go to a higher cost, first-choice institution. If you as a parent have previously discussed what amount they are willing to contribute, it allows your children to make an important decision that will impact them directly."

One Step at a Time

"I think college counseling should be done with a lot of encouragement—and if you break down the process, it doesn't feel so overwhelming. In fact, students are often relieved to hear that what they've already accomplished covers many steps on the path to the future," observes Susan, a mom and college advisor.

Reacting

"I think that one of the things that parents must remember—which I have tried to teach since my eldest daughter went through the college search—is that kids need time to react to schools their own way without any input from parents," suggests Phyllis, an educational consultant. "A gentle 'ah hum' or 'huh' or a terribly unobtrusive neutral sound is far more effective than a comment. I think parents need to trust their kids to do their own reacting and hold off on input until all those first impressions have had a chance to settle in. A parental response, either positive or negative, can produce an oppositional response simply because of adolescence and not because of a school."

See Mail on E-mail

Advice from Cathy, an admission dean and the wife of another dean, "If I have learned one thing this year watching Mary go through the process it's that parents miss out on a lot of information when they don't see the e-mail messages between students and college representatives, namely, coaches, admission people, or student representatives. I have asked Mary to print all e-mail messages she receives so Dave and I can read them and so she can keep them in the folder she has set up for each school. You can learn a lot about the professionalism, sophistication, and education of the representative who is interacting with your child."

Siblings

"Our kids have always been different from the moment they arrived, so it makes sense that they would react to the college search (and landing) process differently. If the kids are close in age, there can be wonderful modeling by the older child, or conversely, behavior that teaches the younger child what not to do when college time comes. What I wish would happen more is for siblings to converse, confer, and support each other through the process. I hear too much silence in families," a high school adjustment counselor observes.

Smarts

Carolyn, a college administrator and mother of two, counsels, "I told my children as they applied to colleges that smart is not what they are but what they will become. Too many children think that an aptitude test or a teacher's assessment or even a college admission offer determines their level of intelligence or predicts future achievement. We're all works in progress and will never run out of things to learn."

Sports

"Our son, Peter, was initially looking at colleges more than 1,000 miles from home," says Gerald. "However, his older brother had picked a college just a two-hour car drive from us and so we were able to continue to attend most of his basketball games. Peter thought that having his parents around for collegiate competitions would be a pretty nice perk, so he narrowed his radius and just considered places closer to home."

Maxine remembers "a friend's child received a golf scholarship at the University of Mississippi. The parent pushed the child to go to Vanderbilt instead. He went and skipped classes to play golf!"

Surprises

Sue remembers, "I was surprised where my children ended up going to school. I thought I had a good idea of what their choices would be and where they might head geographically. After all, who knows children better than parents, right? Wow, was I way off the mark! As a high school junior, my daughter's goal was to find a big campus with lots of action far from home. While she did go about 500 miles from home, she chose a small school in a moderately ho-hum town. However, it was a good fit for her and the educational experience was top notch. Our son surprised us, too. For years he talked about heading to a Big 10 campus, 1,000 miles from home. He's at a campus one-half hour drive from home and about one-tenth the size of Indiana University. But he, too, found a very good fit and is having a positive educational experience. Our daughter looked at 10 schools and our son looked at only two. Each seemed to know what they wanted and needed."

Laurie, a college counselor at an independent school, was amazed that "the one thing I thought I would have is a good vibe about what school was just right for my son, but I didn't. I was learning along with him. His initial list of top choices looked a lot better on paper to both of us than they appeared in person. The way that college staff members treat you—and your child—means a lot. In our case, his top choice fell off a pedestal when we dealt with a pretentious faculty member and condescending admission director. Even if he gets into this highly selective college, I'm not sure I want him to go if that's the way he'll be treated if he enrolls."

Test Scores

Yes, there is life after college entrance exams said one Philadelphia father on the day of his son's Ivy League law school graduation. "When we saw David's

SAT results, we took a detour on the road to Harvard and made tracks to Franklin and Marshall. In retrospect, I can't imagine a better college experience for my son, and he's ended up right about where he was headed back in high school, anyway. I wonder now whether he was better off without those super SAT scores."

The One and Only

Betsy, a college librarian and mother of two, counsels, "I think it's important for students not to focus on just one school, especially if that college is highly selective. The daughter of a colleague was totally focused on the one, perfect choice. She hadn't considered any other options. Fortunately, she got in Early Decision. If she hadn't, I don't know what they would have done. My daughter applied to 10 colleges and likes them all."

Visits

"At every school I visited as a parent, I went to the student newspaper office or library and procured as many back issues as well as the current one and poured over them in an effort to 'read between the lines,' remembers Donna, mother of two and an experienced admission interviewer. "Also, I recommend, if there's time, stopping in town for a coke or gas and having a chat with a few local people about what they think of the college."

Whose Life Is It, Anyway?

Judi, the mom of a son, suggests, "Do remember that it is your child who is going to college, not you. And unless there are major financial considerations, allow him to make the selection. Most young students can tell when the *fit* is right for them and should be allowed to go with their instincts. Once there, let your child determine his own major; please don't push your child into a major you think he should pursue (or, as is more often the case, you wish *you* had pursued)."

"It's not necessary to apply both to the colleges that your child wants to attend and the ones you want him to attend. It's sufficient to apply to the ones he wants to attend. This strategy saves time and money," warns David.

John, a high school counselor, confides, "My daughter is a happy freshman at St. Olaf College in Northfield, Minnesota. I took the college search very seriously and felt that we needed to carefully research each of the 12 to 14 colleges on her list. After visiting a college, she disappointed me by saying,

'Dad, I don't want to look at any more colleges. I've found the one that's right for me.' Although there were many more on *my* list, we stopped looking because it was *her* search after all. She has been in pure heaven ever since."

Mary, a psychiatric nurse and former college instructor warns, "If the college choices you are steering your child toward have more to do with some of your own issues than with the education of your child, get over it. Let your child navigate his or her own course and focus on what's best for your child, not what's best for you."

As soon as you mention that you're going through the admission process with your child, you'll get lots of unsolicited, anecdotal advice in the lines at the supermarket, on the sidelines at athletic games, and at family gatherings. Sort through everything you hear, and remember that every child is unique and every school has advantages and disadvantages. As a parent, you need to trust your instincts. Additionally, as a parent of a young adult, you also need to learn to let go. That's not always easy. It's also hard to accept the fact that the way you want things to be is not always the way they are. Good luck with the process. We hope you learn a lot and that everything works out the best for your child and for you.

If you collect some tips to share along the way, please write to us in care of Peterson's, and we'll keep your words of wisdom in our file.

APPENDIX 1

Checklist/Calendar
for Parents

Keeping on top of college-related deadlines, dates, and things-to-do is one of the toughest parts of the admission process. The list below can help you see the big picture, but (as you've probably learned the hard way, at least once) calendars work best when you check them in advance to see what's ahead, not after the fact, to realize what you've missed.

Before you begin, consider some of these general points:

- Encourage independent reading and writing throughout your child's school career.
- If your child has a special passion or talent (e.g., music, math, fly fishing, hula dancing), try to arrange enrichment opportunities via classes, camps, or private mentoring.
- Don't become obsessed with the college admission process, and don't forget your life—spouse, other children, job, friends, etc.—beyond it.
- You may fret too much about decisions and nag too much about deadlines, but it's not possible to tell your child "I love you" too often.

• 9th Grade

This is the first year that admission officials will see on your child's transcript and thus, a good time to take stock. What strong academic interests should be encouraged? What areas should be strengthened? If your child has any inkling of career goals, consider what prerequisites may exist. This is especially true in scientific and technical fields. Use your school's course listings to sketch out a Comprehensive Academic Program that includes all classes your child will take throughout high school. Think about which extracurricular activities your child plans to continue. Have past passions been outgrown?

September/October

___ Be aware of your child's academic adjustment. Are course levels appropriate?

___ Urge your child to engage in meaningful activity, in and out of school. Consider community service. Begin an Activities Record that lists all participation, along with a brief mention of accomplishments, awards, and leadership positions.

January

___ Evaluate academic progress so far. Are grades up to par? Are course levels on target? Do study habits need improvement?

___ Is your child enjoying extracurricular involvement? If not, assess what changes might be made.

___ Begin thinking about worthwhile summer plans (study, camp, job, volunteer work, travel, etc.).

May/June

___ Evaluate and update Comprehensive Academic Program and Activities Record.

___ Finalize summer plans.

___ Develop a summer reading list.

• 10th Grade

Classes chosen in grade 10 often determine which courses (and course levels) your child will be qualified to take in the important junior and senior years.

September

___ Contact the guidance counselor about a warm-up PSAT/NMSQT for sophomores in October (or ask about PLAN schedule in ACT regions).

___ Ask the guidance department about college fairs in your area and college admission-representative visits to the school. Encourage your child to start investigating by attending one fair and a session or two with representatives at school. *Warning:* This may be too early for many students. Don't push it!

October

____ Save the date for the PSAT/NMSQT.

____ Are first semester classes going well? Extracurriculars?

December

____ Questions about PSAT scores? Contact the guidance counselor. If necessary, discuss strategies for improving weak areas.

January

____ Evaluate academic progress so far. Are grades up to par? Are course levels on target? Do study habits need improvement?

____ Is your child participating in extracurricular activities? If not, reevaluate.

____ Begin thinking about worthwhile summer plans (job, study, camp, volunteer work, travel, etc.).

March

____ Consider whether your child should be taking any SAT II tests (and, in some cases, AP tests) in May or June. Will she or he be completing any subjects this year? (The test most commonly taken by sophomores is biology.)

____ Register for May SAT II tests, if appropriate.

April

____ Register for June SAT II tests, if appropriate.

May/June

____ Save dates for SAT II (or AP) tests, as needed.

____ Oversee registration for next fall's classes and activities. Urge your child to select (or continue) the most challenging classes possible and at least one community service activity.

____ Finalize summer plans.

____ Develop a summer reading list.

Summer

____ Make sure your child has a job or participates in constructive activities *throughout* the summer. Summer study, jobs, and volunteer work always rate high with admission officials.

____ If your child has a career goal in mind, help organize a "shadow day" where he or she spends time with someone at work in that field.

____ The Web provides good (albeit excessive) college entrance information, as well as online applications to many institutions. Summer is a good time for students to check out some of the many sites available and bookmark favorites, without jeopardizing homework time.

• 11th Grade

This year the college search process begins in earnest. Exploration and testing should help you and your child to start developing a list of target schools by spring. Poor grades will not be as easily forgiven as those from previous years, and colleges will look for commitment and accomplishment outside of the classroom.

September

____ Make sure that PSAT/NMSQT registration is handled by guidance staff. (Except in regions where ACT test is prevalent). Ascertain and save the date.

____ Ask the guidance department about college fairs in your area and college admission-representative visits to the school. Encourage your child to attend fairs and sessions with representatives at school.

____ You and your child should begin to familiarize yourselves with guidance office resources.

____ Obtain a Social Security number for you child, if you have not previously done so.

October

____ Make sure PSAT/NMSQT date is on the family calendar. Diplomatically remind your child, if necessary, to read the Student Bulletin and to try the practice questions. Refrain from grilling your child about probable performance as soon as the test is over. (Instead, plan a not-test-related treat.)

____ Schedule a day trip to visit nearby colleges. (Eager beavers will be ready. Other garden-variety college prospects can wait until next spring or summer.) Don't worry if these are places where your child won't apply. The goal is to explore different types of schools. Aim for variety. Discuss which characteristics are attractive and which aren't.

December

____ Questions about PSAT scores? Contact the guidance counselor. If necessary, discuss strategies for improving weak areas. Evaluate different SAT prep options, as needed. (See the end of Chapter 3.)

____ Begin informal brainstorming about possible target colleges, with test results in mind.

____ Take advantage of college students home for vacation. Ask them questions. Ask their parents questions. Ask your child to ask even more questions.

____ Take an introductory look at financial aid forms (see Chapter 5) just to see what you'll need by this time next year.

____ Buy a copy of this book as a holiday gift for every parent on your shopping list.

January

___ Evaluate academic progress so far. Are grades up to par? Are course levels on target? Do study habits need improvement?

___ Begin thinking about worthwhile summer plans (job, study, camp, volunteer work, travel, etc.).

___ Mark projected SAT I & II or ACT test dates on family calendar. Also mark registration deadlines.

February

___ Look ahead to SAT or ACT registration deadlines for the tests your child plans to take. Are you about to miss one? Mark appropriate dates on your calendar. (Some juniors take the SAT I in March. If your child will do so, heed February registration deadline.)

___ Buy a general guidebook to U.S. colleges and universities.

March

___ Consider and plan spring vacation college visits.

___ Begin listing target colleges in a notebook ("The College Bible").

___ Visit college Web sites. Begin calling, writing, or e-mailing target colleges to request publications.

___ Set aside an area for college propaganda. Invest in folders for materials from front-runner schools.

___ Look ahead to SAT or ACT registration deadlines for the tests your child plans to take. Are you about to miss one? Mark appropriate test and registration dates on your calendar.

___ Make sure your child discusses plans to take Advanced Placement exams with teachers and/or guidance counselor, as needed.

___ Discuss senior year classes. Urge your child to include at least one math course or lab science, as well as the most challenging courses possible. Recognize that colleges weigh senior classes and grades as heavily as the junior record.

April

___ Look ahead to SAT or ACT registration deadlines for the tests your child plans to take. Are you about to miss one? Mark appropriate test and registration dates on your calendar.

___ Update Activities Record.

May

___ Look ahead to SAT or ACT (or AP) registration deadlines for the tests your child plans to take. Are you about to miss one? Mark appropriate test and registration dates on your calendar.

___ Assess the need for and affordability of special services such as standardized test prep courses, independent college counselors (see Chapter 2), and private group tour programs (see Chapter 4).

___ Does your child need to take the TOEFL (Test of English as a Foreign Language)? Select date and oversee registration.

June

____ Look ahead to SAT or ACT registration deadlines for the tests your child plans to take. Are you about to miss one? Mark appropriate test and registration dates on your calendar.

___ Take advantage of the summer slow-down by visiting scholarship search and financial aid Web sites or checking out comparable library resources.

Summer

___ Make sure your child has a job or participates in constructive activities throughout most of the summer. Study, jobs, and volunteer work always rate high with admission officials.

___ Consider and plan summer and fall college visits.

___ Oversee standardized test preparation, as needed.

___ Request publications from additional target colleges.

___ Plan and execute supplemental submissions such as audition tapes and art slides/portfolios, if required and/or appropriate.

___ Review and update target college list. Include pros and cons. Make tentative plans for fall visits.

• 12th Grade

This is the year when the college search can feel like a full-time job—with all of the toil, tedium, and triumphs that that implies.

September

___ Plan a special evening out (e.g., dinner at a favorite restaurant) with just the college-bound child. Discuss plans and goals for the months ahead; pros and cons of target schools.

___ Look ahead to SAT or ACT registration deadlines for the tests your child plans to take. Are you about to miss one? Mark appropriate test and registration dates on your calendar.

___ Ask the guidance department about college fairs in your area and college admission-representative visits to the school. Make certain that your child attends fairs and sessions with representatives at school.

___ Visit more college Web sites.

___ Ask about Parents' Night or other high school-sponsored parents' events.

___ Finalize fall college visit plans. Include campus overnights, where possible. Visit!

___ Request additional publications.

____ Determine if your child will be using online or paper applications. If it's the latter, make sure you have them or request them.

October

___ Look ahead to SAT or ACT registration deadlines for the tests your child plans to take. Are you about to miss one? Mark appropriate test and registration dates on your calendar.

___ Discuss Early Decision and Early Action options.

___ Help your child draw up a master schedule of application and financial aid due dates, and put them on the family calendar.

___ Oversee the start of applications. Your child should be considering essay topics and looking for overlap to reduce workload.

___ Make sure your child requests teacher recommendations, as needed.

___ Visit colleges. Include interviews on campus (or with local alumni representatives), if appropriate.

___ Attend college fairs with your child.

___ By this time you might want to laugh about the college admission process. Try renting a video like *Orange County* or *Risky Business.*

___ Plan an "adults only" night out—no college talk, no kids!

November

___ Look ahead to SAT or ACT registration deadlines for the tests your child plans to take. Are you about to miss one? Mark appropriate test and registration dates on your calendar.

___ Nag about early application deadlines, as needed.

___ Reduce target college long list to a short list, where applications will be made.

___ Plan a Thanksgiving break that includes college visits (to almost-empty campuses) or plan a Thanksgiving break where *no one* mentions the word "college."

___ Check up on application completion. Volunteer to proofread, and steel yourself for a wide range of reactions.

December

___ Look ahead to SAT or ACT registration deadlines for the tests your child plans to take. Are you about to miss one? Mark appropriate test and registration dates on your calendar.

___ Get financial aid material from guidance office and Web, and attend planning workshops, if available.

___ Nag about completion of all applications due in January or February.

___ Make sure that teachers and guidance staff are up-to-date with reference forms, and that transcripts are being sent to all short-list colleges.

___ Usher in the new year with a family toast to the future—*whatever* it may bring.

January

___ File income taxes if you can, and then begin filling out financial aid forms. Finish and mail these forms as soon as possible—and never late!

___ Encourage completion of *all* applications, including those with later deadlines. Don't forget to photocopy everything that's put on paper, or print out online materials, and save all in accordion files.

___ Celebrate with the whole family when the last application hits the mailbox.

___ If SATs are being taken this month, are "Rush" scores required? Ask target colleges if you're not certain.

February

___ Unless confirmations have been received, consult colleges by phone or via cyberspace to check on completion of applications. Record the name of any contacts. Track down missing records.

___ WAIT!

March

___ Your wait is nearly over. Some decision letters will arrive this month.

April

___ Take a cold shower and resist the urge to open letters addressed to your child. (Holding them up to the light *is* permissible.) Keep in mind that thin letters aren't always rejections. Some schools send out enrollment forms later.

___ Applaud acceptances; help put rejections in perspective. For example, try saying, "It's an extremely competitive college and your math test scores must have hurt." (But not, "Those admission folks at that school seemed like a bunch of Bozos from the get-go.")

___ Plan crunch-time visits to campuses, as needed, to help prompt final decisions.

___ Compare financial aid decisions, where applicable. Contact financial aid offices with questions. Appeal aid packages, if appropriate.

___ Make sure your child returns wait-list cards, as needed. Contact admission offices to check on wait-list status. Send updated records and other information, if available. Encourage your child to write an upbeat "Please take me, and this is why you should" letter.

___ Is the verdict final? Send the required deposit. Don't dawdle and miss the May 1 deadline or colleges can give away your child's place. Also notify those schools your child *won't* attend, especially if an aid offer was made.

May

____ Make sure your child takes AP exams, if appropriate.

____ Write (or urge your child to write) a thank you note to anyone who may have been especially helpful. Guidance counselors are often unsung heroes. Don't forget teachers who wrote recommendations, scholarship agencies, admission counselors, financial aid officers, secretaries, tours guides, or other students. (Of course this isn't obligatory, but recipients are sure to be pleased and surprised.)

____ Stay abreast of housing choices, etc. When will forms be mailed? Should your child be investigating living situation options? When is freshman orientation? (Some schools have spring and summer programs.) When is course registration?

June

____ Organize a file to keep track of summer mailings from the college. Categories may include orientation, housing, course registration, and finances.

____ Consider summer school for those who want to accelerate or place out of requirements. ALWAYS check with colleges first to make sure credits will count. Get permission in writing when it's questionable.

____ Make sure that a final high school transcript is sent to the college your child will attend. (Most schools should do this automatically.)

____ Dig out some of those masterpieces you've saved since your child's grade school days. Where did the time go?

____ Help your child land a summer job that pays at least $20,000. (That's after taxes.) Call Brooke Shields for details. (She went to Princeton after all.)

APPENDIX 2

Web Site Ready Reference

Advanced Placement Tests

http://apcentral.collegeboard.com

Applications

(*Hint:* Best bet for most online applications: Go to target-college home page and follow links to applications to complete online or download.)

www.petersons.com: Direct links to many applications.

www.commonapp.org: Download Common Application or apply online. Includes list of member schools, application fees, deadlines, etc.

www.review.com: *The Princeton Review* links to member college applications through *Apply!*

www.collegelink.com: Apply to member colleges.

www.embark.com: Apply to member colleges.

Athletics

www.ncaa.org: National Collegiate Athletic Association site includes information about sports programs, eligibility, recruiting rules, etc.

Campus Visits

www.college-visits.com: College Visits offers varied group-tour itineraries, including East Coast, West Coast, Southeast, and Canada.

www.collegeimp.com: College Impressions offers group tours primarily in the Northeast.

Chat and News Sites

www.dailyjolt.com: Select a school from the Jolt membership and log on. Information, while intended for current students, is helpful to prospective students and parents.

www.collegeconfidential.com: Contains many well-indexed admission-related topics. Experts answer questions for free.

www.collegenews.com: Links to many college and university newspapers.

College Admission—General

Many of these sites include not only general information but also links to college home pages, applications, discussion forums, etc.

www.petersons.com: Information on every admission-related topic, plus you can order this book for a friend!

www.collegeboard.com: Includes lots of standardized test and financial aid information.

www.collegeconfidential.com: Links to lots of good info, chats, counseling, etc.

www.review.com: This is *The Princeton Review* site. (See also "Standardize Testing" below.)

www.usnews.com/usnews/edu/college: *U.S. News* college rankings and other information.

www.collegeview.com: Varied topics include schools with special programs.

www.nacac.com: National Association for College Admission Counseling site. Includes college fair information and links to online fairs. Listing of late college vacancies.

www.collegelink.com: Varied topics include anecdotal information, and applications and tips.

College Home Pages (lists of and links to)

www.petersons.com

www.mit.edu:8001/people/cdemello/univ.html

www.utexas.edu/world/univ/

www.universities.com

http://geowww.uibk.ac.at/univ/

Counseling (Independent)

www.educationalconsulting.org: Find a private counselor through the Independent Educational Consultants Association.

www.collegeconfidential.com: Offers a range of online counseling services.

Financial Aid

www.petersons.com: Contains the largest scholarship database available to do scholarship searches. Also has an Education Loan Center to compare and shop for loans, as well as calculators and financial aid resources to estimate expenses and more.

www.ed.gov: U.S. Department of Education Web site with information in Spanish and English.

www.fafsa.ed.gov: Complete the FAFSA online on this site.

www.finaid.org: Financial Aid Information Page sponsored by the National Association of Student Financial Aid Administrators.

www.collegeboard.com: The College Board site with worksheets to estimate family contribution and compare financial aid awards.

www.fastweb.com: Don't miss this one! FastWeb Scholarship Service database of 800,000 private scholarships.

www.collegeparents.org: Information for parents.

www.collegeboard.com/profile: College Scholarship Financial Aid PROFILE®.

www.amsweb.com: Academic Management Services.

www.slsaservices.org: Student Loan Servicing Alliance.

www.salliemae.com: SallieMae, a financial services corporation specializing in funding education.

International Baccalaureate (IB)

www.IBO.org

International Students

www.petersons.com: Search for full-year academic opportunities; ESL programs; and online TOEFL practice tests.

www.nafsa.org: NAFSA, National Association of International Educators.

www.toefl.org: TOEFL, Test of English as a Foreign Language.

Security

www.ope.ed.gov/security/

Standardized Testing

www.petersons.com: Offers general information and even online practice tests.

www.act.org: ACT site. (registration, scores, score-report order forms, test prep materials, etc.)

www.collegeboard.com: College Board SAT Program site. (registration, scores, score-report order forms, test prep materials, etc.)

www.toefl.org: TOEFL information for non-native speakers of English.

www.kaptest.com: *Kaplan, Inc.* test prep information, course schedules, sign up, etc.

www.review.com: *The Princeton Review* test prep information, course schedules, sign up, etc.

www.powerprep.com: Online test-prep information (for a fee *and* free).

Students with Disabilities

www.ahead.org: Association on Higher Education and Disability.

www.heath.gwu.edu: HEATH, the national clearinghouse on postsecondary education for individuals with disabilities.

www.ilru.org: Independent Living Research Utilization.

www.ncil.org: National Council on Independent Living.

"Time Out" Opportunities

www.americorps.org: AmeriCorps information.

www.interimprograms.com: The Center for Interim Programs. (This site, and the two that follow, offer helpful specific suggestions for students looking for worthwhile opportunities when deferring admission or taking time off during college.)

www.takingtimeoff.com: Taking Time Off.

www.timeoutassociates.com: Time Out Associates.

Two-Year Colleges

www.petersons.com: Search for two-year colleges by location, major, GPA, and more.

http://www.cset.sp.utoledo.edu/twoyrcol.html: For help locating two-year schools.

www.aacc.nche.edu: The American Association of Community Colleges.

Index

Peterson's ■ *Panicked
Parents' Guide to College Admissions*